Great Jobs
for
Business
Majors

Great Jobs

for

Business

Majors

Stephen E. Lambert

Series Developers and Contributing Authors
Stephen E. Lambert
Julie Ann DeGalan

VGM Career Horizons
NTC Publishing Group

Library of Congress Cataloging-in-Publication Data

Lambert, Stephen E.
    Great jobs for business majors / Stephen Lambert.
        p.   cm.
    Includes bibliographical references.
    ISBN 0-8442-4357-4
    1. Job hunting.   2. Business students—Employment.   I. Title.
HF5382.7.L347   1996
650.14—dc20   96-3571
                                                                   CIP

Published by VGM Career Horizons
A division of NTC/Contemporary Publishing Group, Inc.
4255 West Touhy Avenue, Lincolnwood (Chicago), Illinois 60712-1975 U.S.A.
Copyright © 1996 by NTC/Contemporary Publishing Group, Inc.
All rights reserved. No part of this book may be reproduced, stored in a retrieval
system, or transmitted in any form or by any means, electronic, mechanical,
photocopying, recording, or otherwise, without the prior written permission of
NTC/Contemporary Publishing Group, Inc.
Printed in the United States of America
International Standard Book Number: 0-8442-4357-4

00 01 02 03 04 05 VP 22 21 20 19 18 17 16 15 14 13 12 11 10 9 8 7 6 5

CONTENTS

Acknowledgments   vi

Dedication   vii

Introduction **Business: All Guarantees Are Off!**   ix

PART ONE. THE JOB SEARCH   1

Chapter 1 **The Self-Assessment**   2

Chapter 2 **The Resume and Cover Letter**   22

Chapter 3 **Researching Careers**   44

Chapter 4 **Networking**   61

Chapter 5 **Interviewing**   74

Chapter 6 **Networking or Interviewing Follow-Up**   83

Chapter 7 **Job Offer Considerations**   88

Chapter 8 **The Graduate School Choice**   93

PART TWO. THE CAREER PATHS   105

Chapter 9 **Introduction to the Business Career Paths**   106

Chapter 10 **Path 1: Sales**   114

Chapter 11 **Path 2: Retailing**   140

Chapter 12 **Path 3: Healthcare**   165

Chapter 13 **Path 4: Nonprofits**   185

Chapter 14 **Path 5: Research Associate A Strategic Approach to the MBA**   219

Additional Resources   244

Index   264

Acknowledgments

Anyone following the yearly additions to the library of *Great Jobs* volumes is aware that with each volume in the series, the list of people deserving of appreciation increases. In writing the *Great Jobs for Business Majors* volume, I have been continually impressed by the generosity of those I have written to, spoken with, and met. The list for this volume is far too extensive to mention each one personally, but I owe special debts of gratitude to two very special individuals.

To Kirsten Giebutowski, many thanks for her superlative editing contribution. Friends for a long time, it's been exciting to have this collaboration. Kirsten, thank you.

To my wife, Barbara Whitney Lambert, I owe a very special thanks for her reading, editing, perceptive comments, and ideas. An educator in her own right, her contributions have become an important part of this book.

Dedication

". . . Knock, Knock."

"Who's there?"

"Candygram!"

For Julie

BUSINESS: ALL GUARANTEES ARE OFF!

*O*ne of the interesting things that happens during college is the self-labeling that occurs because of chosen majors. The art students are seen as "artistic," the computer majors as "techies," the liberal arts as "humanists," and you, the business major, as "realistic" or "materialistic." Of course, these labels are simplifications, generalizations, and, often, just plain wrong. A major *cannot* and *should not* define who you are, or what you do for your career.

Maybe we should begin by defining some terms. Let's start with *business.* If you're a business major or are contemplating majoring in this field, you've heard others say, "Oh, I could never do a desk job" or, "I have no head for figures," or "That stuff is too technical for me" and other expressions of distaste or dislike based on their perceptions of business.

They should meet the business major working at the Metropolitan Opera, the director of community relations for Disneyworld, the individual who buys art to furnish corporate offices, or any of the thousands of businesspeople whose jobs and routines are anything but routine but that are, nonetheless, the stuff of business. Hospitals, universities, art galleries, and conservation societies are among the variety of entities that are businesses.

Business is simply another term for an organized human activity that needs to be managed in order to accomplish its goals. Those activities may be technical, like a software company, or highly artistic, such as a ballet company or symphony orchestra. In fact, you would find it a challenge to identify any vital human activity that seeks to grow, that employs people, and that is engaged in any active enterprise—from education to farming to neuroscience—that does not have a business aspect.

If you haven't thought of business this way, it's an exciting new view. It means that you can look at yourself, your interests, your personality, and your particular talents and try to find some area of business activity (and the choices are almost infinite!) to fit who you are and what you are interested in. That's an exciting prospect.

Exciting and necessary. It's a rough world out there. And that's a message you've encountered from many sources, from your case studies in business school to the evening news on the major networks. Employment is no longer an absolute given, and even the most talented and skilled of workers can lose their jobs through mergers, buyouts, and the kinds of consolidations going on as businesses try to enhance profits through economies of size. To be a contender in this volatile world, you need to have a flexible definition not only of business but of yourself as a business major.

What is a *business major,* exactly? Compared to your liberal arts colleagues, you've had some fairly specific information delivered to you over your four years of college. You've had, for example, accounting, computers, marketing, and organizational behavior courses. You've had opportunities, through case studies, field projects, and presentations, to practice some of these skills. But, you know you're not an accountant, a computer scientists, a marketer, or an organization behaviorist. What are you, then?

Think of a business major as a college graduate who has had broad exposure to all the elements that go into making up the various aspects of human economic endeavor. You've looked at all these various areas in a general way and have an equally general understanding of how these areas interact, yet you are not a specialist and probably don't feel particularly skilled in any business activity.

The jobs outlined in the five career paths covered in *Great Jobs for Business Majors* will provide an overview of some promising areas of employment. As you read these chapters, think about which of these career areas appeals to you. The appeal base will be different for each person. For you, perhaps the most important factors are the skills demanded. Or the most important factors may be the kinds of good or services you'd be working with or the activities you'd be performing. These are all good reasons for pursuing a particular career pathway.

Business majors like yourself often find comfort during their college years in thinking that their major is the most realistic—the most *real world* of all the possible college majors. Business majors will often boast "I'm learning something useful. I can go right to work."

The reality is that most organizations now are working so hard to stay competitive that the new college graduates—even business majors—can represent a time drain these employers cannot afford in the current economic marketplace. Training takes time and money—valuable commodities in today's world. These organizations would prefer to hire individuals who will be fast off the mark and making a contribution immediately.

Of all the many majors available to a college student, business has long held the promise of being the most practical course of study, the major which offers the most real-world applications in the classroom, with course offerings which prepare students for the fastest and easiest transition to jobs after graduation.

Fortunately, much of that thinking remains sound; however, there have been profound and far-reaching changes going on in the business world. The United States, once a leader in electronics manufacture, has seen much of that authority shift to the Pacific Rim. The global economy is also a shrinking economy, and everyone is seeking markets wherever they can be found.

Add to these changes important shifts in the demographics of the global workplace, bringing diversity of ethnicity, gender, and the racial spectrum to all aspects of business. This puts new emphasis and awareness on communication skills, sensitivity, discretion, cultural appreciation, styles of leadership, and team membership skills.

Though some of our newest business texts cover these issues and subjects, the workplace is for many the schoolroom for learning about and coping with the volatility of a changing job climate and workplace environment.

Business education is about content. In the course of a standard four-year business program, you've been exposed to some marketing, economics, management principles, accounting, and organizational behavior. You'll need all of this information. But one area your studies will not explore is how you make your way from the graduation platform into a job that is designed to fit your education and preparation. And, today, more than ever, that journey from classroom to employer is more challenging, more competitive, and less predictable than ever before.

Just look in yesterday's newspaper or at tonight's network news and you will see examples of the way things are changing. Large financial institutions are merging into mega-sized financial institutions. Hospital corporations join to form comprehensive medical-care networks. Smaller colleges become subsumed into larger university organizations. As part of merging, redundancies in positions occur and large numbers (often thousands) of employees lose their jobs. Most of these job losses affect the middle-management level of employee—college educated business majors. As a new college graduate, you need to keep in mind that you are in competition for jobs with these folks.

Plotting a Course for Success

It's easy to be discouraged. You need to remember that one of the best ways to succeed is to anticipate problems and design a strategy for success. If you're determined to surmount these challenges, you'll appreciate the following tips:

1. Don't Rest on Your Major.

One of the most important and continuing changes in the business world today is the trimming down of staff size. Organizations are becoming leaner, and each employee is expected to wear many hats and have diverse skills. Certainly in organizations experiencing a downsizing or merger, the employees who survive personnel cuts most likely are those who can offer the most talent to the firm.

Choosing a marketing, or management, or economics major has put you on a certain educational path. Marketing majors usually only have the basic accounting courses. Management majors may take more math courses than marketing majors. Economics majors certainly receive more economic theory than accounting students. Sometimes, certain business majors are selected to avoid certain courses that are perceived as more difficult. But your required curriculum will not serve as an excuse to an employer who needs you to know more than a little bit about each of these areas.

College has all this knowledge and training in one location. You won't have that luxury again. Take advantage of it, and don't assume your major is a complete meal ticket. Sample other areas of business, and become a well-rounded business student, not just a declared major!

2. Do You Have an Achilles' Heel?

We all have weak spots—areas we feel less than confident about in our abilities. For some, it may be statistics; for others, the analytical skills demanded in interpreting an annual report; for still others, grasping the macroeconomic concepts necessary to make sense of forecasts of Gross National Product, the stock market, or the balance of international trade.

Every addition to today's leaner workforce comes under intense scrutiny and is competing for that position not only with other recent college graduates but with scores of older, more experienced workers as well. You'll feel better about yourself and stronger as a contender if you take steps now, while you're in college, to address these gaps in your education. For those areas in which you are weak, take a general course, ask a professor to recommend some good reading, or seek tutorial assistance from a senior-level student. Do whatever it takes to avoid finding yourself in a situation someday where you'd need to apologize for your ignorance.

3. Use the Classroom as Your Training Ground.

Reading this book is one indication you want to be prepared for the job search. You realize it's going to be rough, and you want to be ready. But the job search is really only the first step in testing your intellectual and personal skills. These days, the job itself can be a continuing exercise in thinking creatively, overcoming challenges, and responding positively to adverse conditions. As Oscar Wilde said,

"In this world there are only two tragedies. One is not getting what one wanted, and the other is getting it."

Wilde realized that we often put so much emphasis on our desire for something that we fail to think carefully about holding on to it. You can't breathe easier once you've got your job. You need to keep learning, meeting deadlines, improving your performance so you remain a valuable employee, deserving of increased responsibility and trust and pay.

Don't wait until the rigors of the job search are staring you in the face. You have the best practice conditions available to you right now. How many of us have sat passively in the classroom, missing opportunity after opportunity to test our thinking, to learn to get our information right, and to present our arguments? Class participation is a superb beginning for the give and take of the world of business. It will teach you to think before you speak, respond evenly and calmly to challenges to your thinking, and to listen and to appreciate the ideas of others. Taking advantage of these classroom opportunities for personal growth may be one of the easiest and yet most important steps you could take to ensure job success!

Treat your teachers as your bosses. Practice your interaction. Ask questions and clarify instructions. Stop by their offices and get to know them outside the classroom. Try and grasp their philosophy of teaching. Let them get to know you. It's good practice for supervisor/employee relations. Such interaction also creates a good basis for letters of reference.

Treat fellow students as colleagues or fellow employees. Make contact with your classmates. Practice and refine your social skills. Your classmates are similar to some of the people you'll be working alongside, and you have a perfect opportunity to develop ease and confidence meeting and learning from all the people who populate your classrooms. Take any group work seriously and realize that any difficulties concerning meeting times, assignments, or leadership roles aren't any different than those you'll encounter on the job. Practice your group skills and contributions now in class for real success in work groups later.

4. Meet Businesspeople.

Don't let your job interviews be your first serious contact with businesspeople. Make the most of your business faculty and their contacts and your career office with their database of alumni in order to meet businesspeople *while* you're studying business. There are many solid reasons why meeting practicing business professionals during your college years is a smart move. You can meet men and women of all ages and backgrounds with a variety of experience, and many will be willing to share those experiences. You'll have a chance to appreciate the diversity present in the world of business and possibly discover some new role models for your own career plans.

5. By All Means, an Internship.

There's no question that an internship is easier said than done. Most are un-paid, and that presents real challenges with the high cost of college today. Many students simply feel they cannot afford to not work for pay during the summer or other breaks from school. Think about this, however: giving up some income now can pay real dividends at graduation time. Many, many internships turn into real jobs for graduates. For others, the internship gives them deeper, more concrete insights into their own skills and an appreciation of the roles they can play in an organization. They are apt to find it easier to relate to people interviewing them, they have more to say, and, as a result of their internship, more to offer. They get hired!

Internships often require a relocation. If you live in a rural area or go to college in a non-metropolitan area, nearby internships will be scarce. The greatest concentration of internships tend to be in and around metropolitan areas where there are more organizations that can afford to train temporary, non-paid additions to their staffs and provide meaningful work for them. You may have to seek the hospitality of a relative or one of your parent's friends or even seek inexpensive temporary housing in order to put yourself where the internships are located. The payoff still applies.

Finding and applying for internships is a monumental task, though not as difficult as finding your first job. Not all good internships are published in directories. Information on some arrive in your business department or career office on broadsheets. Check with both places as well as at your college library. Expect to write many, many cover letters and mail them out with your resume, and be sure and do it early. Many summer internships have January or February application deadlines.

Expect to receive requests for transcripts (both official and unofficial) or requests to complete formal applications that may include essay writing about intent or goals. All of this correspondence must be perfect, because in most cases, interns are chosen on the basis of the written materials submitted as well as phone interviews. Your written work makes your first impression.

The competitiveness of the internships today is good practice and mirrors the competitiveness of the job market in general. Books such as *Internships 96* and *The 100 Best Internships* detail the previous year's competition. Some internships receive 500 applications for three or four available internship spots.

Expect a well-chosen internship experience to stay with you for the rest of your life. That summer or term in an advertising agency, public relations firms, corporate office, government agency, or industrial site will stay with you and become part of your experiential base as long as you are in business. Internships represent a smart move for your future.

SETTING SAIL FOR A BRIGHT FUTURE

We've examined how business has changed and continues to change and the implications of that for you as a business major.

You now understand the responsibility you have to make the most of your remaining college years, and you have some specific techniques to use for that. Some people say college isn't the real world and you can kind of float along, just treading water. I guarantee if you get out and meet some recent alumni of your school, they will assure you that college has the potential for being as real a world as you want to make it and that it can be an important aspect of your preparation for a business career.

Perhaps you are reading this as a junior or even a senior approaching graduation. Your most important goal right now is determining a strategy for finding that job. How do you go about that, considering all you've learned about the changing climate of business?

1. Realize You'll Have Many Careers and Plan for That.

You've seen all the warning signs that, regardless of how talented you are, shifts in employers and employee bases do occur and some people must move on. Those that have the least trouble moving do the following things.

Watch trends. If you're in advertising and you see an increasing use of CD–ROM and interactive advertising on computer, it's a clear sign not only that you need to be developing some skills in that area but that future growth will probably occur in firms that produce those kinds of products and materials. Stay abreast of changes in your field so you have some ready reference points if you do need to jump-start your career.

Understand your needs. Every time we make a job change, we have to address issues such as geographic location, housing options, pay levels, duties and responsibilities, our interest and belief in the nature of the work, our consumption patterns and a thousand other issues that profoundly impact who we are and how we live. Begin to appreciate and understand what you need and what is important to you. That will make job choices and job shifts easier.

As a college career counselor who sees many adult alumni clients, I am too familiar with the economic realities of the job search. The most common lament I hear is "I haven't saved enough money to make a job change" and "I have so much debt I can't afford to take any less with a new job, no matter how great that new job is." These are sad comments on a situation that is easily remedied by reducing consumption and increasing savings.

It is wise to keep your needs as simple as possible and to make sure one of your goals is to have some financial security, for any number of reasons.

Stay alert to the difference between contextual and portable skills. Contextual skills are those understandings, techniques, vocabularies, relationships, and factors directly related to your business but of little value outside your field of work. Portable skills are those talents, knowledge, and techniques that can move from job to job. You need both to succeed, but you want to pay attention to the balance.

If you're doing fund-raising for a major conservation group, everything you know about wetlands preservation, federal legislation to preserve wildlife habitats, public access to wetlands, and influential people in the conservation movement are all part of your contextual base for expertise in this area. You can't raise money and talk authoritatively to potential donors unless you know this context and know it well. However, if you lose your job for whatever reason, unless you stay in conservation, it will not be the contextual skills that are important, it will be the portable skills.

The portable skills are your fund-raising ability, your ability to do special event planning and promotion, your publicity and public relations talents, your "friend-raising" techniques and success stories, your ability to direct volunteer efforts and provide meaningful work assignments for them, your talent at creating attractive brochures, letters, and other public communications, and your presentation skills. These talents and techniques are those that you will carry from job to job, no matter what the particular context of that job.

Pay attention to what you're learning on the job, and maintain a good balance between context and portability. If your firm is offering training in database management, you might not think of taking advantage of it because you aren't currently using databases. However, this kind of training is a portable skill and may be a valuable credential on your resume at some future point. Take advantage of your firm's training opportunities and add to your portable skills. You'll be a more talented employee and a more viable job applicant in the future.

PART ONE

THE JOB SEARCH

CHAPTER ONE

THE SELF-ASSESSMENT

elf-assessment is the process by which you begin to acknowledge your own particular blend of education, experiences, values, needs, and goals. It provides the foundation for career planning and the entire job search process. Self-assessment involves looking inward and asking yourself what can sometimes prove to be difficult questions. This self-examination should lead to an intimate understanding of your personal traits, your personal values, your consumption patterns and economic needs, your longer-term goals, your skill base, your preferred skills, and your underdeveloped skills.

You come to the self-assessment process knowing yourself well in some of these areas, but you may still be uncertain about other aspects. You may be well aware of your consumption patterns, but have you spent much time specifically identifying your longer-term goals, or your personal values as they relate to work? No matter what level of self-assessment you have undertaken to date, it is now time to clarify all of these issues and questions as they relate to the job search.

The knowledge you gain in the self-assessment process will guide the rest of your job search. In this book, you will learn about all of the following tasks:

❑ Writing resumes

❑ Exploring possible job titles

❑ Identifying employment sites

❑ Networking

❑ Interviewing

❑ Following up

❑ Evaluating job offers

In each of these steps, you will rely on and return often to the understanding gained through your self-assessment. Any individual seeking employment must be able and willing to express to potential recruiters and interviewers throughout the job search these facets of his or her personality. This communication allows you to show the world who you are so that together with employers you can determine whether there will be a workable match with a given job or career path.

How to Conduct a Self-Assessment

The self-assessment process goes on naturally all the time. People ask you to clarify what you mean, or you make a purchasing decision, or you begin a new relationship. You react to the world and the world reacts to you. How you understand these interactions and any changes you might make because of them are part of the natural process of self-discovery. There is, however, a more comprehensive and efficient way to approach self-assessment with regard to employment.

Because self-assessment can become a complex exercise, we have distilled it into a seven-step process that provides an effective basis for undertaking a job search. The seven steps include the following:

1. Understanding your personal traits

2. Identifying your personal values

3. Calculating your economic needs

4. Exploring your longer-term goals

5. Enumerating your skill base

6. Recognizing your preferred skills

7. Assessing skills needing further development

As you work through your self-assessment, you might want to create a worksheet similar to the one shown in Exhibit 1.1. Or you might want to keep a journal of the thoughts you have as you undergo this process. There will be many opportunities to revise your self-assessment as you start down the path of seeking a career.

STEP 1 Understanding Your Personal Traits

Each person has a unique personality that he or she brings to the job search process. Gaining a better understanding of your personal traits can help you evaluate job and career choices. Identifying these traits, then finding employment that allows you to draw on at least some of them can create a rewarding and fulfilling work experience. If potential employment doesn't allow you to use these preferred traits, it is important to decide whether you can find other ways to express them or

Exhibit 1.1

Self-Assessment Worksheet

STEP 1. Understand Your Personal Traits

The personal traits that describe me are:
(Include all of the words that describe you.)

The ten personal traits that most accurately describe me are:
(List these ten traits.)

STEP 2. Identify Your Personal Values

Working conditions that are important to me include:
(List working conditions that would have to exist for you to accept a position.)

The values that go along with my working conditions are:
(Write down the values that correspond to each working condition.)

Some additional values I've decided to include are:
(List those values you identify as you conduct this job search.)

STEP 3. Calculate Your Economic Needs

My estimated minimum annual salary requirement is:
(Write the salary you have calculated based on your budget.)

Starting salaries for the positions I'm considering are:
(List the name of each job you are considering and the associated starting salary.)

STEP 4. Explore Your Longer-Term Goals

My thoughts on longer-term goals right now are:
(Jot down some of your longer-term goals as you know them right now.)

continued

continued

STEP 5. Enumerate Your Skill Base

The general skills I possess are:
(List the skills that underlie tasks you are able to complete.)

The specific skills I possess are:
(List more technical or specific skills that you possess and indicate your level of expertise.)

General and specific skills that I want to promote to employers for the jobs I'm considering are:
(List general and specific skills for each type of job you are considering.)

STEP 6. Recognize Your Preferred Skills

Skills that I would like to use on the job include:
(List skills that you hope to use on the job, and indicate how often you'd like to use them.)

STEP 7. Assess Skills Needing Further Development

Some skills that I'll need to acquire for the jobs I'm considering include:
(Write down skills listed in job advertisements or job descriptions that you don't currently possess.)

I believe I can build these skills by:
(Describe how you plan to acquire these skills.)

whether you would be better off not considering this type of job. Interests and hobbies pursued outside of work hours can be one way to use personal traits you don't have an opportunity to draw on in your work. For example, if you consider yourself an outgoing person and the kinds of jobs you are examining allow little contact with other people, you may be able to achieve the level of interaction that is comfortable for you outside of your work setting. If such a compromise seems impractical or otherwise unsatisfactory, you probably should explore only jobs that provide the interaction you want and need on the job.

Many young adults who are not very confident about their attractiveness to employers will downplay their need for income. They will say, "Money is not all that important if I love my work." But if you begin to document exactly what you need for housing, transportation, insurance, clothing, food, and utilities, you will begin to understand that some jobs cannot meet your financial needs and it doesn't matter how wonderful the job is. If you have to worry each payday about bills and other financial obligations, you won't be very effective on the job. Begin now to be honest with yourself about your needs.

Inventorying Your Personal Traits. Begin the self-assessment process by creating an inventory of your personal traits. Using the list in Exhibit 1.2, decide which of these personal traits describe you.

Exhibit 1.2

Personal Traits

Active	Critical	Generous
Accurate	Curious	Gentle
Adaptable	Daring	Good-natured
Adventurous	Decisive	Helpful
Affectionate	Deliberate	Honest
Aggressive	Detail-oriented	Humorous
Ambitious	Determined	Idealistic
Analytical	Discreet	Imaginative
Appreciative	Dominant	Impersonal
Artistic	Eager	Independent
Brave	Easygoing	Individualistic
Businesslike	Efficient	Industrious
Calm	Emotional	Informal
Capable	Empathetic	Innovative
Caring	Energetic	Intellectual
Cautious	Excitable	Intelligent
Cheerful	Expressive	Introverted
Clean	Extroverted	Intuitive
Competent	Fair-minded	Inventive
Confident	Farsighted	Jovial
Conscientious	Feeling	Just
Conservative	Firm	Kind
Considerate	Flexible	Liberal
Cool	Formal	Likable
Cooperative	Friendly	Logical
Courageous	Future-oriented	

continued

continued

Loyal	Precise	Serious
Mature	Principled	Sincere
Methodical	Private	Sociable
Meticulous	Productive	Spontaneous
Mistrustful	Progressive	Strong
Modest	Quick	Strong-minded
Motivated	Quiet	Structured
Objective	Rational	Subjective
Observant	Realistic	Tactful
Open-minded	Receptive	Thorough
Opportunistic	Reflective	Thoughtful
Optimistic	Relaxed	Tolerant
Organized	Reliable	Trusting
Original	Reserved	Trustworthy
Outgoing	Resourceful	Truthful
Patient	Responsible	Understanding
Peaceable	Reverent	Unexcitable
Personable	Sedentary	Uninhibited
Persuasive	Self-confident	Verbal
Pleasant	Self-controlled	Versatile
Poised	Self-disciplined	Wholesome
Polite	Sensible	Wise
Practical	Sensitive	

Focusing on Selected Personal Traits. Of all the traits you identified from the list in Exhibit 1.2, select the ten you believe most accurately describe you. If you are having a difficult time deciding, think about which words people who know you well would use to describe you. Keep track of these ten traits.

Considering Your Personal Traits in the Job Search Process. As you begin exploring jobs and careers, watch for matches between your personal traits and the job descriptions you read. Some jobs will require many personal traits you know you possess, and others will not seem to match those traits.

....

Working in sales, for example, will draw upon your reserves of creativity, poise, and sociability. Sales is essentially problem-solving, not persuasion. Your ability to listen attentively, analyze problems, and perscribe solutions will be far more important personal traits for success than fast-talking and pressure tactics. Professional sales calls for self-discipline and excellent time management skills since you often work autonomously. Sales positions for business graduates often require the mastery of sophisticated product information. Attention to detail and memory are also important attributes for this work.

....

Your ability to respond to changing conditions, decision-making ability, productivity, creativity, and verbal skills all have a bearing on your success in and enjoyment of your work life. To better guarantee success, be sure to take the time needed to understand these traits in yourself.

STEP 2   Identifying Your Personal Values

Your personal values affect every aspect of your life, including employment, and they develop and change as you move through life. Values can be defined as principles that we hold in high regard, qualities that are important and desirable to us. Some values aren't ordinarily connected to work (love, beauty, color, light, marriage, family, or religion), and others are (autonomy, cooperation, effectiveness, achievement, knowledge, and security). Our values determine, in part, the level of satisfaction we feel in a particular job.

Defining Acceptable Working Conditions.   One facet of employment is the set of working conditions that must exist for someone to consider taking a job.

Each of us would probably create a unique list of acceptable working conditions, but items that might be included on many people's lists are the amount of money you would need to be paid, how far you are willing to drive or travel, the amount of freedom you want in determining your own schedule, whether you would be working with people or data or things, and the types of tasks you would be willing to do. Your conditions might include statements of working conditions you will *not* accept; for example, you might not be willing to work at night or on weekends or holidays.

If you were offered a job tomorrow, what conditions would have to exist for you to realistically consider accepting the position? Take some time and make a list of these conditions.

Realizing Associated Values.   Your list of working conditions can be used to create an inventory of your values relating to jobs and careers you are exploring. For example, if one of your conditions stated that you wanted to earn at least $25,000 per year, the associated value would be financial gain. If another condition was that you wanted to work with a friendly group of people, the value that goes along with

---

Exhibit 1.3

Work Values

Achievement	Development	Physical activity
Advancement	Effectiveness	Power
Adventure	Excitement	Precision
Attainment	Fast pace	Prestige
Authority	Financial gain	Privacy
Autonomy	Helping	Profit
Belonging	Humor	Recognition
Challenge	Improvisation	Risk
Change	Independence	Security
Communication	Influencing others	Self-expression
Community	Intellectual stimulation	Solitude
Competition	Interaction	Stability
Completion	Knowledge	Status
Contribution	Leading	Structure
Control	Mastery	Supervision
Cooperation	Mobility	Surroundings
Creativity	Moral fulfillment	Time freedom
Decision making	Organization	Variety

---

that might be belonging or interaction with people. Exhibit 1.3 provides a list of commonly held values that relate to the work environment; use it to create your own list of personal values.

Relating Your Values to the World of Work. As you read the job descriptions in this book and in other suggested resources, think about the values associated with that position.

....

> For example, in sales, your duties may include calling on clients, explaining products and/or services you offer, arranging delivery, and/or installing and providing follow-up services after the sale.

....

If you were thinking about a career in this field, or any other field you're exploring, at least some of the associated values should match those you extracted from your list of working conditions. Take a second look at any values that don't match up. How important are they to you? What will happen if they are not satisfied on the job? Can you incorporate those personal values elsewhere? Your answers need to be brutally honest. As you continue your exploration, be sure to add to your list any additional values that occur to you.

STEP 3 Calculating Your Economic Needs

Each of us grew up in an environment that provided for certain basic needs, such as food and shelter, and, to varying degrees, other needs that we now consider basic, such as cable TV, reading materials, or an automobile. Needs such as privacy, space, and quiet, which at first glance may not appear to be monetary needs, may add to housing expenses and so should be considered as you examine your economic needs. For example, if you place a high value on a large, open living space for yourself, it would be difficult to satisfy that need without an associated high housing cost, especially in a densely populated city environment.

As you prepare to move into the world of work and become responsible for meeting your own basic needs, it is important to consider the salary you will need to be able to afford a satisfying standard of living. The three-step process outlined here will help you plan a budget, which in turn will allow you to evaluate the various career choices and geographic locations you are considering. The steps include (1) developing a realistic budget, (2) examining starting salaries, and (3) using a cost-of-living index.

Developing a Realistic Budget. Each of us has certain expectations for the kind of life-style we want to maintain. In order to begin the process of defining your economic needs, it will be helpful to determine what you expect to spend on routine monthly expenses. These expenses include housing, food, transportation, entertainment, utilities, loan repayments, and revolving charge accounts. A worksheet that details many of these expenses is shown in Exhibit 1.4. You may not currently spend for certain items, but you probably will have to once you begin supporting yourself. As you develop this budget, be generous in your estimates, but keep in mind any items that could be

---

Exhibit 1.4

Estimated Monthly Expenses Worksheet

		Could Reduce Spending? (Yes/No)
Cable	$ _____	_____
Child care	_____	_____
Clothing	_____	_____

continued

continued

		Could Reduce Spending? (Yes/No)
Educational loan repayment	_____	_____
Entertainment	_____	_____
Food	_____	_____
At home	_____	_____
Meals out	_____	_____
Gifts	_____	_____
Housing		
Rent/mortgage	_____	_____
Insurance	_____	_____
Property taxes	_____	_____
Medical insurance	_____	_____
Reading materials		
Newspapers	_____	_____
Magazines	_____	_____
Books	_____	_____
Revolving loans/charges	_____	_____
Savings	_____	_____
Telephone	_____	_____
Transportation		
Auto payment	_____	_____
Insurance	_____	_____
Parking	_____	_____
—or		
Cab/train/bus fare	_____	_____
Utilities		
Electric	_____	_____
Gas	_____	_____
Water/sewer	_____	_____
Vacations	_____	_____
Miscellaneous expense 1	_____	_____
Expense: _____		
Miscellaneous expense 2	_____	_____
Expense: _____		
Miscellaneous expense 3	_____	_____
Expense: _____		

TOTAL MONTHLY EXPENSES: _____

YEARLY EXPENSES (Monthly expenses x 12): _____

INCREASE TO INCLUDE TAXES (Yearly expenses x 1.35): _____ =
MINIMUM ANNUAL SALARY REQUIREMENT _____

reduced or eliminated. If you are not sure about the cost of a certain item, talk with family or friends who would be able to give you a realistic estimate.

If this is new or difficult for you, start to keep a log of expenses right now. You may be surprised at how much you actually spend each month for food or stamps or magazines. Household expenses and personal grooming items can often loom very large in a budget, as can auto repairs or home maintenance.

Income taxes must also be taken into consideration when examining salary requirements. State and local taxes vary by location, so it is difficult to calculate exactly the effect of taxes on the amount of income you need to generate. To roughly estimate the gross income necessary to generate your minimum annual salary requirement, multiply the minimum salary you have calculated (see Exhibit 1.4) by a factor of 1.35. The resulting figure will be an approximation of what your gross income would need to be, given your estimated expenses.

Examining Starting Salaries. Starting salaries for each of the career tracks are provided throughout this book. These salary figures can be used in conjunction with the cost-of-living index (discussed in the next section) to determine whether you would be able to meet your basic economic needs in a given geographic location.

Using a Cost-of-Living Index. If you are thinking about trying to get a job in a geographic region other than the one where you now live, understanding differences in the cost of living will help you come to a more informed decision about making a move. By using a cost-of-living index, you can compare salaries offered and the cost of living in different locations with what you know about the salaries offered and the cost of living in your present location.

Many variables are used to calculate the cost-of-living index, including housing expenses, groceries, utilities, transportation, health care, clothing, entertainment, local income taxes, and local sales taxes. Cost-of-living indices can be found in many resources, such as *Equal Employment Opportunity Bimonthly, Places Rated Almanac,* or *The Best Towns in America.* They are constantly being recalculated based on changes in costs.

....

If you lived in Cleveland, Ohio, for example, and you were interested in working as a sales representative for a consumer goods firm, you would earn, on average, $20,784 annually. But let's say you're also thinking about moving to either New York, Los Angeles, or Denver. You know you can live on $20,784 in Cleveland, but you want to be able to equal that salary in the other locations you're considering. How much will you need to earn in those locations to do this? Figuring the cost of living for each city will show you.

Let's walk through this example. In any cost-of-living index, the number 100 represents the national average cost of living, and each city is assigned an index number based on current prices in that city for the items included in the index (housing, food, etc.). In the index we used, New York was assigned the number 213.3, Los Angeles' index was 124.6, Denver's was 100.0, and Cleveland's index was 114.3. In other words, it costs more than twice as much to live in New York as it does in Denver. We can set up a table to determine exactly how much you would have to earn in each of these cities to have the same buying power that you have in Cleveland.

Job: Sales Representative

CITY	INDEX	EQUIVALENT SALARY
$\dfrac{\text{New York}}{\text{Cleveland}}$	$\dfrac{213.3}{114.3}$	x $20,784 = $38,785 in New York
$\dfrac{\text{Los Angeles}}{\text{Cleveland}}$	$\dfrac{124.6}{114.3}$	x $20,784 = $22,656 in Los Angeles
$\dfrac{\text{Denver}}{\text{Cleveland}}$	$\dfrac{100.0}{114.3}$	x $20,784 = $18,199 in Denver

---

You would have to earn $38,785 in New York, $22,656 in Los Angeles, and $18,199 in Denver to match the buying power of $20,784 in Cleveland.

If you would like to determine whether it's financially worthwhile to make any of these moves, one more piece of information is needed: the salaries of sales representatives in these other cities. The *American Salaries and Wages Survey* (3rd edition) reports the following average salary information for sales representatives in their 1995 edition:

Region	Annual Salary	Salary Equivalent to Ohio	Change In Buying Power
Mid Atlantic (including New York)	$29,030	$38,785	–$9,755
West (including Los Angeles)	$23,070	$22,656	+$ 414
Mountain Plains (including Denver)	$22,862	$18,199	+$3,863
Midwest (including Cleveland)	$20,784	—	—

If you moved to New York City and secured employment as a sales representative in consumer goods, you would not be able to maintain a lifestyle similar to the one you led in Cleveland; in fact, you would almost have to add almost fifty percent to your income to maintain a similar lifestyle in New York. The same would not be true for a move to Los Angeles or Denver. You would increase your buying power given the rate of pay and cost of living in these cities.

....

You can work through a similar exercise for any type of job you are considering and for many locations when current salary information is available. It will be worth your time to undertake this analysis if you are seriously considering a relocation. By doing so you will be able to make an informed choice.

STEP 4 Exploring Your Longer-Term Goals

There is no question that when we first begin working, our goals are to use our skills and education in a job that will reward us with employment, income, and status relative to the preparation we brought with us to this position. If we are not being paid as much as we feel we should for our level of education, or if job demands don't provide the intellectual stimulation we had hoped for, we experience unhappiness and, as a result, often seek other employment.

Most jobs we consider "good" are those that fulfill our basic "lower-level" needs of security, food, clothing, shelter, income, and productive work. But even when our basic needs are met and our jobs are secure and productive, we as individuals are constantly changing. As we change, the demands and expectations we place on our jobs may change. Fortunately, some jobs grow and change with us, and this explains why some people are happy throughout many years in a job.

But more often people are bigger than the jobs they fill. We have more goals and needs than any job could fulfill. These are "higher-level" needs of self-esteem, companionship, affection, and an increasing desire to feel we are employing ourselves in the most effective way possible. Not all of these higher-level needs can be fulfilled through employment, but for as long as we are employed, we increasingly demand that our jobs play their part in moving us along the path to fulfillment.

Another obvious but important fact is that we change as we mature. Although our jobs also have the potential for change, they may not change as frequently or as markedly as we do. There are increasingly fewer one-job, one-employer careers; we must think about a work future that may involve voluntary or forced moves from employer to employer. Because of that very real possibility, we need to take advantage of the opportunities in each position we hold to acquire skills and competencies that will keep us viable and attractive as employees in a job market that is not only increasingly technology/computer dependent, but also is populated with more and more small, self-transforming organizations rather than the large, seemingly stable organizations of the past.

It may be difficult in the early stages of the job search to determine whether the path you are considering can meet these longer-term goals. Reading about career paths and individual career histories in your field can be very helpful in this regard. Meeting and talking with individuals further along in their careers can be enlightening as well. Older workers can provide valuable guidance on "self-managing" your career, which will become an increasingly valuable skill in the future. Some of these ideas may seem remote as you read this now, but you should be able to appreciate the need to ensure that you are growing, developing valuable new skills, and researching other employers who might be interested in your particular skills package.

....

If you are considering a position in retailing, you would gain a better perspective on this career if you could talk to an entry-level associate buyer, a more senior and experienced department head or branch store manager, and finally, a vice president for sales merchandising or store operations who has a considerable work history in the retail sector. Each will have a different perspective, unique concerns, and an individual set of value priorities.

....

STEP 5   Enumerating Your Skill Base

In terms of the job search, skills can be thought of as capabilities that can be developed in school, at work, or by volunteering and then used in specific job settings. Many studies have documented the kinds of skills that employers seek in entry-level applicants. For example, some of the most desired skills for individuals interested in the teaching profession include the ability to interact effectively with students one on one, to manage a classroom, to adapt to varying situations as necessary, and to get involved in school activities. Business employers have also identified important qualities, including enthusiasm for the employer's product or service, a businesslike mind, the ability to follow written or verbal instructions, the ability to demonstrate self-control, the confidence to suggest new ideas, the ability to communicate with all members of a group, awareness of cultural differences, and loyalty, to name just a few. You will find that many of these skills are also in the repertoire of qualities demanded in your college major.

In order to be successful in obtaining any given job, you must be able to demonstrate that you possess a certain mix of skills that will allow you to carry out the duties required by that job. This skill mix will vary a great deal from job to job; to determine the skills necessary for the jobs you are seeking, you can read job advertisements or more generic job descriptions, such as those found later in this book. If you want to be effective in the job search, you must directly show employers that you possess the skills needed to be successful in filling the position. These skills will initially be described on your resume and then discussed again during the interview process.

Skills are either general or specific. General skills are those that are developed throughout the college years by taking classes, being employed, and getting involved in other related activities such as volunteer work or campus organizations. General skills include the ability to read and write, to perform computations, to think critically, and to communicate effectively. Specific skills are also acquired on the job and in the classroom, but they allow you to complete tasks that require specialized knowledge. Computer programming, drafting, language translating, and copy editing are just a few examples of specific skills that may relate to a given job.

In order to develop a list of skills relevant to employers, you must first identify the general skills you possess, then list specific skills you have to offer, and, finally, examine which of these skills employers are seeking.

Identifying Your General Skills.   Because you possess or will possess a college degree, employers will assume that you can read and write, perform certain basic computations, think critically, and communicate effectively. Employers will want to see that you have acquired these skills, and they will want to know which additional general skills you possess.

One way to begin identifying skills is to write an experiential diary. An experiential diary lists all the tasks you were responsible for completing for each job you've held and then outlines the skills required to do those tasks. You may list several skills for any given task. This diary allows you to distinguish between the tasks you performed and the underlying skills required to complete those tasks. Here's an example:

Tasks	Skills
Answering telephone	Effective use of language, clear diction, ability to direct inquiries, ability to solve problems
Waiting on tables	Poise under conditions of time and pressure, speed, accuracy, good memory, simultaneous completion of tasks, sales skills

For each job or experience you have participated in, develop a worksheet based on the example shown here. On a resume, you may want to describe these skills rather than simply listing tasks. Skills are easier for the employer to appreciate, especially when your experience is very different from the employment you are seeking. In addition to helping you identify general skills, this experiential diary will prepare you to speak more effectively in an interview about the qualifications you possess.

Identifying Your Specific Skills. It may be easier to identify your specific skills, because you can definitely say whether you can speak other languages, program a computer, draft a map or diagram, or edit a document using appropriate symbols and terminology.

Using your experiential diary, identify the points in your history where you learned how to do something very specific, and decide whether you have a beginning, intermediate, or advanced knowledge of how to use that particular skill. Right now, be sure to list *every* specific skill you have, and don't consider whether you like using the skill. Write down a list of specific skills you have acquired and the level of competence you possess—beginning, intermediate, or advanced.

Relating Your Skills to Employers. You probably have thought about a couple of different jobs you might be interested in obtaining, and one way to begin relating the general and specific skills you possess to potential employer needs is to read actual advertisements for these types of positions (see Part II for resources listing actual job openings).

....

For example, you might be interested in working as a financial analyst for an investment banking firm, prior to returning to graduate school for your MBA (Masters in

Business Administration). A typical job listing might read, "conduct financial analysis, economic evaluations, and profitability studies pertaining to new business opportunities. Bachelors degree in business and excellent PC skills required. Experience with venture financing preferred." If you then used any one of a number of general sources of information that described the job of financial analyst, you would find additional information. Financial analysts also track and report on competitive information, manage multiple projects simultaneously, interpret financial data, and advise management about trends.

Begin building a comprehensive list of required skills with the first job description you read. Exploring advertisements for and descriptions of several types of related positions will reveal an important core of skills that are necessary for obtaining the type of work you're interested in. In building this list, include both general and specific skills.

Following is a sample list of skills needed to be successful as a financial analyst in investment banking. These items were extracted from general resources and actual job listings.

Job: Financial Analyst/Investment Banking

General Skills	Specific Skills
Accounting	Estimate company
Reading	worth
Gathering information	Track market data
Decision making	Analyze income
Meeting deadlines	statements
Attending meetings	Evaluate alternatives
Collaborating on	Generate color
projects	graphics
Entering data into	Use annual reports
computer	Generate ratios
Writing	Master various
	software packages
	Edit presentations

On separate sheets of paper, try to generate a comprehensive list of required skills for at least one job you are considering.

> The list of general skills that you develop for a given career path would be valuable for any number of jobs you might apply for. Many of the specific skills would also be transferable to other types of positions. For example, tracking market data is a required skill for market analysts, consultants, product managers, and would be helpful for marketing managers, as well.
>
> ....

Now review the list of skills you developed and check off those skills that *you know you possess* and that are required for jobs you are considering. You should refer to these specific skills on the resume that you write for this type of job. See Chapter 2 for details on resume writing.

STEP 6   Recognizing Your Preferred Skills

In the previous section, you developed a comprehensive list of skills that relate to particular career paths that are of interest to you. You can now relate these to skills that you prefer to use. We all use a wide range of skills (some researchers say individuals have a repertoire of about 500 skills), but we may not be particularly interested in using all of them in our work. There may be some skills that come to us more naturally or that we use successfully time and time again and that we want to continue to use; these are best described as our preferred skills. For this exercise, use the list of skills that you developed for the previous section and decide which of them you are *most interested in using* in future work and how often you would like to use them. You might be interested in using some skills only occasionally, while others you would like to use more regularly. You probably also have skills that you hope you can use constantly.

As you examine job announcements, look for matches between this list of preferred skills and the qualifications described in the advertisements. These skills should be highlighted on your resume and discussed in job interviews.

STEP 7   Assessing Skills Needing Further Development

Previously you developed a list of general and specific skills required for given positions. You already possess some of these skills; those that remain to be developed are your underdeveloped skills.

If you are just beginning the job search, there may be gaps between the qualifications required for some of the jobs being considered and skills you possess. These are your underdeveloped skills. The thought of having to admit to and talk about these underdeveloped skills, especially in a job interview, is a frightening one. One way to put a healthy perspective on this subject is to target and relate your exploration of underdeveloped skills to the types of positions you are seeking. Recognizing these shortcomings and planning to overcome them with either on-the-job training or additional formal education can be a positive way to address the concept of underdeveloped skills.

On your worksheet or in your journal, make a list of up to five general or specific skills required for the positions you're interested in that you *don't currently possess*. For each item, list an idea you have for specific action you could take to acquire that skill. Do some brainstorming to come up with possible actions. If you have a hard time generating ideas, talk to people currently working in this type of position, professionals in your college career services office, trusted friends, family members, or members of related professional associations.

If, for example, you are interested in a job for which you don't have some specific required experience, you could locate training opportunities such as classes or workshops offered through a local college or university, community college, or club or association that would help you build the level of expertise you need for the job.

You might have noticed in this book that many excellent positions for your major demand computer skills. These computer skills were probably not part of your required academic preparation. While it is easy for the business world to see the direct link between oral and written communication and high technology, some college departments have been markedly reluctant to add this dimension to their curriculums. What can you do now? If you're still in college, take what computer courses you can before you graduate. If you've already graduated, look at evening programs, continuing education courses, or tutorial programs that may be available commercially. Developing a modest level of expertise will encourage you to be more confident in suggesting to potential employers that you can continue to add to your skill base on the job.

In Chapter 5 on interviewing, we will discuss in detail how to effectively address questions about underdeveloped skills. Generally speaking, though, employers want genuine answers to these types of questions. They want you to reveal "the real you," and they also want to see how you answer difficult questions. In taking the positive, targeted approach discussed above, you show the employer that you are willing to continue to learn and that you have a plan for strengthening your job qualifications.

USING YOUR SELF-ASSESSMENT

Exploring entry-level career options can be an exciting experience if you have good resources available and will take the time to use them. Can you effectively complete the following tasks?

1. Understand and relate your personality traits to career choices

2. Define your personal values

3. Determine your economic needs

4. Explore longer-term goals

5. Understand your skill base

6. Recognize your preferred skills

7. Express a willingness to improve on your underdeveloped skills

If so, then you can more meaningfully participate in the job search process by writing a more effective resume, finding job titles that represent work you are interested in doing, locating job sites that will provide the opportunity for you to use your strengths and skills, networking in an informed way, participating in focused interviews, getting the most out of follow-up contacts, and evaluating job offers to find those that create a good match between you and the employer. The remaining chapters guide you through these next steps in the job search process. For many job seekers, this process can take anywhere from three months to a year to implement. The time you will need to put into your job search will depend on the type of job you want and the geographic location where you'd like to work. Think of your effort as a job in itself, requiring you to set aside time each week to complete the needed work. Carefully undertaken efforts may reduce the time you need for your job search.

CHAPTER TWO

THE RESUME AND COVER LETTER

The task of writing a resume may seem overwhelming if you are unfamiliar with this type of document, but there are some easily understood techniques that can and should be used. This section was written to help you understand the purpose of the resume, the different types of resume formats available, and how to write the sections of information traditionally found on a resume. We will present examples and explanations that address questions frequently posed by people writing their first resume or updating an old resume.

Even within the formats and suggestions given below, however, there are infinite variations. True, most resumes follow one of the outlines suggested below, but you should feel free to adjust the resume to suit your needs and make it expressive of your life and experience.

WHY WRITE A RESUME?

The purpose of a resume is to convince an employer that you should be interviewed. You'll want to present enough information to show that you can make an immediate and valuable contribution to an organization. A resume is not an in-depth historical or legal document; later in the job search process you'll be asked to document your entire work history on an application form and attest to its validity. The resume should, instead, highlight relevant information pertaining directly to the organization that will receive the document or the type of position you are seeking.

We will discuss four types of resumes in this chapter: chronological resume, functional resume, targeted resume, and the broadcast letter. The reasons for using one type of resume over another and the typical format for each are addressed in the following sections.

THE CHRONOLOGICAL RESUME

The chronological resume is the most common of the various resume formats and therefore the format that employers are most used to receiving. This type of resume is easy to read and understand because it details the chronological progression of jobs you have held. (See Exhibit 2.1.) It begins with your most recent employment and works back in time. If you have a solid work history, or experience that provided growth and development in your duties and responsibilities, a chronological resume will highlight these achievements. The typical elements of a chronological resume include the heading, a career objective, educational background, employment experience, activities, and references.

The Heading

The heading consists of your name, address, and telephone number. Recently it has come to include fax numbers and electronic mail addresses as well. We suggest that you spell out your full name and type it in all capital letters in bold type. After all, *you* are the focus of the resume! If you have a current as well as a permanent address and you include both in the heading, be sure to indicate until what date your current address will be valid. The two-letter state abbreviation should be the only abbreviation that appears in your heading. Don't forget to include the zip code with your address and the area code with your telephone number.

The Objective

As you formulate the wording for this part of your resume, keep the following points in mind.

The Objective Focuses the Resume. Without a doubt, this is the most challenging part of the resume for most resume writers. Even for individuals who have quite firmly decided on a career path, it can be difficult to encapsulate all they want to say in one or two brief sentences. For job seekers who are unfocused or unclear about their intentions, trying to write this section can inhibit the entire resume writing process.

Recruiters tell us, time and again, that the objective creates a frame of reference for them. It helps them see how you express your goals and career focus. In

Exhibit 2.1

Chronological Resume

MARIANNE FLAMAND

Duchess Hall #801	2068 Lincoln
Indiana University	Montreal, P.Q.
Bloomington, IN 01234	H3H 1H9
(317) 555-1234	Canada
(until May 1996)	(514) 555-6798

OBJECTIVE

Entry-level position in healthcare administration. Special interest in managed care sales and contracting.

EDUCATION

Bachelor of Science Degree in Business Management
Indiana University, Bloomington, Indiana, May 1996
Concentration: Human Resources Management
Minor: Psychology

EXPERIENCE

Intern. Humana Hospital Corporation, August, GA, Summer 1995
A rotating internship throughout the corporate office divisions, including human resources, marketing, strategic planning, accounting and finance. Portfolio of projects completed during the internship available upon request.

Staff. Admission, Discharge and Transfer Services, Westwood Hospital, Montreal, Canada, Summers, 1993–94.
Increasing responsibility in this busy department of a 250-bed general hospital assisting in the administration of admission and discharge services. Extensive information systems experience. No patient contact in this position.

Line Cook. KiWi Kitchen, Burlington, VT, Summer 1992
Short order cook for popular breakfast and lunch eatery catering

continued

continued

to the upscale market. Emphasis on high quality, well presented meals. Attention to detail, portion control critical.

COMMUNITY SERVICE
Volunteer, Medical Records Department, Spear Hospital, Spear, IN
Intake Processor, Student Red Cross Blood Drive (three years)
Indiana University

REFERENCES
A selection of both personal and professional references are available upon request.

---

addition, the statement may indicate in what ways you can immediately benefit an organization. Given the importance of the objective, every point covered in the resume should relate to it. If information doesn't relate, it should be omitted. With the word processing technology available today, each resume can and should be tailored for individual employers or specific positions that are available.

Choose an Appropriate Length.   Because of the brevity necessary for a resume, you should keep the objective as short as possible. Although objectives of only four or five words often don't show much direction, objectives that take three full lines would be viewed as too wordy and might possibly be ignored.

Consider Which Type of Objective Statement You Will Use.   There are many ways to state an objective, but generally there are four forms this statement can take: (1) a very general statement; (2) a statement focused on a specific position; (3) a statement focused on a specific industry; or (4) a summary of your qualifications. In our contacts with employers, we often hear that many resumes don't exhibit any direction or career goals, so we suggest avoiding general statements when possible.

1. General Objective Statement.   General objective statements look like the following:

- ❏ An entry-level educational programming coordinator position

- ❏ An entry-level marketing position

This type of objective would be useful if you know what type of job you want but you're not sure which industries interest you.

2. Position-Focused Objective.   Following are examples of objectives focusing on a specific position:

- ❏ To obtain the position of Conference Coordinator at State College

- ❏ To obtain a position as Assistant Editor at *Time* magazine

When a student applies for an advertised job opening, this type of focus can be very effective. The employer knows that the applicant has taken the time to tailor the resume specifically for this position.

3. Industry-Focused Objective.   Focusing on a particular industry in an objective could be stated as follows:

- ❏ To begin a career as a sales representative in the cruise line industry

4. Summary of Qualifications Statement.   The summary of qualifications can be used instead of an objective or in conjunction with an objective. The purpose of this type of statement is to highlight relevant qualifications gained through a variety of experiences. This type of statement is often used by individuals with extensive and diversified work experience. An example of a qualifications statement follows:

....

A degree in business management and four years of progressively increasing job responsibility in every department of a local bank have prepared me to begin a career as a business manager for a medical practice that values thoroughness and attention to detail.

....

Support Your Objective.   A resume that contains any one of these types of objective statements should then go on to demonstrate why you are qualified to get the position. Listing academic degrees can be one way to indicate qualifications. Another demonstration would be in the way previous experiences, both volunteer and paid, are described. Without this kind of documentation in the body of the resume, the objective looks unsupported. Think of the resume as telling a connected story about you. All the elements should work together to form a coherent picture that ideally should relate to your statement of objective.

Education

This section of your resume should indicate the exact name of the degree you will receive or have received, spelled out completely with no abbreviations.

The degree is generally listed after the objective, followed by the institution name and address, and then the month and year of graduation. This section could also include your academic minor, grade point average (GPA), and appearance on the Dean's List or President's List.

If you have enough space, you might want to include a section listing courses related to the field in which you are seeking work. The best use of a "related courses" section would be to list some course work that is not traditionally associated with the major. Perhaps you took several computer courses outside your degree that will be helpful and related to the job prospects you are entertaining. Several education section examples are shown here:

···

❏ Bachelor of Science Degree in Management
State University, Boulder, Colorado, 1996
Concentration: Human Resource Management

❏ Bachelor of Science Degree in Business Management
State College, Columbus, OH, May 1996
Minor: Computer Scienc

❏ Bachelor of Science Degree in Management Science
Community College, Summit, New Jersey, 1996
General Management Option
Minor in Economics,

An example of a format for a related courses section follows:

RELATED COURSES	
Labor Management Relations	Corporate Finance
Business Computer Applications	Personnel Management
Real Estate Investment and Development	Business Research Design

···

Experience

The experience section of your resume should be the most substantial part and should take up most of the space on the page. Employers want to see what kind of work history you have. They will look at your range of experiences, longevity in jobs, and specific tasks you are able to complete. This section may also be called "work experience," "related experience," "employment history," or "employment." No matter what you call this section, some important points to remember are the following:

1. **Describe your duties** as they relate to the position you are seeking.

2. **Emphasize major responsibilities** and indicate increases in responsibility. Include all relevant employment experiences: summer, part-time, internships, cooperative education, or self-employment.

3. **Emphasize skills,** especially those that transfer from one situation to another. The fact that you coordinated a student organization, chaired meetings, supervised others, and managed a budget leads one to suspect that you could coordinate other things as well.

4. **Use descriptive job titles** that provide information about what you did. A "Student Intern" should be more specifically stated as, for example, "Magazine Operations Intern." "Volunteer" is also too general; a title like "Peer Writing Tutor" would be more appropriate.

5. **Create word pictures** by using active verbs to start sentences. Describe *results* you have produced in the work you have done.

A limp description would say something like the following: "My duties included helping with production, proofreading, and editing. I used a word processing package to alter text." An action statement would be stated as follows: "Coordinated and assisted in the creative marketing of brochures and seminar promotions, becoming proficient in WordPerfect."

Remember, an accomplishment is simply a result, a final measurable product that people can relate to. A duty is not a result, it is an obligation—every job holder has duties. For an effective resume, list as many results as you can. To make the most of the limited space you have and to give your description impact, carefully select appropriate and accurate descriptors from the list of action words in Exhibit 2.2.

Exhibit 2.2

Resume Action Verbs

Achieved	Collected	Converted
Acted	Communicated	Coordinated
Administered	Compiled	Corrected
Advised	Completed	Created
Analyzed	Composed	Decreased
Assessed	Conceptualized	Defined
Assisted	Condensed	Demonstrated
Attained	Conducted	Designed
Balanced	Consolidated	Determined
Budgeted	Constructed	Developed
Calculated	Controlled	Directed

continued

continued

Documented	Learned	Received
Drafted	Lectured	Recommended
Edited	Led	Recorded
Eliminated	Maintained	Reduced
Ensured	Managed	Reinforced
Established	Mapped	Reported
Estimated	Marketed	Represented
Evaluated	Met	Researched
Examined	Modified	Resolved
Explained	Monitored	Reviewed
Facilitated	Negotiated	Scheduled
Finalized	Observed	Selected
Generated	Obtained	Served
Handled	Operated	Showed
Headed	Organized	Simplified
Helped	Participated	Sketched
Identified	Performed	Sold
Illustrated	Planned	Solved
Implemented	Predicted	Staffed
Improved	Prepared	Streamlined
Increased	Presented	Studied
Influenced	Processed	Submitted
Informed	Produced	Summarized
Initiated	Projected	Systematized
Innovated	Proposed	Tabulated
Instituted	Provided	Tested
Instructed	Qualified	Transacted
Integrated	Quantified	Updated
Interpreted	Questioned	Verified
Introduced	Realized	

Here are some traits that employers tell us they like to see:

❑ Teamwork

❑ Energy and motivation

❑ Learning and using new skills

❑ Demonstrated versatility

❑ Critical thinking

❑ Understanding how profits are created

❑ Displaying organizational acumen

- ❑ Communicating directly and clearly, in both writing and speaking
- ❑ Risk taking
- ❑ Willingness to admit mistakes
- ❑ Manifesting high personal standards

SOLUTIONS TO FREQUENTLY ENCOUNTERED PROBLEMS

Repetitive Employment with the Same Employer

EMPLOYMENT: **The Foot Locker,** Portland, Oregon. Summer 1991, 1992, 1993. Initially employed in high school as salesclerk. Due to successful performance, asked to return next two summers at higher pay with added responsibility. Ranked as the #2 salesperson the first summer and #1 the next two summers. Assisted in arranging eye-catching retail displays; served as manager of other summer workers during owner's absence.

A Large Number of Jobs

EMPLOYMENT: Recent Hospitality Industry Experience: Affiliated with four upscale hotel/restaurant complexes (September 1991–February 1994), where I worked part- and full-time as a waiter, bartender, disc jockey, and bookkeeper to produce income for college.

Several Positions with the Same Employer

EMPLOYMENT: Coca-Cola Bottling Co., Burlington, VT, 1991–94. In four years, I received three promotions, each with increased pay and responsibility.

Summer Sales Coordinator: Promoted to hire, train, and direct efforts of add-on staff of 15 college-age route salespeople hired to meet summer peak demand for product.

Sales Administrator: Promoted to run home office sales desk, managing accounts and associated delivery schedules for professional sales force of ten people. Intensive phone work, daily interaction with all personnel, and strong knowledge of product line required.

Route Salesperson: Summer employment to travel and tourism industry sites using Coke products. Met specific schedule demands, used good communication skills with wide variety of customers, and demonstrated strong selling skills. Named salesperson of the month for July and August of that year.

QUESTIONS RESUME WRITERS OFTEN ASK

How Far Back Should I Go in Terms of Listing Past Jobs?

Usually, listing three or four jobs should suffice. If you did something back in high school that has a bearing on your future aspirations for employment, by all means list the job. As you progress through your college career, high school jobs may be replaced on the resume by college employment.

Should I Differentiate between Paid and Nonpaid Employment?

Most employers are not initially as concerned about how much you were paid. They are anxious to know how much responsibility you held in your past employment. There is no need to specify that your work was volunteer if you had significant responsibilities.

How Should I Represent My Accomplishments or Work-Related Responsibilities?

Succinctly, but fully. In other words, give the employer enough information to arouse curiosity, but not so much detail that you leave nothing to the imagination. Besides, some jobs merit more lengthy explanations than others. Be sure to convey any information that can give an employer a better understanding of the depth of your involvement at work. Did you supervise others? How many? Did your efforts result in a more efficient operation? How much did you increase efficiency? Did you handle a budget? How much? Were you promoted in a short time? Did you work two jobs at once or 15 hours per week after high school? Where appropriate, quantify.

Should the Work Section Always Follow the Education Section on the Resume?

Always lead with your strengths. If your past work closely relates to the employment you now seek, put this section after the objective. Or, if you are weak on the academic side but have a surplus of good work experiences, consider reversing the order of your sections to lead with employment, followed by education.

How Should I Present My Activities, Honors, Awards, Professional Societies, and Affiliations?

This section of the resume can add valuable information for an employer to consider if used correctly. The rule of thumb for information in this section is to include only those activities that are in some way relevant to the objective stated on your resume. If you can draw a valid connection between your activities and your objective, include them; if not, leave them out.

Granted, this is hard to do. Center on the championship basketball team or coordinator of the biggest homecoming parade ever held are roles that have meaning for you and represent personal accomplishments you'd like to share. But the resume is a brief document, and the information you provide on it should help the employer make a decision about your job eligibility. Including personal details can be confusing and could hurt your candidacy. Limiting your activity list to a few very significant experiences can be very effective.

If you are applying for a position as a safety officer, your certificate in Red Cross lifesaving skills or CPR would be related and valuable. You would want to include it. If, however, you are applying for a job as a junior account executive in an advertising agency, that information would be unrelated and superfluous. Leave it out.

Professional affiliations and honors should *all* be listed; especially important are those related to your job objective. Social clubs and activities need not be a part of your resume unless you hold a significant office or you are looking for a position related to your membership. Be aware that most prospective employers' principle concerns are related to your employability, not your social life. If you have any, publications can be included as an addendum to your resume.

The focus of the resume is your experience and education. It is not necessary to describe your involvement in activities. However, if your resume needs to be lengthened, this section provides the freedom either to expand on or mention only briefly the contributions you have made. If you have made significant contributions (e.g., an officer of an organization or a particularly long tenure with a group), you may choose to describe them in more detail. It is not always necessary to include the dates of your memberships with your activities the way you would include job dates.

There are a number of different ways in which to present additional information. You may give this section a number of different titles. Assess what you want to list, and then use an appropriate title. Do not use extracurricular activities. This terminology is scholastic, not professional, and therefore not appropriate. The following are two examples:

❏ ACTIVITIES: Society for Technical Communication, Student Senate, Student Admissions Representative, Senior Class Officer

❏ ACTIVITIES: • Society for Technical Communication Member
 • Student Senator
 • Student Admissions Representative
 • Senior Class Officer

The position you are looking for will determine what you should or should not include. *Always* look for a correlation between the activity and the prospective job.

How Should I Handle References?

The use of references is considered a part of the interview process, and they should never be listed on a resume. You would always provide references to a potential employer if requested to, so it is not even necessary to include this section on the resume if room does not permit. If space is available, it is acceptable to include one of the following statements:

❑ REFERENCES: Furnished upon request.

❑ REFERENCES: Available upon request.

Individuals used as references must be protected from unnecessary contacts. By including names on your resume, you leave your references unprotected. Overuse and abuse of your references will lead to less-than-supportive comments. Protect your references by giving out their names only when you are being considered seriously as a candidate for a given position.

THE FUNCTIONAL RESUME

The functional resume departs from a chronological resume in that it organizes information by specific accomplishments in various settings: previous jobs, volunteer work, associations, etc. This type of resume permits you to stress the substance of your experiences rather than the position titles you have held. (See Exhibit 2.3.) You should consider using a functional resume if you have held a series of similar jobs that relied on the same skills or abilities.

Exhibit 2.3

Functional Resume

KIRSTEN A. GIEBUTOWSKI

Blair Hall, Room 233   Stinson Lake Road
Emerson College   Brattleboro, VT 44116
Boston, MA 02134   (802) 555-0000
(617) 444-9999
(until May 1996)

OBJECTIVE
A position as an entry-level buyer (associate buyer) for a major department or specialty goods store that will build upon my past retail experience and business education.

continued

continued

CAPABILITIES
- High energy, task oriented, decision maker
- Strong market orientation
- Excellent quantitative and analytical skills

SELECTED ACCOMPLISHMENTS

MERCHANDISING: Four years of progressively more challenging retail exposure, including display, signage, pricing, vendor relations, inventory, and extensive customer contact. Extensive exposure to store operations and special merchandising events. Work assignments in both soft and hard goods.

ADVERTISING/MARKETING: Considerable exposure to design, execution, and placement of retail advertisement in newspapers. Thoroughly familiar with coop advertising fees and considerations. Designed marketing/advertising zero-based budget for small, local retail jewelry store as part of my senior business thesis. Owner reported documented 27% increase in traffic based on direct response mechanism.

LEADERSHIP: Vice President, American Marketing Association college chapter for 1995–96. Co-chair of sorority annual book sale. Alternate member, local Chamber of Commerce business development team 1994–96.

AWARDS
Employee of the month (8 times over three years)
Dean's List (six semesters)
American Marketing Association Advertising Team Award, 1995

EMPLOYMENT HISTORY
Carolina Dress Shop, Bridge St., Brattleboro, VT 1992–96
Mystery Books, (part-time), Winslow St., Brattleboro, VT 1995–96
Career Office (student worker), Emerson College, 1994–96

EDUCATION
Bachelor of Science in Business Management
Emerson College, Boston, Massachusetts, May 1996

REFERENCES
Provided upon request.

The Objective

A functional resume begins with an objective that can be used to focus the contents of the resume.

Specific Accomplishments

Specific accomplishments are listed on this type of resume. Examples of the types of headings used to describe these capabilities might include sales, counseling, teaching, communication, production, management, marketing, or writing. The headings you choose will directly relate to your experience and the tasks that you carried out. Each accomplishment section contains statements related to your experience in that category, regardless of when or where it occurred. Organize the accomplishments and the related tasks you describe in their order of importance as related to the position you seek.

Experience or Employment History

Your actual work experience is condensed and placed after the specific accomplishments section. It simply lists dates of employment, position titles, and employer names.

Education

The education section of a functional resume is identical to that of the chronological resume, but it does not carry the same visual importance because it is placed near the bottom of the page.

References

Because actual reference names are never listed on a resume, this section is optional if space does not permit.

THE TARGETED RESUME

The targeted resume focuses on specific work-related capabilities you can bring to a given position within an organization. (See Exhibit 2.4.) It should be sent to an individual within the organization who makes hiring decisions about the position you are seeking.

The Objective

The objective on this type of resume should be targeted to a specific career or position. It should be supported by the capabilities, accomplishments, and achievements documented in the resume.

Exhibit 2.4

Targeted Resume

ART S. MALIK

Norton Bagley House
Rollins College
Park, FL 78544
(914) 555-2901
(Until May 1996)

266 Chase Avenue
Winter Park, FL 78543
(914) 555-2443

JOB TARGET

Financial Analyst position in an investment bank or investment banking department of a large commercial bank.

CAPABILITIES

- Proven team skills
- Familiar with a variety of computer software, including spreadsheets
- Strong quantitative skills/practiced in research techniques
- Excellent communicator, both written and orally

ACHIEVEMENTS

- Entertainment contract negotiator for College Union, 1995–96
- Created student team to assist local senior citizens with income tax preparation
- Marketed my own line of imprinted mugs to campus organizations

WORK HISTORY

1996–Present (part-time)	Data Analyst, Moosilake National Bank, Winter Park, FL • Using established databases, respond to a variety of account information needs
1994–1996	Student Worker, Reference Desk, Rollins College Library, Winter Park, FL • Work with professional reference librarians to respond to information requests from students, faculty, staff, and townspeople
1993–1996 (summers)	Recreation Leader, Winter Park Parks Department, FL • Increasing responsibilities for children's program

continued

---

continued

EDUCATION

Bachelor of Science in Management with Finance Option
Rollins College
Minor: English

Capabilities

Capabilities should be statements that illustrate tasks you believe you are capable of based on your accomplishments, achievements, and work history. Each should relate to your targeted career or position. You can stress your qualifications rather than your employment history. This approach may require research to obtain an understanding of the nature of the work involved and the capabilities necessary to carry out that work.

Accomplishments/Achievements

This section relates the various activities you have been involved in to the job market. These experiences may include previous jobs, extracurricular activities at school, internships, and part-time summer work.

Experience

Your work history should be listed in abbreviated form and may include position title, employer name, and employment dates.

Education

Because this type of resume is directed toward a specific job target and an individual's related experience, the education section is not prominently located at the top of the resume as is done on the chronological resume.

THE BROADCAST LETTER

The broadcast letter is used by some job seekers in place of a resume and cover letter. (See Exhibit 2.5.) The purpose of this type of document is to make a number of potential employers aware of the availability and expertise of the job seeker. Because the broadcast letter is mass-mailed (500–600 employers), the amount of work required may not be worth the return for many people. If you choose to mail out a broadcast letter, you can expect to receive a response from 2–5 percent, at best, of the organizations that receive your letter.

This type of document is most often used by individuals who have an extensive and quantifiable work history. College students often do not have the

Exhibit 2.5

Broadcast Letter

TRICIA A. SWAIN
27 Parker Street
Rumney, Illinois 60615
(812) 555-1844

Mr. Niles Lee Perkins, Administrator   June 6, 1996
Webster Nursing Homes, Inc.
Box 270, Rt. 109
Danvers, MA 29401

Dear Mr. Perkins:

I am writing to you because your organization may be in need of an administrator with my experience, education, and training. My longterm goal is to work in a management role in the area of patient admissions, discharge, and transfer services, developing and delivering quality of care with a strong "bottom line" orientation. Today's healthcare marketplace challenges us to continue to provide the highest level of patient services within the confines of increasingly restrictive third-party payments. I feel well prepared to contribute to your excellent management team as they work hard to keep Webster Nursing Homes ahead of tomorrow's health care challenges. Some highlights of my experience that might particularly interest you include:

- A serious interest in healthcare. I have volunteered more than 400 hours in the medical records department of my local hospital and served as college representative to the board of directors.

- My internship with a major hospital in the state focused on queuing problems and delays in operating room scheduling. My recommendations were adopted.

- As a peer counselor here on campus, I have developed excellent listening and counseling skills, qualities I feel are crucial to today's healthcare administrator.

- I have excellent research, analytical, and computer software skills, including database and spreadsheet experience. My writing has been consistently recognized throughout college for its clarity and style.

I received my bachelor of science degree in business management from White Mountain College in May of 1996.

continued

---

continued

It would be a pleasure to review my qualifications with you in a personal interview at some mutually convenient time. I will call your office at the end of next week to make arrangements. I look forward to discussing career opportunities with Webster Nursing Homes, Inc.

Sincerely,

Tricia A. Swain

---

credentials and work experience to support using a broadcast letter, and most will find it difficult to effectively quantify a slim work history.

A broadcast letter is generally five paragraphs (one page) long. The first paragraph should immediately gain the attention of the reader and state some unusual accomplishment or skill that would be of benefit to the organization. The second paragraph states the reason for the letter. Details of the sender's work history are revealed in the third paragraph. Education and other qualifications or credentials are then described. Finally, the job seeker indicates what he or she will do to follow up on the letter, which usually is a follow-up call 1–2 weeks after the letter is sent.

RESUME PRODUCTION AND OTHER TIPS

If you have the option and convenience of using a laser printer, you may want to initially produce a limited number of copies in case you want or need to make changes on your resume.

Resume paper color should be carefully chosen. You should consider the types of employers who will receive your resume and the types of positions for which you are applying. Use white or ivory paper for traditional or conservative employers, or for higher-level positions.

Black ink on sharply white paper can be harsh on the reader's eyes. Think about an ivory or cream paper that will provide less contrast and be easier to read. Pink, green, and blue tints should generally be avoided.

Many resume writers buy packages of matching envelopes and cover sheet stationery that, although not absolutely necessary, does convey a professional impression.

If you'll be producing many cover letters at home, be sure you have high-quality printing equipment, whether it be computerized or standard typewriter equipment. Learn standard envelope formats for business and retain a copy of every cover letter you send out. You can use it to take notes of any telephone conversations that may occur.

If attending a job fair, women generally can fold their resume in thirds lengthwise and find it fits into a clutch bag or envelope-style purse. Both men and women will have no trouble if they carry a briefcase. For men without a briefcase, carry the resume in a nicely covered legal-size pad holder or fold it in half lengthwise and place it inside your suitcoat pocket, taking care it doesn't "float" outside your collar.

THE COVER LETTER

The cover letter provides you with the opportunity to tailor your resume by telling the prospective employer how you can be a benefit to the organization. It will allow you to highlight aspects of your background that are not already discussed in your resume and that might be especially relevant to the organization you are contacting or to the position you are seeking. Every resume should have a cover letter enclosed when you send it out. Unlike the resume, which may be mass-produced, a cover letter is most effective when it is individually typed and focused on the particular requirements of the organization in question.

A good cover letter should supplement the resume and motivate the reader to review the resume. The format shown in Exhibit 2.6 is only a suggestion to help you decide what information to include in writing a cover letter.

Begin the cover letter with your street address 12 lines down from the top. Leave three to five lines between the date and the name of the person to whom

---

Exhibit 2.6

Cover Letter Format

Your Street Address
Your Town, State, Zip
Phone Number
Date

continued

continued

Name
Title
Organization
Address

Dear _____:

First Paragraph. In this paragraph, state the reason for the letter, name the specific position or type of work you are applying for, and indicate from which resource (career development office, newspaper, contact, employment service) you learned of the opening. The first paragraph can also be used to inquire about future openings.

Second Paragraph. Indicate why you are interested in the position, the company, its products or services, and what you can do for the employer. If you are a recent graduate, explain how your academic background makes you a qualified candidate. Try not to repeat the same information found in the resume.

Third Paragraph. Refer the reader to the enclosed resume for more detailed information.

Fourth Paragraph. In this paragraph, say what you will do to follow up on your letter. For example, state that you will call by a certain date to set up an interview or to find out if the company will be recruiting in your area. Finish by indicating your willingness to answer any questions they may have. Be sure you have provided your phone number.

Sincerely,

Type your name

Enclosure

you are addressing the cover letter. Make sure you leave one blank line between the salutation and the body of the letter and between each paragraph.

After typing "Sincerely," leave four blank lines and type your name. This should leave plenty of room for your signature. A sample cover letter is shown in Exhibit 2.7.

The following are guidelines that will help you write good cover letters:

1. Be sure to type your letter; ensure there are no misspellings.

Exhibit 2.7

Sample Cover Letter

---

13 Locust Street
San Diego, CA 98021
(312) 555-1111
October 12, 1995

Mr. Ken Kochien
Director of Development
Nature Conservancy Preserves
22 Main Street
Lockport, CA 98772

Dear Mr. Kochien:

In May of 1996, I will graduate from the San Diego campus of University College with a bachelor's degree in business management. I read of your opening for a capital campaign manager in *Community Jobs* (April 1966), and I am very interested in the possibilities it offers. I am writing to explore the opportunity for employment with the Nature Conservancy Preserves.

The advertisement indicated that you were looking for someone capable of coordinating meetings, producing campaign materials and donor acknowledgments. I believe my resume outlines a work and education history that you will find interesting and relevant. Beginning with office duties and logistics for a renowned science conference for two summers early in high school, I gained some advertising and graphics experience with a local newspaper and my writing skills were polished working on our college weekly newspaper. Courses in psychology have added to my major course work and I had some excellent relevant experience working in our campus admissions office. I am productive, focused, and capable of producing high quality work under time constraints.

continued

continued

As you will see by the enclosed resume, I have had exposure to considerable technology here at college and am thoroughly familiar with all the software and database systems you mention in your ad. In addition, I have good spreadsheet experience and my word processing skills are excellent.

I would like to meet with you to discuss how my education and experience would be consistent with your needs. I will contact your office next week to discuss the possibility of an interview. In the meantime, if you have any questions or require additional information, please contact me at my home, (312) 555-9201.

Sincerely,

Mary Campbell
Enclosure

2. Avoid unusual typefaces, such as script.

3. Address the letter to an individual, using the person's name and title. To obtain this information, call the company. If answering a blind newspaper advertisement, address the letter "To Whom It May Concern" or omit the salutation.

4. Be sure your cover letter directly indicates the position you are applying for and tells why you are qualified to fill it.

5. Send the original letter, not a photocopy, with your resume. Keep a copy for your records.

6. Make your cover letter no more than one page.

7. Include a phone number where you can be reached.

8. Avoid trite language and have someone read it over to react to its tone, content, and mechanics.

9. For your own information, record the date you send out each letter and resume.

CHAPTER THREE

RESEARCHING CAREERS

Many business majors made their degree choice with the expectation that their degree would be the ticket to employment after graduation. But "business" is a vast field, populated with tens of thousands of job titles you have never heard before. You know that a business major has given you an overview of management, marketing, accounting, economics, and organizational behavior. However, you still may be confused as to exactly what kind of jobs you can do with your degree and what kinds of organizations will hire you. Are sales jobs only reserved for marketing majors? Where does a business major fit into a hospital or a museum, a department store chain or an environmental learning center?

WHAT DO THEY CALL THE JOB YOU WANT?

There is every reason to be unaware. One reason for confusion is perhaps a mistaken assumption that a college education provides job training. In most cases, it does not. Of course, applied fields such as engineering, management, or education provide specific skills for the workplace, whereas most liberal arts degrees simply provide an education. A liberal arts education exposes you to numerous fields of study and teaches you quantitative reasoning, critical thinking, writing, and speaking, all of which can be successfully applied to a number of different job fields. But it still remains up to you to choose a job field and to learn how to articulate the benefits of your education in a way the employer will appreciate.

As indicated in Chapter 1 on self-assessment, your first task is to understand and value what parts of that education you enjoyed and were good at and would continue to enjoy in your life's work. Did your writing courses encourage you in your ability to express yourself in writing? Did you enjoy the research process and did you find your work was well received? Did you enjoy any of your required quantitative subjects like algebra or calculus?

The answers to questions such as these provide clues to skills and interests you bring to the employment market over and above the credential of your degree. In fact, it is not an overstatement to suggest that most employers who demand a college degree immediately look beyond that degree to you as a person and your own individual expression of what you like to do and think you can do for them, regardless of your major.

Collecting Job Titles

The world of employment is a big place, and even seasoned veterans of the job hunt can be surprised about what jobs are to be found in what organizations. You need to become a bit of an explorer and adventurer and be willing to try a variety of techniques to begin a list of possible occupations that might use your talents and education. Once you have a list of possibilities that you are interested in and qualified for, you can move on to find out what kinds of organizations have these job titles.

....

Not every employer seeking to hire someone with a business degree may be equally desirable to you. Some employment environments may be more attractive to you than others. A business major considering sales could do that as an inside sales representative, outside sales representative, or telemarketing representative selling anything from complex pharmaceuticals to book-binding equipment. Though income production might be exactly the same, each environment presents a different "culture" with associated norms in the pace of work, the interaction with customers, and the background and training of those you'll work with or encounter on the job. Your job title might be the same in each situation, but not all situations present the same "fit" for you.

If you majored in business and enjoyed the in-class presentations you did as part of your degree and have developed some

> strong communications skills, you might naturally think sales. But business majors with these same skills and interests go on to work as human resource professionals, training and development specialists, public relations executives, development officers and fund raisers and advertising account managers. Each job title in this list can be found in a variety of settings.

....

Take training, for example. Trainers write policy and procedural manuals and actively teach to assist all levels of employees in mastering various tasks and work-related systems. Trainers exist in all large corporations, banks, consumer goods manufacturers, medical diagnostic equipment firms, sales organizations, and any organization that has processes or materials that need to be presented to and learned by the staff.

In reading job descriptions or want ads for any of these positions, you would find your four-year degree a "must." However, the academic major might be less important than your own individual skills in critical thinking, analysis, report writing, public presentations, and interpersonal communication. Even more important than thinking or knowing you have certain skills is your ability to express those skills concretely and the examples you use to illustrate them to an employer.

The best beginning to a job search is to create a list of job titles you might want to pursue, learn more about the nature of the jobs behind those titles, and then discover what kinds of employers hire for those positions. In the following section, we'll teach you how to build a job title directory to use in your job search.

Developing a Job Title Directory That Works for You

A job title directory is simply a complete list of all the job titles you are interested in, are intrigued by, or think you are qualified for. Combining the understanding gained through self-assessment with your own individual interests and the skills and talents you've acquired with your degree, you'll soon start to read and recognize a number of occupational titles that seem right for you. There are several resources you can use to develop your list, including computer searches, books, and want ads.

Computerized Interest Inventories. One way to begin your search is to identify a number of jobs that call for your degree and the particular skills and interests you identified as part of the self-assessment process. There are on the market excellent interactive computer career guidance programs to help you produce such selected lists of possible job titles. Most of these are available at high schools and colleges and at some larger town and city libraries. Two of the industry leaders are SIGI and DISCOVER. Both allow you to enter interests, values, educational background, and other information to produce lists of possible occupations and industries. Each of the resources listed here will produce different job title lists. Some job titles will appear again and again, while others will be unique to a particular source. Investigate them all!

Reference Books.   Books on the market that may be available through your local library or career counseling office also suggest various occupations related to a number of majors. The following are only two of the many good books on the market: *What Can I Do with a Major In . . . ? How to Choose and Use Your College Major,* by Lawrence R. Malnig with Anita Malnig, and *The Occupational Thesaurus. What Can I Do with a Major In . . . ?* lists job titles by academic major and identifies those jobs by their *Dictionary of Occupational Titles* (DOT) code (see following discussion).

....

For Business majors, approximately 82 job titles are listed. Some are familiar ones, such as sales agent or retail manager, hospital administrator and financial analyst. Others are interestingly different, such as import–export agent, job analyst, or conciliator.

The *Occupational Thesaurus* is another good resource, which essentially lists job title possibilities under general categories. So, if as a business major you discovered retail manager as a job title in the book *What Can I Do with a Major in . . . ?,* you can then go to the *Occupational Thesaurus,* which lists scores of jobs under that title. Under "Merchandising" there is a list of over 40 associated job titles, including inventory control, operations management, economic forecasting, customer relations, and new business research. If retail management was a suggested job title for you, this source adds some depth by suggesting a number of different occupational settings.

....

Each job title deserves your consideration. Like the layers of an onion, the search for job titles can go on and on! As you spend time doing this activity, you are actually learning more about the value of your degree. What's important in your search at this point is not to become critical or selective, but rather to develop as long a list of possibilities as you can. Every source used will help you add new and potentially exciting jobs to your growing list.

Want Ads.   It has been well publicized that newspaper want ads represent only about 10–15 percent of the current job market. Nevertheless, the Sunday want ads can be a great help to you in your search. Although they may not be the best place to look for a job, they can teach the job seeker much about the job market and provide a good education in job descriptions, duties and responsibilities, active industries, and some indication of the volume of job traffic. For our purposes, they are a good source for job titles to add to your list.

Read the Sunday want ads in a major market newspaper for several Sundays in a row. Circle and then cut out any and all ads that interest you and seem to call for something close to your education and experience. Remember, because want ads are written for what an organization *hopes* to find, you don't have to meet absolutely every criterion. However, if certain requirements are stated as absolute minimums and you cannot meet them, it's best not to waste your time.

A recent examination of *The Boston Sunday Globe* reveals the following possible occupations for a liberal arts major with some computer skills and limited prior work experience. (This is only a partial list of what was available.)

❏ Admissions representative	❏ Technical writer
❏ Salesperson	❏ Personnel trainee
❏ Compliance director	❏ GED examiner
❏ Assistant principal gifts writer	❏ Direct mail researcher
❏ Public relations officer	❏ Associate publicist

After performing this exercise for a few Sundays, you'll find you have collected a new library of job titles.

The Sunday want ad exercise is important because these jobs are out in the marketplace. They truly exist, and people with your qualifications are being sought to apply. What's more, many of these advertisements describe the duties and responsibilities of the job advertised and give you a beginning sense of the challenges and opportunities such a position presents. Some will indicate salary, and that will be helpful as well. This information will better define the jobs for you and provide some good material for possible interviews in that field.

Exploring Job Descriptions

Once you've arrived at a solid list of possible job titles that interest you and for which you believe you are somewhat qualified, it's a good idea to do some research on each of these jobs. The preeminent source for such job information is the *Dictionary of Occupational Titles,* or DOT. This directory lists every conceivable job and provides excellent up-to-date information on duties and responsibilities, interactions with associates, and day-to-day assignments and tasks. These descriptions provide a thorough job analysis, but they do not consider the possible employers or the environments in which this job may be performed. So, although a position as public relations officer may be well defined in terms of duties and responsibilities, it does not explain the differences in doing public relations work in a college or a hospital or a factory or a bank. You will need to look somewhere else for work settings.

Learning More about Possible Work Settings

After reading some job descriptions, you may choose to edit and revise your list of job titles once again, discarding those you feel are not suitable and keeping those that continue to hold your interest. Or you may wish to keep your list intact and see where these jobs may be located. For example, if you are interested in public relations and you appear to have those skills and the requisite education, you'll want to know what organizations do public relations. How can you find that out? How much income does someone in public relations make a year and what is the employment potential for the field of public relations?

To answer these and many other good questions about your list of job titles, we will direct you to any of the following resources: *Careers Encyclopedia, Career Information Center, College to Career: The Guide to Job Opportunities,* and the *Occupational Outlook Handbook.* Each of these books, in a different way, will help to put the job titles you have selected into an employer context. *VGM'S Handbook for Business and Management Careers* shows detailed career descriptions for over 50 fields. Entries include complete information on duties and responsibilities for individual careers and detailed entry-level requirements. There is information on working conditions and promotional opportunities as well. Salary ranges and career outlook projections are also provided. Perhaps the most extensive discussion is found in the *Occupational Outlook Handbook,* which gives a thorough presentation of the nature of the work, the working conditions, employment statistics, training, other qualifications, and advancement possibilities as well as job outlook and earnings. Related occupations are also detailed, and a select bibliography is provided to help you find additional information.

Continuing with our public relations example, your search through these reference materials would teach you that the public relations jobs you find attractive are available in larger hospitals, financial institutions, most corporations (both consumer goods and industrial goods), media organizations, and colleges and universities.

Networking to Get the Complete Story

You now have not only a list of job titles but also, for each of these job titles, a description of the work involved and a general list of possible employment settings in which to work. You'll want to do some reading and keep talking to friends, colleagues, teachers, and others about the possibilities. Don't neglect to ask if the career office at your college maintains some kind of alumni network. Often such alumni networks will connect you with another graduate from the college who is working in the job title or industry you are seeking information about. These career networkers offer what assistance they can. For some, it is a full day "shadowing" the alumnus as he or she goes about the job. Others offer partial day visits, tours, informational interviews, resume reviews, job postings, or, if distance prevents a visit, telephone interviews. As fellow graduates, they'll be frank and informative about their own jobs and prospects in their field.

Take them up on their offer and continue to learn all you can about your own personal list of job titles, descriptions, and employment settings. You'll probably continue to edit and refine this list as you learn more about the realities of the job, the possible salary, advancement opportunities, and supply and demand statistics.

In the next section, we'll describe how to find the specific organizations that represent these industries and employers, so that you can begin to make contact.

WHERE ARE THESE JOBS, ANYWAY?

Having a list of job titles that you've designed around your own career interests and skills is an excellent beginning. It means you've really thought about who you are and what you are presenting to the employment market. It has caused you to think seriously about the most appealing environments to work in, and you have identified some employer types that represent these environments.

The research and the thinking that you've done this far will be used again and again. It will be helpful in writing your resume and cover letters, in talking about yourself on the telephone to prospective employers, and in answering interview questions.

Now is a good time to begin to narrow the field of job titles and employment sites down to some specific employers to initiate the employment contact.

Finding Out Which Employers Hire People Like You

This section will provide tips, techniques, and specific resources for developing an actual list of specific employers that can be used to make contacts. It is only an outline that you must be prepared to tailor to your own particular needs and according to what you bring to the job search. Once again, it is important to stress the need to communicate with others along the way exactly what you're looking for and what your goals are for the research you're doing. Librarians, employers, career counselors, friends, friends of friends, business contacts, and bookstore staff will all have helpful information on geographically specific and new resources to aid you in locating employers who'll hire you.

Identifying Information Resources

Your interview wardrobe and your new resume may have put a dent in your wallet, but the resources you'll need to pursue your job search are available for free (although you might choose to copy materials on a machine instead of taking notes by hand). The categories of information detailed here are not hard to find and are yours for the browsing.

Numerous resources described in this section will help you identify actual employers. Use all of them or any others that you identify as available in your geographic area. As you become experienced in this process, you'll quickly figure out which information sources are helpful and which are not. If you live in a rural area, a well-planned day trip to a major city that includes a college career office, a large college or city library, state and federal employment centers, a chamber of commerce office, and a well-stocked bookstore can produce valuable results.

There are many excellent resources available to help you identify actual job sites. They are categorized into employer directories (usually indexed by product lines and geographic location), geographically based directories (designed to highlight particular cities, regions, or states), career-specific directories (e.g., *Sports Market Place,* which lists tens of thousands of firms involved with sports), periodicals and newspapers, targeted job posting publications, and videos. This is by no means meant to be a complete list of resources, but rather a starting point for identifying useful resources.

Working from the more general references to highly specific resources, we will provide a basic list to help you begin your search. Many of these you'll find easily available. In some cases, reference librarians and others will suggest even better materials for your particular situation. Start to create your own customized bibliography of job search references. Use copying services to save time and to allow you to carry away information about organization mission, location, company officers, phone numbers, and addresses.

Employer Directories.   There are many employer directories available to give you the kind of information you need for your job search. Some of our favorites are listed here, but be sure to ask the professionals you are working with to make additional suggestions.

❑ *America's Corporate Families* identifies many major U.S. ultimate parent companies and displays corporate family linkage of subsidiaries and divisions. Businesses can be identified by their industrial code.

❑ *Million Dollar Directory: America's Leading Public and Private Companies* lists about 160,000 companies.

❑ *Moody's* various manuals are intended as guides for investors, so they contain a history of each company. Each manual contains a classification of companies by industries and products.

❑ *Standard and Poor's Register of Corporations* contains listings for 45,000 businesses, some of which are not listed in the *Million Dollar Directory*.

❑ *Job Seeker's Guide to Private and Public Companies* profiles 15,000 employers in four volumes, each covering a different geographic region. Company entries include contact information, business descriptions, and application procedures.

❑ *The Career Guide: Dun's Employment Opportunities Directory* includes more than 5,000 large organizations, including hospitals and local governments. Profiles include an overview and history of the employer as well as opportunities, benefits, and contact names. It contains geographic and industrial indexes and indexes by discipline or internship availability. This guide also includes a state-by-state list of professional personnel consultants and their specialties.

❑ *Professional's Job Finder/Government Job Finder/Non-Profits Job Finder* are specific directories of job services, salary surveys, and periodical listings in which to find advertisements for jobs in the professional, government, or not-for-profit sector.

❑ *Opportunities in Nonprofit Organizations* is a VGM career series edition that opens up the world of not-for-profit by helping you match your interest profile to the aims and objectives of scores of nonprofit employers in business, education, health and medicine, social welfare, science and technology, and many others. There is also a special section on fundraising and development career paths.

❑ *The 100 Best Companies to Sell For* lists companies by industry and provides contact information and describes benefits and corporate culture.

❑ *The 100 Best Companies to Work For in America* rates organizations on several factors including opportunities, job security, and pay.

❑ *Companies That Care* lists organizations that the authors believe are family-friendly. One index organizes information by state.

❑ *Infotrac CD-ROM Business Index* covers business journals and magazines as well as news magazines and can provide information on public and private companies.

❑ *ABI/INFORM On Disc* (CD-ROM) indexes articles in over 800 journals.

Geographically Based Directories.   The Job Bank series published by Bob Adams, Inc. contains detailed entries on each area's major employers, including business activity, address, phone number, and hiring contact name. Many listings specify educational backgrounds being sought in potential employees. Each volume contains a solid discussion of each city's or state's major employment sectors. Organizations are also indexed by industry. Job Bank volumes are available for the following places: Atlanta, Boston, Chicago, Denver, Dallas–Ft. Worth, Florida, Houston, Ohio, St. Louis, San Francisco, Seattle, Los Angeles, New York, Detroit, Philadelphia, Minneapolis, the Northwest, and Washington, D.C.

National Job Bank lists employers in every state, along with contact names and commonly hired job categories. Included are many small companies often overlooked by other directories. Companies are also indexed by industry. This publication provides information on educational backgrounds sought and lists company benefits.

Career-Specific Directories.   VGM publishes a number of excellent series detailing careers for college graduates. In the *Professional Career Series* are guides to careers in the following fields, among others:

❑ Advertising

❑ Communications

❑ Business

❑ Computers

❑ Health Care

❑ High Tech

Each provides an excellent discussion of the industry, educational requirements for jobs, salary ranges, duties, and projected outlooks for the field.

Another VGM series, *Opportunities In . . .,* has an equally wide range of titles relating to your major, such as the following:

❑ *Opportunities in Banking*

❑ *Opportunities in Insurance*

❑ *Opportunities in Sports and Athletics*

❑ *Opportunities in Journalism*

❑ *Opportunities in Marketing*

❑ *Opportunities in Television and Radio*

Sports Market Place (Sportsguide) lists organizations by sport. It also describes trade/professional associations, college athletic organizations, multi-sport publications, media contacts, corporate sports sponsors, promotion/event/athletic management services, and trade shows.

Periodicals and Newspapers.   Several sources are available to help you locate which journals or magazines carry job advertisements in your field. Other resources help you identify opportunities in other parts of the country.

❑ *Where the Jobs Are: A Comprehensive Directory of 1200 Journals Listing Career Opportunities* links specific occupational titles to corresponding periodicals that carry job listings for your field.

❑ *Social & Behavioral Sciences Jobs Handbook* contains a periodicals matrix organized by academic discipline and highlights periodicals containing job listings.

❑ *National Business Employment Weekly* compiles want ads from four regional editions of the *Wall Street Journal.* Most are business and management positions.

❑ *National Ad Search* reprints ads from 75 metropolitan newspapers across the country. Although the focus is on management positions, technical and professional postings are also included. *Caution:* Watch deadline dates carefully on listings, because deadlines may have already passed by the time the ad is printed.

❑ *The Federal Jobs Digest* and *Federal Career Opportunities* list government positions.

❑ *World Chamber of Commerce Directory* lists addresses for chambers worldwide, state boards of tourism, convention and visitors' bureaus, and economic development organizations.

This list is certainly not exhaustive; use it to begin your job search work.

Targeted Job Posting Publications.   Although the resources that follow are national in scope, they are either targeted to one medium of contact (telephone), focused on specific types of jobs, or are less comprehensive than the sources previously listed.

❑ *Job Hotlines USA* pinpoints over 1,000 hard-to-find telephone numbers for companies and government agencies that use prerecorded job messages and listings. Very few of the telephone numbers listed are toll-free, and sometimes recordings are long, so callers beware!

❑ *The Job Hunter* is a national biweekly newspaper listing business, arts, media, government, human services, health, community-related, and student services job openings.

❑ *Current Jobs for Graduates* is a national employment listing for liberal arts professions, including editorial positions, management opportunities, museum work, teaching, and nonprofit work.

❑ *Environmental Opportunities* serves environmental job interests nationwide by listing administrative, marketing, and human resources positions along with education-related jobs and positions directly related to a degree in an environmental field.

❑ *Y National Vacancy List* shows YMCA professional vacancies, including development, administration, programming, membership, and recreation postings.

❑ *ARTSearch* is a national employment service bulletin for the arts, including administration, managerial, marketing, and financial management jobs.

❑ *Community Jobs* is an employment newspaper for the nonprofit sector that provides a variety of listings, including project manager, canvas director, government relations specialist, community organizer, and program instructor.

❑ *College Placement Council Annual: A Guide to Employment Opportunities for College Graduates* is an annual guide containing solid job-hunting information and, more importantly, displaying ads from large corporations actively seeking recent college graduates in all majors. Company profiles provide brief descriptions and available employment opportunities. Contact names and addresses are given. Profiles are indexed by organization name, geographic location, and occupation.

Videos. You may be one of the many job seekers who like to get information via a medium other than paper. Many career libraries, public libraries, and career centers in libraries carry an assortment of videos that will help you learn new techniques and get information helpful in the job search. A small sampling of the multitude of videos now available includes the following:

❑ *The Skills Search* (20 min.) discusses three types of skills important in the workplace, how to present the skills in an interview, and how to respond to problem questions.

❑ *Effective Answers to Interview Questions* (35 min.) presents two real-life job seekers and shows how they realized the true meaning of interview questions and formulated positive answers.

❑ *Employer's Expectations* (33 min.) covers three areas that are important to all employers: appearance, dependability, and skills.

❑ *The Tough New Labor Market of the 1990s* (30 min.) presents labor market facts as well as suggestions on what job seekers should do to gain employment in this market.

❑ *Dialing for Jobs: Using the Phone in the Job Search* (30 min.) describes how to use the phone effectively to gain information and arrange interviews by following two new graduates as they learn and apply techniques.

Locating Information Resources

An essay by John Case that appeared in the *Boston Globe* (August 25, 1993) alerts both new and seasoned job seekers that the job market is changing, and the old guarantees of lifelong employment no longer hold true. Some of our major corporations, which were once seen as the most prestigious of employment destinations, are now laying off thousands of employees. Middle management is especially hard hit in downsizing situations. On the other side of the coin, smaller, more entrepreneurial firms are adding employees and realizing enormous profit margins. The geography of the new job market is unfamiliar, and the terrain is much harder to map. New and smaller firms can mean different kinds of jobs and new job titles. The successful job seeker will keep an open mind about where he or she might find employment and what that employment might be called.

In order to become familiar with this new terrain, you will need to undertake some research, which can be done at any of the following locations:

❑ Public libraries

❑ Business organizations

❑ Employment agencies

❑ Bookstores

❑ Career libraries

Each one of these places offers a collection of resources that will help you get the information you need.

As you meet and talk with service professionals at all these sites, be sure to let them know what you're doing. Inform them of your job search, what you've already accomplished, and what you're looking for. The more people who know you're job seeking, the greater the possibility that someone will have information or know someone who can help you along your way.

Public Libraries.   Large city libraries, college and university libraries, and even well-supported town library collections contain a variety of resources to help you conduct a job search. It is not uncommon for libraries to have separate "vocational choices" sections with books, tapes, and associated materials relating to job search and selection. Some are now even making resume creation software available for use by patrons.

Some of the publications we name throughout this book are expensive reference items that are rarely purchased by individuals. In addition, libraries carry a wide range of newspapers and telephone yellow pages as well as the usual array of books. If resources are not immediately available, many libraries have loan arrangements with other facilities and can make information available to you relatively quickly.

Take advantage of not only the reference collections, but also the skilled and informed staff. Let them know exactly what you are looking for, and they'll have their own suggestions. You'll be visiting the library frequently, and the reference staff will soon come to know who you are and what you're working on. They'll be part of your job search network!

Business Organizations. Chambers of Commerce, Offices of New Business Development, Councils on Business and Industry, Small Business Administration (SBA) offices, and professional associations can all provide geographically specific lists of companies and organizations that have hiring needs. They also have an array of other available materials, including visitors' guides and regional fact books that provide additional employment information.

These agencies serve to promote local and regional businesses and ensure their survival and success. Although these business organizations do not advertise job openings or seek employees for their members, they may be very aware of staffing needs among their member firms. In your visits to each of these locations, spend some time with the personnel getting to know who they are and what they do. Let them know of your job search and your intentions regarding employment. You may be surprised and delighted at the information they may provide.

Employment Agencies. Employment agencies, including state and federal employment offices, professional "head hunters" or executive search firms, and some private career counselors can provide direct leads to job openings. Don't overlook these resources. If you are mounting a complete job search program and want to ensure that you are covering the potential market for employers, consider the employment agencies in your territory. Some of these organizations work contractually with several specific firms and may have access that is unavailable to you. Others may be particularly well informed about supply and demand in particular industries or geographic locations.

In the case of professional (commercial) employment agencies, which include those executive recruitment firms labeled "head hunters," you should be cautious about entering into any binding contractual agreement. Before doing so, be sure to get the information you need to decide whether their services can be of use to you. Questions to ask include the following: Who pays the fee when employment is obtained? Are there any other fees or costs associated with this service? What is their placement rate? Can you see a list of previous clients and can you talk to any for references? Do they typically work with entry-level job seekers? Do they tend to focus on particular kinds of employment or industries?

A few cautions are in order, however, when you work with professional agencies. Remember, the professional employment agency is, in most cases, paid by the hiring organization. Naturally, their interest and attention is largely directed to the employer, not to the candidate. Of course, they want to provide good candidates to guarantee future contracts, but they are less interested in the job seeker than the employer.

For teacher candidates, there are a number of good placement firms that charge the prospective teacher, not the employer. This situation has evolved over time as a result of supply and demand and financial structuring of most school systems, which cannot spend money on recruiting teachers. Usually these firms charge a nonrefundable administrative fee and, upon successful placement, require a fee based on percentage of salary, which may range from 10–20 percent of annual compensation. Often, this can be repaid over a number of months. Check your contract carefully.

State and federal employment offices are no-fee services that maintain extensive "job boards" and can provide detailed specifications for each job advertised and help with application forms. Because government employment application forms are detailed, keep a master copy along with copies of all additional documentation (resumes, educational transcripts, military discharge papers, proof of citizenship, etc.). Successive applications may require separate filings. Visit these offices as frequently as you can, because most deal with applicants on a "walk-in" basis and will not telephone prospective candidates or maintain files of job seekers. Check your telephone book for the address of the nearest state and federal offices.

One type of employment service that causes much confusion among job seekers is the outplacement firm. Their advertisements tend to suggest they will put you in touch with the "hidden job market." They use advertising phrases such as "We'll work with you until you get that job," or "Maximize your earnings and career opportunities." In fact, if you read the fine print on these ads, you will notice these firms must state they are "Not an employment agency." These firms are, in fact, corporate and private outplacement counseling agencies whose work involves resume editing, counseling to provide leads for jobs, interview skills training, and all the other aspects of hiring preparation. They do this for a fee, sometimes in the thousands of dollars, which is paid by you, the client. Some of these firms have good reputations and provide excellent materials and techniques. Most, however, provide a service you as a college student or graduate can receive free from your alma mater or through a reciprocity agreement between your college and a college or university located closer to your current address.

Bookstores.   Any well-stocked bookstore will carry some job search books that are worth buying. Some major stores will even have an extensive section devoted to materials, including excellent videos, related to the job search process. Several possibilities are listed in following sections. You will also find copies of local newspapers and business magazines. The one advantage that is provided by resources purchased at a bookstore is that you can read and work with the information in the comfort of your own home and do not have to conform to the hours of operation of a library, which can present real difficulties if you are working full time as you seek employment. A few minutes spent browsing in a bookstore might be a beneficial break from your job search activities and turn up valuable resources.

Career Libraries.   Career libraries, which are found in career centers at colleges and universities and sometimes within large public libraries, contain a unique blend of the job search resources housed in other settings. In addition, career libraries often purchase a number of job listing publications, each of which targets a specific industry or type of job. You may find job listings specifically for entry-level positions for liberal arts majors. Ask about job posting newsletters or newspapers specifically focused on careers in the area that most interests you. Each center will be unique, but you are certain to discover some good sources of jobs.

Most college career libraries now hold growing collections of video material on specific industries and on aspects of your job search process, including dress and appearance, how to manage the luncheon or dinner interview, how to be effective at a job fair, and many other specific titles. Some larger corporations produce handsome video materials detailing the variety of career paths and opportunities available in their organizations.

Some career libraries also house computer-based career planning and information systems. These interactive computer programs help you to clarify your values and interests and will combine that with your education to provide possible job titles and industry locations. Some even contain extensive lists of graduate school programs.

One specific kind of service a career library will be able to direct you to is computerized job search services. These services, of which there are many, are run by private companies, individual colleges, or consortiums of colleges. They attempt to match qualified job candidates with potential employers. The candidate submits a resume (or an application) to the service. This information (which can be categorized into hundreds of separate "fields" of data) is entered into a computer database. Your information is then compared with the information from employers about what they desire in a prospective employee. If there is a "match" between what they want and what you have indicated you can offer, the job search service or the employer will contact you directly to continue the process.

Computerized job search services can complement an otherwise complete job search program. They are *not*, however, a substitute for the kinds of activities described in this book. They are essentially passive operations that are random in nature. If you have not listed skills, abilities, traits, experiences, or education *exactly* as an employer has listed its needs, there is simply no match.

Consult with the staff members at the career libraries you use. These professionals have been specifically trained to meet the unique needs you present. Often you can just drop in and receive help with general questions, or you may want to set up an appointment to speak one-on-one with a career counselor to gain special assistance.

Every career library is different in size and content, but each can provide valuable information for the job search. Some may even provide some limited counseling. If you have not visited the career library at your college or alma mater, call and ask if these collections are still available for your use. Be sure to ask about other services that you can use as well.

If you are not near your own college as you work on your job search, call the career office and inquire about reciprocal agreements with other colleges that are closer to where you live. Very often, your own alma mater can arrange for you to use a limited menu of services at another school. This typically would include access to a career library and job posting information and might include limited counseling.

CHAPTER FOUR

NETWORKING

N etworking is the process of deliberately establishing relationships to get career-related information or to alert potential employers that you are available for work. Networking is critically important to today's job seeker for two reasons: it will help you get the information you need, and it can help you find out about *all* of the available jobs.

Getting the Information You Need

Networkers will review your resume and give you candid feedback on its effectiveness. They will talk about the job you are looking for and give you a candid appraisal of how they see your strengths and weaknesses. If they have a good sense of the industry or the employment sector for that job, you'll get their feelings on future trends in the industry as well. Some networkers will be very candid about salaries, job hunting techniques, and suggestions for your job search strategy. Many have been known to place calls right from the interview desk to friends and associates that might be interested in you. Each networker will make his or her own contribution, and each will be valuable.

Because organizations must evolve to adapt to current global market needs, the information provided by decision makers within various organizations will be critical to your success as a new job market entrant. For example, you might learn about the concept of virtual organizations from a networker. Virtual organizations are those that are temporarily established to take advantage of fast-changing opportunities and then dissolved. This concept is being discussed and implemented by chief executive officers of many organizations, including Corning, Apple, and Digital. Networking can help you find out about this and other trends currently affecting the industries under your consideration.

Finding Out about All of the Available Jobs

Secondly, not every job that is available at this very moment is advertised for potential applicants to see. This is called the *hidden job market*. Only 15–20 percent of all jobs are formally advertised, which means that 80–85 percent of available jobs do not appear in published channels. Networking will help you become more knowledgeable about all the employment opportunities available during your job search period.

Although someone you might talk to today doesn't know of any openings within his or her organization, tomorrow or next week or next month an opening may occur. If you've taken the time to show an interest in and knowledge of their organization, if you've shown the company representative how you can help achieve organizational goals and that you can fit into the organization, you'll be one of the first candidates considered for the position.

Networking: A Proactive Approach

Networking is a proactive rather than a reactive approach. You, as a job seeker, are expected to initiate a certain level of activity on your own behalf; you cannot afford to simply respond to jobs listed in the newspaper. Being proactive means building a network of contacts that includes informed and interested decision makers who will provide you with up-to-date knowledge of the current job market and increase your chances of finding out about employment opportunities appropriate for your interests, experience, and level of education.

An old axiom of networking says, "You are only two phone calls away from the information you need." In other words, by talking to enough people, you will quickly come across someone who can offer you help. Start with your professors. Each of them probably has a wide circle of contacts. In their work and travel they might have met someone who can help you or direct you to someone who can.

Control and the Networking Process

In deliberately establishing relationships, the process of networking begins with you in control—*you* are contacting specific individuals. As your network expands and you establish a set of professional relationships, your search for information or jobs will begin to move outside of your total control. A part of the networking process involves others assisting you by gathering information for you or recommending you as a possible job candidate. As additional people become a part of your networking system, you will have less knowledge about activities undertaken on your behalf; you will undoubtedly be contacted by individuals whom you did not initially approach. If you want to function effectively in surprise situations, you must be prepared at all times to talk with strangers about the informational or employment needs that motivated you to become involved in the networking process.

PREPARING TO NETWORK

In deliberately establishing relationships, maximize your efforts by organizing your approach. Five specific areas in which you can organize your efforts include reviewing your self-assessment, reviewing your research on job sites and organizations, deciding who it is you want to talk to, keeping track of all your efforts, and creating your self-promotion tools.

Review Your Self-Assessment

Your self-assessment is as important a tool in preparing to network as it has been in other aspects of your job search. You have carefully evaluated your personal traits, personal values, economic needs, longer-term goals, skill base, preferred skills, and underdeveloped skills. During the networking process you will be called upon to communicate what you know about yourself and relate it to the information or job you seek. Be sure to review the exercises that you completed in the self-assessment section of this book in preparation for networking. We've explained that you need to assess what skills you have acquired from your major that are of general value to an employer and to be ready to express those in ways employers can appreciate as useful in their own organizations.

Review Researching Job Sites and Organizations

In addition, individuals assisting you will expect that you'll have at least some background information on the occupation or industry of interest to you. Refer to the appropriate sections of this book and other relevant publications to acquire the background information necessary for effective networking. They'll explain how to identify not only the job titles that might be of interest to you, but also what kinds of organizations employ people to do that job. You will develop some sense of working conditions and expectations about duties and responsibilities—all of which will be of help in your networking interviews.

Decide Who It Is You Want to Talk To

Networking cannot begin until you decide who it is that you want to talk to and, in general, what type of information you hope to gain from your contacts. Once you know this, it's time to begin developing a list of contacts. Five useful sources for locating contacts are described here.

College Alumni Network.   Most colleges and universities have created a formal network of alumni and friends of the institution who are particularly interested in helping currently enrolled students and graduates of their alma mater gain employment-related information.

> Because the business major covers such a broad spectrum of human activity, you'll find business majors employed in every sector of the economy: government, business, and nonprofit. The diversity of employment as evidenced by an alumni list from your college or university should be encouraging and informative to the Business graduate. Among such a diversified group, there are likely to be scores you would enjoy talking with and perhaps could meet. Some might be working quite far from you, but that does not preclude a telephone call or exchange of correspondence.

It is usually a simple process to make use of an alumni network. You need only visit the alumni or career office at your college or university and follow the procedure that has been established. Often, you will simply complete a form indicating your career goals and interests and you will be given the names of appropriate individuals to contact. In many cases, staff members will coach you on how to make the best use of the limited time these alumni contacts may have available for you.

Alumni networkers may provide some combination of the following services: day-long shadowing experiences, telephone interviews, in-person interviews, information on relocating to given geographic areas, internship information, suggestions on graduate school study, and job vacancy notices.

> What a valuable experience! If you are interested in a nonprofit administrative position, you may be concerned about your degree preparation and whether you would be considered eligible to work in this field. Spending a day with an alumnus who works as an administrator for a nonprofit, asking questions about his or her educational preparation and training, will give you a more concrete view of the possibilities for your degree. Observing firsthand how this person does the job and exactly what the job entails is a far better decision criteria for you than just reading on the subject could possibly provide.

Present and Former Supervisors.   If you believe you are on good terms with present or former job supervisors, they may be an excellent resource for providing information or directing you to appropriate resources that would have information related to your current interests and needs. Additionally, these supervisors probably belong to professional organizations, which they might be willing to utilize to get information for you.

···

If, for example, you were interested in working as a buyer or merchandise manager for a major department store, and you are currently working on the wait staff of a local restaurant, talk with your supervisor or the owner. He or she may belong to the local Chamber of Commerce, whose director might have information on members affiliated with retail stores in your area. You would probably be able to obtain the names and business telephone numbers of those people, which would allow you to begin the networking process.

···

Employers in Your Area. Although you may be interested in working in a geographic location different from the one where you currently reside, don't overlook the value of the knowledge and contacts those around you are able to provide. Use the local telephone directory and newspaper to identify the types of organizations you are thinking of working for or professionals who have the kinds of jobs you are interested in. Recently, a call made to a local hospital's financial administrator for information on working in health care financial administration yielded more pertinent information on training seminars, regional professional organizations, and potential employment sites than a national organization was willing to provide.

Employers in Geographic Areas Where You Hope to Work. If you are thinking about relocating, identifying prospective employers or informational contacts in this new location will be critical to your success. Many resources are available to help you locate contact names. These include the yellow pages directory, the local newspapers, local or state business publications, and local Chambers of Commerce.

Professional Associations and Organizations. Professional associations and organizations can provide valuable information in several areas: career paths that you may not have considered, qualifications relating to those career choices, publications that list current job openings, and workshops or seminars that will enhance your professional knowledge and skills. They can also be excellent sources for background information on given industries: their health, current problems, and future challenges.

There are several excellent resources available to help you locate professional associations and organizations that would have information to meet your needs. Two especially useful publications are the *Encyclopedia of Associations* and the *National Trade and Professional Associations of the United States.*

Keep Track of All Your Efforts

It can be difficult, almost impossible, to remember all the details related to each contact you make during the networking process, so you will want to develop a record-keeping system that works for you. Formalize this process by using a notebook or index cards to organize the information you gather. Begin by creating a list of the people or organizations you want to contact. Record the contact's name, address, telephone number, and what information you hope to gain. Each entry might look something like this:

Contact Name	Address	Phone #	Purpose
Mr. Tim Keefe	Wrigley Bldg.		
Dir. of Mines	Suite 72	555-8906	Resume screen

Once you have created this initial list, it will be helpful to keep more detailed information as you begin to actually make the contacts. Using the Network Contact Record form in Exhibit 4.1, keep good information on all your network contacts. They'll appreciate your recall of details of your meetings and conversations, and the information will help you to focus your networking efforts.

Exhibit 4.1

Network Contact Record

Name: Be certain your spelling is absolutely correct.

Title: Pick up a business card to be certain of the correct title.

Employing organization: Note any parent company or subsidiaries.

Business mailing address: This is often different from the street address.

Business telephone number: Include area code/alternative numbers/fax.

Source for this contact: Who referred you, and what is their relationship?

continued

---

continued

Date of call or letter: Use plenty of space here to record multiple phone calls or visits, other employees you may have met, names of secretaries/ receptionists, etc.

Content of discussion: Keep enough notes here to remind you of the substance of your visits and telephone conversations in case some time elapses between contacts.

Follow-up necessary to continue working with this contact:
Your contact may request that you send them some materials or direct you to contact an associate. Note any such instructions or assignments in this space.

Name of additional networker: Here you would record the names
Address: and phone numbers of additional
Phone: contacts met at this employer's
Name of additional networker: site. Often you will be introduced to
Address: many people, some of whom may
Phone: indicate a willingness to help in
Name of additional networker: your job search.
Address:
Phone:

Date thank-you note written: May help to date your next contact.

Follow-up action taken: Phone calls, visits, additional notes.

Other miscellaneous notes: Record any other additional interaction you may find is important to remember in working with this networking client. You will want this form in front of you when telephoning or just before and after a visit.

Create Your Self-Promotion Tools

There are two types of promotional tools that are used in the networking process. The first is a resume and cover letter, and the second is a one-minute "infomercial," which may be given over the telephone or in person.

Techniques for writing an effective resume and cover letter are covered in Chapter 2. Once you have reviewed that material and prepared these important documents, you will have created one of your self-promotion tools.

The one-minute infomercial will demand that you begin tying your interests, abilities, and skills to the people or organizations you want to network with. Think about your goal for making the contact to help you understand what you should say about yourself. You should be able to express yourself easily and convincingly. If, for example, you are contacting an alumna of your institution to obtain the names of possible employment sites in a distant city, be prepared to discuss why you are interested in moving to that location, the types of jobs you are interested in, and the skills and abilities you possess that will make you a qualified candidate.

To create a meaningful one-minute infomercial, write it out, practice it if it will be a spoken presentation, rewrite it, and practice it again if necessary until expressing yourself comes easily and is convincing.

Here's a simplified example of an infomercial for use over the telephone:

．．．

Hello, Mr. Billow? My name is Mindy Howard. I am a recent graduate of West Coast College, and I wish to enter the healthcare field. I feel confident I have many of the skills I understand are valued for administrators in healthcare. I have a strong quantitative background, with good research and computer skills. In addition, I have excellent interpersonal skills and am known as a compassionate, caring individual. I understand these are valuable traits in your line of work!

Mr. Billow, I'm calling you because I still need more information about the healthcare field and where I might fit in. I'm hoping you'll have time to sit down with me for about half an hour and discuss your perspective on careers in healthcare administration with me. There are so many possible employers to approach, and I am seeking some advice on which might be the best bet for my particular combination of skills and experience.

Would you be willing to do that for me? I would greatly appreciate it. I am available most mornings, if that's convenient for you.

．．．

Other effective self-promotion tools include portfolios for those in the arts, writing professions, or teaching. Portfolios show examples of work, photographs of projects or classroom activities, or certificates and credentials that are job related. There may not be an opportunity to use the portfolio during an interview, and it is not something that should be left with the organization. It is designed to be explained and displayed by the creator. However, during some networking meetings, there may be an opportunity to illustrate a point or strengthen a qualification by exhibiting the portfolio.

BEGINNING THE NETWORKING PROCESS

Set the Tone for Your Contacts

It can be useful to establish "tone words" for any communications you embark upon. Before making your first telephone call or writing your first letter, decide what you want your contact to think of you. If you are networking to try to obtain a job, your tone words might include works like *genuine, informed,* and *self-knowledgeable.* When trying to acquire information, your tone words may have a slightly different focus, such as *courteous, organized, focused,* and *well spoken.* Use the tone words you establish for your contacts to guide you through the networking process.

Honestly Express Your Intentions

When contacting individuals, it is important to be honest about your reasons for making the contact. Establish your purpose in your own mind and be able and ready to articulate it concisely. Determine an initial agenda, whether it be informational questioning or self-promotion, present it to your contact, and be ready to respond immediately. If you don't adequately prepare before initiating your contacts, you may find yourself at a disadvantage if you're asked to immediately begin your informational interview or self-promotion during the first phone conversation or visit.

Start Networking within Your Circle of Confidence

Once you have organized your approach—by utilizing specific researching methods, creating a system for keeping track of the people you will contact, and developing effective self-promotion tools—you are ready to begin networking. The best place to begin networking is by talking with a group of people you trust and feel comfortable with. This group is usually made up of your family, friends, and career counselors. No matter who is in this inner circle, they will have a special interest in seeing you succeed in your job search. In addition, because they will be easy to talk to, you should try taking some risks in terms of practicing your information-seeking approach. Gain confidence in talking about the strengths you bring to an organization and the underdeveloped skills you feel hinder your candidacy. Be sure to review the section on self-assessment for tips on approaching each of these areas. Ask for critical but constructive feedback from the people in your circle of confidence on the letters you write and the one-minute infomercial you have developed. Evaluate whether you want to make the changes they suggest, then practice the changes on others within this circle.

Stretch the Boundaries of Your Networking Circle of Confidence

Once you have refined the promotional tools you will use to accomplish your networking goals, you will want to make additional contacts. Because you will not know most of these people, it will be a less comfortable activity to undertake. The practice that you gained with your inner circle of trusted friends should have prepared you to now move outside of that comfort zone.

It is said that any information a person needs is only two phone calls away, but the information cannot be gained until you (1) make a reasonable guess about who might have the information you need and (2) pick up the telephone to make the call. Using your network list that includes alumni, instructors, supervisors, employers, and associations, you can begin preparing your list of questions that will allow you to get the information you need. Review the question list shown below and then develop a list of your own.

Questions You Might Want to Ask

1. In the position you now hold, what do you do on a typical day?

2. What are the most interesting aspects of your job?

3. What part of your work do you consider dull or repetitious?

4. What were the jobs you had that led to your present position?

5. How long does it usually take to move from one step to the next in this career path?

6. What is the top position to which you can aspire in this career path?

7. What is the next step in *your* career path?

8. Are there positions in this field that are similar to your position?

9. What are the required qualifications and training for entry-level positions in this field?

10. Are there specific courses a student should take to be qualified to work in this field?

11. What are the entry-level jobs in this field?

12. What types of training are provided to persons entering this field?

13. What are the salary ranges your organization typically offers to entry-level candidates for positions in this field?

14. What special advice would you give a person entering this field?

15. Do you see this field as a growing one?

16. How do you see the content of the entry-level jobs in this field changing over the next two years?

17. What can I do to prepare myself for these changes?

18. What is the best way to obtain a position that will start me on a career in this field?

19. Do you have any information on job specifications and descriptions that I may have?

20. What related occupational fields would you suggest I explore?

21. How could I improve my resume for a career in this field?

22. Who else would you suggest I talk to, both in your organization and in other organizations?

Questions You Might Have to Answer

In order to communicate effectively, you must anticipate questions that will be asked of you by the networkers you contact. Review the list below and see if you can easily answer each of these questions. If you cannot, it may be time to revisit the self-assessment process.

1. Where did you get my name, or how did you find out about this organization?

2. What are your career goals?

3. What kind of job are you interested in?

4. What do you know about this organization and this industry?

5. How do you know you're prepared to undertake an entry-level position in this industry?

6. What course work have you taken that is related to your career interests?

7. What are your short-term career goals?

8. What are your long-term career goals?

9. Do you plan to obtain additional formal education?

10. What contributions have you made to previous employers?

11. Which of your previous jobs have you enjoyed the most, and why?

12. What are you particularly good at doing?

13. What shortcomings have you had to face in previous employment?

14. What are your three greatest strengths?

15. Describe how comfortable you feel with your communication style.

General Networking Tips

Make Every Contact Count. Setting the tone for each interaction is critical. Approaches that will help you communicate in an effective way include politeness, being appreciative of time provided to you, and being prepared and thorough. Remember, *everyone* within an organization has a circle of influence, so be prepared to interact effectively with each person you encounter in the networking process, including secretarial and support staff. Many information or job seekers have thwarted their own efforts by being rude to some individuals they encountered as they networked because they made the incorrect assumption that certain persons were unimportant.

Sometimes your contacts may be surprised at their ability to help you. After meeting and talking with you, they might think they have not offered much in the way of help. A day or two later, however, they may make a contact that would be useful to you and refer you to it.

With Each Contact, Widen Your Circle of Networkers. Always leave an informational interview with the names of at least two more people who can help you get the information or job that you are seeking. Don't be shy about asking for additional contacts; networking is all about increasing the number of people you can interact with to achieve your goals.

Make Your Own Decisions. As you talk with different people and get answers to the questions you pose, you may hear conflicting information or get conflicting suggestions. Your job is to listen to these "experts" and decide what information and which suggestions will help you achieve *your* goals. Only implement those suggestions that you believe will work for you.

SHUTTING DOWN YOUR NETWORK

As you achieve the goals that motivated your networking activity—getting the information you need or the job you want—the time will come to inactivate all or parts of your network. As you do so, be sure to tell your primary supporters about your change in status. Call or write to each one of them and give them as many details about your new status as you feel is necessary to maintain a positive relationship.

Because a network takes on a life of its own, activity undertaken on your behalf will continue even after you cease your efforts. As you get calls or are contacted in some fashion, be sure to inform these networkers about your change in status, and thank them for assistance they have provided.

Information on the latest employment trends indicates that workers will change jobs or careers several times in their lifetime. If you carefully and thoughtfully conduct your networking activities now, you will have solid experience when you need to network again.

CHAPTER FIVE

INTERVIEWING

Certainly, there can be no one part of the job search process more fraught with anxiety and worry than the interview. Yet seasoned job seekers welcome the interview and will often say, "Just get me an interview and I'm on my way!" They understand that the interview is crucial to the hiring process and equally crucial for them, as job candidates, to have the opportunity of a personal dialogue to add to what the employer may already have learned from a resume, cover letter, and telephone conversations.

Believe it or not, the interview is to be welcomed, and even enjoyed! It is a perfect opportunity for you, the candidate, to sit down with an employer and express yourself and display who you are and what you want. Of course, it takes thought and planning and a little strategy; after all, it *is* a job interview! But it can be a positive, if not pleasant, experience and one you can look back on and feel confident about your performance and effort.

For many new job seekers, a job, any job, seems a wonderful thing. But seasoned interview veterans know that the job interview is an important step for both sides—the employer and the candidate—to see what each has to offer and whether there is going to be a "fit" of personalities, work styles, and attitudes. And it is this concept of balance in the interview, that both sides have important parts to play, that holds the key to success in mastering this aspect of the job search strategy.

Try to think of the interview as a conversation between two interested and equal partners. You both have important, even vital, information to deliver and to learn. Of course, there's no denying the employer has some leverage, especially in the initial interview for recruitment or any interview scheduled by the candidate and not the recruiter. That should not prevent the interviewee from seeking to play an equal part in what should be a fair exchange of information. Too often the untutored candidate allows the interview to become one-sided. The employer asks all the questions and the candidate simply responds. The ideal would be for two mutually interested parties to sit down and discuss possibilities for each. For this is a *conversation of significance,* and it requires pre-interview preparation, thought about the tone of the interview, and planning of the nature and details of the information to be exchanged.

PREPARING FOR THE INTERVIEW

Most initial interviews are about 30 minutes long. Given the brevity, the information that is exchanged ought to be important. The candidate should be delivering material that the employer cannot discover on the resume and, in turn, the candidate should be learning things about the employer that he or she could not otherwise find out. After all, if you have only 30 minutes, why waste time on information that is already published? Not all the information exchanged is factual, and both sides will learn much from what they see of each other, as well. How the candidate looks, speaks, and acts is important to the employer. The employer's attention to the interview and awareness of the candidate's resume, the setting, and the quality of information presented are important to the candidate.

Just as the employer has every right to be disappointed when a prospect is late for the interview, looks unkempt, and seems ill prepared to answer fairly standard questions, the candidate may be disappointed with an interviewer who isn't ready for the meeting, hasn't learned the basic resume facts, and is constantly interrupted for telephone calls. In either situation, there's good reason to feel let down.

There are many elements to a successful interview, and some of them are not easy to describe or prepare for. Sometimes there is just a chemistry between interviewer and interviewee that brings out the best in both, and a good exchange takes place. But there is much the candidate can do to pave the way for success in terms of his or her resume, personal appearance, goals, and interview strategy—each of which we will discuss. However, none of this preparation is as important as the time and thought the candidate gives to personal self-assessment.

Self-Assessment

Neither a stunning resume nor an expensive, well-tailored suit can compensate for candidates who do not know what they want, where they are going, or why they are interviewing with a particular employer. Self-assessment, the process by which we begin to know and acknowledge our own particular blend of education, experiences, needs, and goals is not something that can be sorted out the weekend before a major interview. Of all the elements of interview preparation, this one requires the longest lead time and cannot be faked.

Because the time allotted for most interviews is brief, it is all the more important for job candidates to understand and express succinctly why they are there and what they have to offer. This is not a time for undue modesty or for braggadocio, either; but it is a time for a compelling, reasoned statement of why you feel that you and this employer might make a good match. It means you have to have thought about your skills, interests, and attributes; related those to your life experiences and your own history of challenges and opportunities; and determined what that indicates about your strengths, preferences, values, and areas needing further development.

A common complaint of employers is that many candidates didn't take advantage of the interview time, didn't seem to know why they were there or what they wanted. When asked to talk about themselves and their work-related skills and attributes, employers don't want to be faced with shyness or embarrassed laughter; they need to know about you so they can make a fair determination of you and your competition. If you lose the opportunity to make a case for your employability, you can be certain the person ahead of you has or the person after you will, and it will be on the strength of those impressions that the employer will hire.

If you need some assistance with self-assessment issues, refer to Chapter 1. Included are suggested exercises that can be done as needed, such as making up an experiential diary and extracting obvious strengths and weaknesses from past experiences. These simple, pen-and-paper assignments will help you look at past activities as collections of tasks with accompanying skills and responsibilities. Don't overlook your high school or college career office, as well. Many offer personal counseling on self-assessment issues and may provide testing instruments such as the Myers-Briggs Type Indicator (MBTI)®, the Harrington-O'Shea Career Decision Making® System (CDM), the Strong Interest Inventory (SII)®, or any of a wide selection of assessment tools that can help you clarify some of these issues prior to the interview stage of your job search.

The Resume

Resume preparation has been discussed in detail, and some basic examples of various types were provided. In this section, we want to concentrate on how best to use your resume in the interview. In most cases, the employer will have seen the resume prior to the interview, and, in fact, it may well have been the quality of that resume that secured the interview opportunity.

An interview is a conversation, however, and not an exercise in reading. So, if the employer hasn't seen your resume and you have brought it along to the interview, wait until asked or until the end of the interview to offer it. Otherwise, you may find yourself staring at the back of your resume and simply answering "Yes" and "No" to a series of questions drawn from that document.

Sometimes an interviewer is not prepared and does not know or recall the contents of the resume and may use the resume to a greater or lesser degree as a "prompt" during the interview. It is for you to judge what that may indicate about the individual doing the interview or the employer. If your interviewer seems surprised by the scheduled meeting, relies on the resume to an inordinate degree, and seems otherwise unfamiliar with your background, this lack of preparation for the hiring process could well be a symptom of general management disorganization or may simply be the result of poor planning on the part of one individual. It is your responsibility as a potential employee to be aware of these signals and make your decisions accordingly.

··

In any event, it is perfectly acceptable for you to get the conversation back to a more interpersonal style by saying something like, "Mr. Smith, you might be interested in some recent experience I gained in a volunteer position at our local hospital that is not detailed on my resume. May I tell you about it?" This can return the interview to two people talking to each other, not one reading and the other responding.

··

By all means, bring at least one copy of your resume to the interview. Occasionally, at the close of an interview, an interviewer will express an interest in circulating a resume to several departments, and you could then offer to provide those. Sometimes, an interview appointment provides an opportunity to meet others in the organization who may express an interest in you and your background, and it may be helpful to follow that up with a copy of your resume. Our best advice, however, is to keep it out of sight until needed or requested.

Appearance

Although many of the absolute rules that once dominated the advice offered to job candidates about appearance have now been moderated significantly, conservative is still the watchword unless you are interviewing in a fashion-related industry. For men, conservative translates into a well-cut dark suit with appropriate tie, hosiery, and dress shirt. A wise strategy for the male job seeker looking for a good but not expensive suit would be to try the men's department of a major department store. They usually carry a good range of sizes, fabrics, and prices; offer professional sales help; provide free tailoring; and have associated departments for putting together a professional look.

For women, there is more latitude. Business suits are still popular, but they have become more feminine in color and styling with a variety of jacket and skirt lengths. In addition to suits, better quality dresses are now worn in many environments and, with the correct accessories, can be most appropriate. Company literature, professional magazines, the business section of major newspapers, and television interviews can all give clues about what is being worn in different employer environments.

Both men and women need to pay attention to issues such as hair, jewelry, and make-up; these are often what separates the candidate in appearance from the professional work force. It seems particularly difficult for the young job seeker to give up certain hair styles, eyeglass fashions, and jewelry habits, yet those can be important to the employer, who is concerned with your ability to successfully make the transition into the organization. Candidates often find the best strategy is to dress conservatively until they find employment. Once employed and familiar with the norms within your organization, you can begin to determine a look that you enjoy, works for you, and fits your organization.

Choose clothes that suit your body type, fit well, and flatter you. Feel good about the way you look! The interview day is not the best for a new hairdo, a new pair of shoes, or any other change that will distract you or cause you to be self-conscious. Arrive a bit early to avoid being rushed, and ask the receptionist to direct you to a restroom for any last-minute adjustments of hair and clothes.

Employer Information

Whether your interview is for graduate school admission, an overseas corporate position, or a reporter position with a local newspaper, it is important to know something about the employer or the organization. Keeping in mind that the interview is relatively brief and that you will hopefully have other interviews with other organizations, it is important to keep your research in proportion. If secondary interviews are called for, you will have additional time to do further research. For the first interview, it is helpful to know the organization's mission, goals, size, scope of operations, etc. Your research may uncover recent areas of challenge or particular successes that may help to fuel the interview. Use the "Where Are These Jobs, Anyway?" section of Chapter 3, your library, and your career or guidance office to help you locate this information in the most efficient way possible. Don't be shy in asking advice of these counseling and guidance professionals on how best to spend your preparation time. With some practice, you'll soon learn how much information is enough and which kinds of information are most useful to you.

INTERVIEW CONTENT

We've already discussed how it can help to think of the interview as an important conversation—one that, as with any conversation, you want to find pleasant and interesting and leaves you with a good feeling. But because this conversation is especially important, the information that's exchanged is critical to its success. What do you want them to know about you? What do you need to know about them? What interview technique do you need to particularly pay attention to? How do you want to manage the close of the interview? What steps will follow in the hiring process?

Except for the professional interviewer, most of us find interviewing stressful and anxiety-provoking. Developing a strategy before you begin interviewing will help you relieve some stress and anxiety. One particular strategy that has worked for many and may work for you is interviewing by objective. Before you interview, write down 3–5 goals you would like to achieve for that interview. They may be technique goals: smile a little more, have a firmer handshake, be sure to ask about the next stage in the interview process before I leave, etc. They may be content-oriented goals: find out about the company's current challenges and opportunities, be sure to speak of my recent research writing experiences or foreign travel, etc. Whatever your goals, jot down a few of them as goals for this interview.

Most people find that, in trying to achieve these few goals, their interviewing technique becomes more organized and focused. After the interview, the most common question friends and family ask is, "How did it go?" With this technique, you have an indication of whether you met *your* goals for the meeting, not just some vague idea of how it went. Chances are, if you accomplished what you wanted to, it informed the quality of the entire interview. As you continue to interview, you will want to revise your goals to continue improving your interview skills.

Now, add to the concept of the significant conversation the idea of a beginning, a middle, and a closing and you will have two thoughts that will give your interview a distinctive character. Be sure to make your introduction warm and cordial. Say your full name (and if it's a difficult-to-pronounce name, help the interviewer to pronounce it) and make certain you know your interviewer's name and how to pronounce it. Most interviews begin with some "soft talk" about the weather, chat about the candidate's trip to the interview site, national events, etc. This is done as a courtesy, to relax both you and the interviewer, to get you talking, and to generally try to defuse the atmosphere of excessive tension. Try to be yourself, engage in the conversation, and don't try to second-guess the interviewer. This is simply what it appears to be—casual conversation.

Once you and the interviewer move on to exchange more serious information in the middle part of the interview, the two most important concerns become your ability to handle challenging questions and your success at asking meaningful ones. Interviewer questions will probably fall into one of three categories: personal assessment and career direction, academic background, and knowledge of the employer. The following are some examples of questions in each category:

Personal Assessment and Career Direction

1. How would you describe yourself?

2. What motivates you to put forth your greatest effort?

3. In what kind of work environment are you most comfortable?

4. What do you consider to be your greatest strengths and weaknesses?

5. How well do you work under pressure?

6. What qualifications do you have that make you think you will be successful in this career?

7. Will you relocate? What do you feel would be the most difficult aspect of relocating?

8. Are you willing to travel?

9. Why should I hire you?

Academic Assessment

1. Why did you select your college or university?

2. What changes would you make at your alma mater?

3. What led you to choose your major?

4. What subjects did you like best and least? Why?

5. If you could, how would you plan your academic study differently? Why?

6. Describe your most rewarding college experience.

7. How has your college experience prepared you for this career?

8. Do you think that your grades are a good indication of your ability to succeed with this organization?

9. Do you have plans for continued study?

Knowledge of the Employer

1. If you were hiring a graduate of your school for this position, what qualities would you look for?

2. What do you think it takes to be successful in an organization like ours?

3. In what ways do you think you can make a contribution to our organization?

4. Why did you choose to seek a position with this organization?

The interviewer wants a response to each question but is also gauging your enthusiasm, preparedness, and willingness to communicate. In each response you should provide some information about yourself that can be related to the employer's needs. A common mistake is to give too much information. Answer each question completely, but be careful not to run on too long with extensive details or examples.

Questions about Underdeveloped Skills

Most employers interview people who have met some minimum criteria of education and experience. They interview candidates to see who they are, to learn what kind of personality they exhibit, and to get some sense of how this person might fit into the existing organization. It may be that you are asked about skills the employer hopes to find and that you have not documented. Maybe it's grant-writing experience, knowledge of the European political system, or a knowledge of the film world.

To questions about skills and experiences you don't have, answer honestly and forthrightly and try to offer some additional information about skills you do have. For example, perhaps the employer is disappointed you have no grant-writing experience. An honest answer may be as follows:

> No, unfortunately, I was never in a position to acquire those skills. I do understand something of the complexities of the grant-writing process and feel confident that my attention to detail, careful reading skills, and strong writing would make grants a wonderful challenge in a new job. I think I could get up on the learning curve quickly.

The employer hears an honest admission of lack of experience but is reassured by some specific skill details that do relate to grant writing and a confident manner that suggests enthusiasm and interest in a challenge.

For many students, questions about their possible contribution to an employer's organization can prove challenging. Because your education has probably not included specific training for a job, you need to review your academic record and select capabilities you have developed in your major that an employer can appreciate. For example, perhaps you read well and can analyze and condense what you've read into smaller, more focused pieces. That could be valuable. Or maybe you did some serious research and you know you have valuable investigative skills. Your public speaking might be highly developed and you might use visual aids appropriately and effectively. Or maybe your skill at correspondence, memos, and messages is effective. Whatever it is, you must take it out of the academic context and put it into a new, employer-friendly context so your interviewer can best judge how you could help the organization.

Exhibiting knowledge of the organization will, without a doubt, show the interviewer that you are interested enough in the available position to have done some legwork in preparation for the interview. Remember, it is not necessary to know every detail of the organization's history, but rather to have a general knowledge about why it is in business and how the industry is faring.

Sometime during the interview, generally after the midway point, you'll be asked if you have any questions for the interviewer. Your questions will tell the employer much about your attitude and your desire to understand the organization's expectations so you can compare it to your own strengths. The following are some selected questions you might want to ask:

1. What are the main responsibilities of the position?

2. What are the opportunities and challenges associated with this position?

3. Could you outline some possible career paths beginning with this position?

4. How regularly do performance evaluations occur?

5. What is the communication style of the organization? (meetings, memos, etc.)

6. Describe a typical day for me in this position.

7. What kinds of opportunities might exist for me to improve my professional skills within the organization?

8. What have been some of the interesting challenges and opportunities your organization has recently faced?

Most interviews draw to a natural closing point, so be careful not to prolong the discussion. At a signal from the interviewer, wind up your presentation, express your appreciation for the opportunity, and be sure to ask what the next stage in the process will be. When can you expect to hear from them? Will they be conducting second-tier interviews? If you're interested and haven't heard, would they mind a phone call? Be sure to collect a business card with the name and phone number of your interviewer. On your way out, you might have an opportunity to pick up organizational literature you haven't seen before.

With the right preparation—a thorough self-assessment, professional clothing, and employer information, you'll be able to set and achieve the goals you have established for the interview process.

CHAPTER SIX

NETWORKING OR INTERVIEWING FOLLOW-UP

Quite often, there is a considerable time lag between interviewing for a position and being hired, or, in the case of the networker, between your phone call or letter to a possible contact and the opportunity of a meeting. This can be frustrating. "Why aren't they contacting me?" "I thought I'd get another interview, but no one has telephoned." "Am I out of the running?" You don't know what is happening.

CONSIDER THE DIFFERING PERSPECTIVES

Of course, there is another perspective—that of the networker or hiring organization. Organizations are complex, with multiple tasks that need to be accomplished each day. Hiring is but one discrete activity that does not occur as frequently as other job assignments. The hiring process might have to take second place to other, more immediate organizational needs. Although it may be very important to you and it is certainly ultimately significant to the employer, other issues such as fiscal management, planning and product development, employer vacation periods, or financial constraints, may prevent an organization or individual within that organization from acting on your employment or your request for information as quickly as you or they would prefer.

Use Your Communication Skills

Good communication is essential here to resolve any anxieties, and the responsibility is on you, the job or information seeker. Too many job seekers and networkers offer as an excuse that they don't want to "bother" the organization by writing letters or calling. Let us assure you here and now, once and for all, that if you are troubling an organization by over-communicating, someone will indicate that situation to you quite clearly. If not, you can only assume you are a worthwhile prospect and the employer appreciates being reminded of your availability and interest in them. Let's look at follow-up practices in both the job interview process and the networking situation separately.

Following Up on the Employment Interview

A brief thank-you note following an interview is an excellent and polite way to begin a series of follow-up communications with a potential employer with whom you have interviewed and want to remain in touch. It should be just that—a thank-you for a good meeting. If you failed to mention some fact or experience during your interview that you think might add to your candidacy, you may use this note to do that. However, this should be essentially a note whose overall tone is appreciative and, if appropriate, indicative of a continuing interest in pursuing any opportunity that may exist with that organization. It is one of the few pieces of business correspondence that may be handwritten, but always use plain, good-quality, monarch-size paper.

If, however, at this point you are no longer interested in the employer, the thank-you note is an appropriate time to indicate that. You are under no obligation to identify any reason for not continuing to pursue employment with that organization, but if you are so inclined to indicate your professional reasons (pursuing other employers more akin to your interests, looking for greater income production than this employer can provide, a different geographic location than is available, etc.), you certainly may. It should not be written with an eye to negotiation, for it will not be interpreted as such.

As part of your interview closing, you should have taken the initiative to establish lines of communication for continuing information about your candidacy. If you asked permission to telephone, wait a week following your thank-you note, then telephone your contact simply to inquire how things are progressing on your employment status. The feedback you receive here should be taken at face value. If your interviewer simply has no information, he or she will tell you so and indicate whether you should call again and when. Don't be discouraged if this should continue over some period of time.

If during this time something occurs that you think improves or changes your candidacy (some new qualification or experience you may have had), including any offers from other organizations, by all means telephone or write to inform the employer about this. In the case of an offer from a competing but less desirable or equally desirable organization, telephone your contact, explain what has happened, express your real interest in the organization, and inquire whether some determination on your employment might be made before you must respond to this other offer. If the organization is truly interested in you, they may be moved to make a decision about your candidacy. Equally possible is the scenario in which they are not yet ready to make a decision and so advise you to take the offer that has been presented. Again, you have no ethical alternative but to deal with the information presented in a straightforward manner.

When accepting other employment, be sure to contact any employers still actively considering you and inform them of your new job. Thank them graciously for their consideration. There are many other job seekers out there just like you who will benefit from having their candidacy improved when others bow out of the race. Who knows, you might, at some future time, have occasion to interact professionally with one of the organizations with whom you sought employment. How embarrassing to have someone remember you as the candidate who failed to notify them of taking a job elsewhere!

In all of your follow-up communications, keep good notes of who you spoke with, when you called, and any instructions that were given about return communications. This will prevent any misunderstandings and provide you with good records of what has transpired.

Following Up on the Network Contact

Far more common than the forgotten follow-up after an interview is the situation where a good network contact is allowed to lapse. Good communications are the essence of a network, and follow-up is not so much a matter of courtesy here as it is a necessity. In networking for job information and contacts, you are the active network link. Without you, and without continual contact from you, there is no network. You and your need for employment is often the only shared element between members of the network. Because network contacts were made regardless of the availability of any particular employment, it is incumbent upon the job seeker, if not simple common sense, that unless you stay in regular communication with the network, you will not be available for consideration should some job become available in the future.

This brings up the issue of responsibility, which is likewise very clear. The job seeker initiates network contacts and is responsible for maintaining those contacts; therefore, the entire responsibility for the network belongs with him or her. This becomes patently obvious if the network is left unattended. It very shortly falls out of existence, as it cannot survive without careful attention by the networker.

A variety of ways are open to you to keep the lines of communication open and to attempt to interest the network in you as a possible employee. You are limited only by your own enthusiasm for members of the network and your creativity. However, you as a networker are well advised to keep good records of whom you have met and spoken with in each organization. Be sure to send thank-you notes to anyone who has spent any time with you, be it a quick tour of a department or a sit-down informational interview. All of these communications should, in addition to their ostensible reason, add some information about you and your particular combination of strengths and attributes.

You can contact your network at any time to convey continued interest, to comment on some recent article you came across concerning an organization, to add information about your training or changes in your qualifications, to ask advice or seek guidance in your job search, or to request referrals to other possible network opportunities. Sometimes just a simple note to network members reminding them of your job search, indicating that you have been using their advice, and noting that you are still actively pursuing leads and hope to continue to interact with them is enough to keep communications alive.

Because networks have been abused in the past, it's important that your conduct be above reproach. Networks are exploratory options, they are not back-door access to employers. The network works best for someone who is exploring a new industry or making a transition into a new area of employment and who needs to find information or to alert people to their search activity. Always be candid and direct with contacts in expressing the purpose of your call or letter and your interest in their help or information about their organization. In follow-up contacts, keep the tone professional and direct. Your honesty will be appreciated, and people will respond as best they can if your qualifications appear to meet their forthcoming needs. The network does not owe you anything, and that tone should be clear to each person you meet.

FEEDBACK FROM FOLLOW-UPS

A network contact may prove to be miscalculated. Perhaps you were referred to someone and it became clear that your goals and their particular needs did not make a good match. Or the network contact may simply not be in a position to provide you with the information you are seeking. Or in some unfortunate situations, the contact may become annoyed by being contacted for this purpose. In such a situation, many job seekers simply say "Thank you" and move on.

If the contact is simply not the right contact, but the individual you are speaking with is not annoyed by the call, it might be a better tactic to express regret that the contact was misplaced and then express to the contact what you are seeking and ask for their advice or possible suggestions as to a next step. The more people who are aware you are seeking employment, the better your chances of connecting, and that is the purpose of a network. Most people in a profession have excellent knowledge of their field and varying amounts of expertise on areas near to or tangent to their own. Use their expertise and seek some guidance before you dissolve the contact. You may be pleasantly surprised.

Occasionally, networkers will express the feeling that they have done as much as they can or provided all the information that is available to them. This may be a cue that they would like to be released from your network. Be alert to such attempts to terminate, graciously thank the individual by letter, and move on in your network development. A network is always changing, adding and losing members, and you want the network to be composed of only those who are actively interested in supporting your interests.

A Final Point on Networking for Business Majors

In any field a business major might consider as a potential career path, your contacts will be critically evaluating all your written and oral communications. For some job seekers, this may be more crucial that others. Many of the jobs in the career paths that follow do, however, emphasize communication skills. This should be a welcome demand, as your study of business has involved writing papers, research reports, and some classroom presentations—all of which have helped polish your communication style.

In your telephone communications, interview presentations, and follow-up correspondence, your written and spoken use of English will be part of the portfolio of impressions you create in those you meet along the way.

CHAPTER SEVEN

JOB OFFER CONSIDERATIONS

for many recent college graduates, the thrill of their first job and, for some, the most substantial regular income they have ever earned seems an excess of good fortune coming at once. To question that first income or be critical in any way of the conditions of employment at the time of the initial offer seems like looking a gift horse in the mouth. It doesn't seem to occur to many new hires even to attempt to negotiate any aspect of their first job. And, as many employers who deal with entry-level jobs for recent college graduates will readily confirm, the reality is that there simply isn't much movement in salary available to these new college recruits. The entry-level hire generally does not have an employment track record on a professional level to provide any leverage for negotiation. Real negotiations on salary, benefits, retirement provisions, etc., come to those with significant employment records at higher income levels.

Of course, the job offer is more than just money. It can be comprised of geographic assignment, duties and responsibilities, training, benefits, health and medical insurance, educational assistance, car allowance or company vehicle, and a host of other items. All of this is generally detailed in the formal letter that presents the final job offer. In most cases, this is a follow-up to a personal phone call from the employer representative who has been principally responsible for your hiring process.

That initial telephone offer is certainly binding as a verbal agreement, but most firms follow up with a detailed letter outlining the most significant parts of your employment contract. You may certainly choose to respond immediately at the time of the telephone offer (which would be considered a binding oral contract), but you will also be required to formally answer the letter of offer with a letter of acceptance, restating the salient elements of the employer's description of your position, salary, and benefits. This ensures that both parties are clear on the terms and conditions of employment and remuneration and any other outstanding aspects of the job offer.

IS THIS THE JOB YOU WANT?

Most new employees will write this letter of acceptance back, glad to be in the position to accept employment. If you've worked hard to get the offer, and the job market is tight, other offers may not be in sight, so you will say "Yes, I accept!" What is important here is that the job offer you accept be one that does fit your particular needs, values, and interests as you've outlined them in your self-assessment process. Moreover, it should be a job that will not only use your skills and education, but also challenge you to develop new skills and talents.

Jobs are sometimes accepted too hastily, for the wrong reasons and without proper scrutiny by the applicant. For example, an individual might readily accept a sales job only to find the continual rejection by potential clients unendurable. An office worker might realize within weeks the constraints of a desk job and yearn for more activity. Employment is an important part of our lives. It is, for most of our adult lives, our most continuous productive activity. We want to make good choices based on the right criteria.

If you have a low tolerance for risk, a job based on commission will certainly be very anxiety provoking. If being near your family is important, issues of relocation could present a decision crisis for you. If you're an adventurous person, a job with frequent travel would provide needed excitement and be very desirable. The importance of income, the need to continue your education, your personal health situation—all of these have an impact on whether the job you are considering will ultimately meet your needs. Unless you've spent some time understanding and thinking about these issues, it will be difficult to evaluate offers you do receive.

More importantly, if you make a decision that you cannot tolerate and feel you must leave that job, you will then have both unemployment and self-esteem issues to contend with. These will combine to make the next job search tough going, indeed. So make your acceptance a carefully considered decision.

NEGOTIATING YOUR OFFER

It may be that there is some aspect of your job offer that is not particularly attractive to you. Perhaps there is no relocation allotment to help you move your possessions and this presents some financial hardship for you. It may be that the medical and health insurance is less than you had hoped. Your initial assignment may be different than you expected, either in its location or in the duties and responsibilities that comprise it. Or it may simply be that the salary is less than you anticipated. Other considerations may be your official starting date of employment, vacation time, evening hours, dates of training programs or schools, etc.

If you are considering not accepting the job because of some item or items in the job offer "package" that do not meet your needs, you should know that most employers emphatically wish that you would bring that issue to their attention. It may be that the employer can alter it to make the offer more agreeable for you. In some cases, it cannot be changed. In any event, the employer would generally like to have the opportunity to try to remedy a difficulty rather than risk losing a good potential employee over an issue that might have been resolved. After all, they have spent time and funds in securing your services, and they certainly deserve an opportunity to resolve any possible differences.

Honesty is the best approach in discussing any objections or uneasiness you might have over the employer's offer. Having received your formal offer in writing, contact your employer representative and indicate your particular dissatisfaction in a straightforward manner. For example, you might explain that, while very interested in being employed by this organization, the salary (or any other benefit) is less than you have determined you require. State the terms you do need, and listen to the response. You may be asked to put this in writing, or you may be asked to hold off until the firm can decide on a response. If you are dealing with a senior representative of the organization, one who has been involved in hiring for some time, you may get an immediate response or a solid indication of possible outcomes.

Perhaps the issue is one of relocation. Your initial assignment is in the Midwest, and because you had indicated a strong West Coast preference, you are surprised at the actual assignment. You might simply indicate that, while you understand the need for the company to assign you based on its needs, you are disappointed and had hoped to be placed on the West Coast. You could inquire if that were still possible and, if not, would it be reasonable to expect a West Coast relocation in the future.

If your request is presented in a reasonable way, the employer will not see this as jeopardizing your offer. If they can agree to your proposal, they will. If not, they will simply tell you so, and you may choose to continue your candidacy with them or remove yourself from consideration as a possible employee. The choice will be up to you.

Some firms will adjust benefits within their parameters to meet the candidate's need if at all possible. If a candidate requires a relocation cost allowance, he or she may be asked to forgo tuition benefits for the first year to accomplish this adjustment. An increase in life insurance may be adjusted by some other benefit trade-off; perhaps a family dental plan is not needed. In these decisions, you are called upon, sometimes under time pressure, to know how you value these issues and how important each is to you.

Many employers find they are more comfortable negotiating for candidates who have unique qualifications or who bring especially needed expertise to the organization. Employers hiring large numbers of entry-level college graduates may be far more reluctant to accommodate any changes in offer conditions. They are well supplied with candidates with similar education and experience, so that if rejected by one candidate, they can draw new candidates from an ample labor pool.

COMPARING OFFERS

With only about 40 percent of recent college graduates employed three months after graduation, many graduates do not get to enjoy the experience of entertaining more than one offer at a time. The conditions of the economy, the job seekers' particular geographic job market, and their own needs and demands for certain employment conditions may not provide more than one offer at a time. Some job seekers may feel that no reasonable offer should go unaccepted, for the simple fear there won't be another.

In a tough job market, or if the job you seek is not widely available, or when your job search goes on too long and becomes difficult to sustain financially and emotionally, it may be necessary to accept an offer. The alternative is continued unemployment. Even here, when you feel you don't have a choice, you can at least understand that in accepting this particular offer, there may be limitations and conditions you don't appreciate. At the time of acceptance, there were no other alternatives, but the new employee can begin to use that position to gain the experience and talent to move toward a more attractive position.

Sometimes, however, more than one offer is received at one time, and the candidate has the luxury of choice. If the job seeker knows what he or she wants and has done the necessary self-assessment honestly and thoroughly, it may be clear that one of the offers conforms more closely to those expressed wants and needs.

However, if, as so often happens, the offers are similar in terms of conditions and salary, the question then becomes which organization might provide the necessary climate, opportunities, and advantages for your professional development and growth. This is the time when solid employer research and astute questioning during the interviews really pays off. How much did you learn about the employer through your own research and skillful questioning? When the interviewer asked during the interview, "Now, I'm sure you must have many questions?" did you ask the kinds of questions that would help resolve a choice between one organization and another? Just as an employer must decide among numerous applicants, so must the applicant learn to assess the potential employer. Both are partners in the job search.

RENEGING ON AN OFFER

An especially disturbing occurrence for employers and career counseling professionals is when a student formally (either orally or by written contract) accepts employment with one organization and later reneges on the agreement and goes with another employer.

There are all kinds of rationalizations offered for this unethical behavior. None of them satisfies. The sad irony is that what the job seeker is willing to do to the employer—make a promise and then break it—he or she would be outraged to have done to them—have the job offer pulled. It is a very bad way to begin a career. It suggests the individual has not taken the time to do the necessary self-assessment and self-awareness exercises to think and judge critically. The new offer taken may, in fact, be no better or worse than the one refused. Job candidates should be aware that there have been incidents of legal action following job candidates reneging on an offer. This adds a very sour note to what should be a harmonious beginning of a lifelong adventure.

CHAPTER EIGHT

THE GRADUATE SCHOOL CHOICE

The reasons for continuing one's education in graduate school can be as varied and unique as the individuals electing this course of action. Many continue their studies at an advanced level because they simply find it difficult to end the educational process. They love what they are learning and want to learn more and continue their academic exploration.

....

Continuing to work with a particular subject, such as the dynamics of organizational behavior in an increasingly diverse workforce; and thinking, studying, and writing critically on what others have discovered can provide excitement, challenge, and serious work. Some Business majors have loved this aspect of their academic work and want to continue that activity.

Others go on to graduate school for purely practical reasons. They have examined employment prospects in their field of study and all indications are that a graduate degree is required. For example, you have a B.S. in business, no particular "hard" skills, and many of the jobs you're interested in seem to demand an MBA (masters in business administration). You sense your opportunities to work at the level you prefer to in business would be limited without an MBA. Be certain to read Chapter Fourteen for a strategy to approach the graduate school decision.

Alumni who are working in the fields you are considering can be a good source of what degree level the field demands. Ask your college career office for some alumni names and give them a telephone call. Prepare some questions on specific job prospects in their field at each degree level. A thorough examination of the marketplace and talking to employers and professors will give you a sense of the scope of employment for a bachelor's, master's, or doctoral degree.

College teaching will require an advance degree. The more senior executive positions in the career paths outlined in this book will require advanced education and perhaps some particular specialization in a subject area (finance, human resources, etc.).

CONSIDER YOUR MOTIVES

The answer to the question of "Why graduate school?" is a personal one for each applicant. Nevertheless, it is important to consider your motives carefully. Graduate school involves additional time out of the employment market, a high degree of critical evaluation, significant autonomy as you pursue your studies, and considerable financial expenditure. For some students in doctoral programs, there may be additional life choice issues, such as relationships, marriage, and parenthood that may present real challenges while in a program of study. You would be well advised to consider the following questions as you think about your decision to continue your studies.

Are You Postponing Some Tough Decisions by Going to School?

Graduate school is not a place to go to avoid life's problems. There is intense competition for graduate school slots and for the fellowships, scholarships, and financial aid available. This competition means extensive interviewing, resume submission, and essay writing that rivals corporate recruitment. Likewise, the graduate school process is a mentored one in which faculty stay aware of and involved in the academic progress of their students and continually challenge the quality of their work. Many graduate students are called upon to participate in teaching and professional writing and research as well.

In other words, this is no place to hide from the spotlight. Graduate students work very hard and much is demanded of them individually. If you elect to go to graduate school to avoid the stresses and strains of the "real world," you will find no safe place in higher academics. Vivid accounts, both fiction and nonfiction, have depicted quite accurately the personal and professional demands of graduate school work.

The selection of graduate studies as a career option should be a positive choice—something you *want* to do. It shouldn't be selected as an escape from other, less attractive or more challenging options, nor should it be selected as the option of last resort (i.e., "I can't do anything else; I'd better just stay in school."). If you're in some doubt about the strength of your reasoning about continuing in school, discuss the issues with a career counselor. Together you can clarify your reasoning, and you'll get some sound feedback on what you're about to undertake.

On the other hand, staying on in graduate school because of a particularly poor employment market and a lack of jobs at entry-level positions has proven to be an effective "stalling" strategy. If you can afford it, pursuing a graduate degree immediately after your undergraduate education gives you a year or two to "wait out" a difficult economic climate while at the same time acquiring a potentially valuable credential.

Have You Done Some "Hands-on" Reality Testing?

There are experiential options available to give some reality to your decision-making process about graduate school. Internships or work in the field can give you a good idea about employment demands, conditions, and atmosphere.

••

An MBA is the frequent choice of business majors who hope to enhance their career. You'll want to read chapter fourteen in this book to understand how you can make the most of both your graduate education and your career, if the MBA is in your plans. Publications like the *Wall Street Journal's Managing Your Career* newspaper often contain articles that continue the public discussions over the wisdom of the MBA choice.

For business majors who want to take their graduate education to the doctoral level, with an eye to college teaching or research, the need for some "hands-on" reality testing is vital. Begin with your own college professors and ask them to talk to you about their own educational and career paths to their current teaching posts. They will have had actual experience with the current market for Ph.D.s in business.

Whether it's an MBA or a Ph.D. in business that is in your
future, the kind of reality tests that come through internships,
co-op experiences, and, most importantly, talking to people
who have attained the kinds of careers you are seeking will give
you the best kind of information to make your decision.

Do You Need an Advanced Degree to Work in Your Field?

Certainly there are fields such as law, psychiatry, medicine, and college teaching that demand advanced degrees. Is the field of employment you're considering one that also puts a premium on an advanced degree? You may be
surprised. Read the want ads in a number of major Sunday newspapers for
positions you would enjoy. How many of those require an advanced degree?

Retailing, for example, has always put a premium on what people can do, rather than how much education they have had. Successful people in retailing come
from all academic preparations. A Ph.D. in English may bring only prestige to the
individual employed as a magazine researcher. It may not bring a more senior position or better pay. In fact, it may disqualify you for some jobs because an employer might believe you will be unhappy to be overqualified for a particular position.
Or your motives in applying for the work may be misconstrued, and the employer
might think you will only be working at this level until something better comes
along. None of this may be true for you, but it comes about because you are working outside of the usual territory for that degree level.

When economic times are especially difficult, we tend to see stories featured about individuals with advanced degrees doing what is considered un-
suitable work, such as the Ph.D. in English driving a cab or the Ph.D. in
chemistry waiting tables. Actually, this is not particularly surprising when you
consider that as your degree level advances, the job market narrows apprecia-
bly. At any one time, regardless of economic circumstances, there are only so
many jobs for your particular level of expertise. If you cannot find employment for your advanced degree level, chances are you will be considered suspect for many other kinds of employment and may be forced into temporary
work far removed from your original intention.

Before making an important decision such as graduate study, learn your options
and carefully consider what you want to do with your advanced degree. Ask yourself whether it is reasonable to think you can achieve your goals. Will there be jobs
when you graduate? Where will they be? What will they pay? How competitive
will the market be at that time, based on current predictions?

If you're uncertain about the degree requirements for the fields you're interested in, you should check a publication such as the U.S. Department of
Labor's *Occupational Outlook Handbook*. Each entry has a section on training

and other qualifications that will indicate clearly what the minimum educational requirement is for employment, what degree is the standard, and what employment may be possible without the required credential.

For example, for physicists and astronomers, a doctoral degree in physics or a closely related field is essential. Certainly this is the degree of choice in academic institutions. However, the *Occupational Outlook Handbook* also indicates what kinds of employment may be available to individuals holding a master's or even a bachelor's degree in physics.

Have You Compared Your Expectations of What Graduate School Will Do for You with What It Has Done for Alumni of the Program You're Considering?

Most colleges and universities perform some kind of postgraduate survey of their students to ascertain where they are employed, what additional education they have received, and what levels of salary they are enjoying. Ask to see this information either from the university you are considering applying to or from your own alma mater, especially if it has a similar graduate program. Such surveys often reveal surprises about occupational decisions, salaries, and work satisfaction. This information may affect your decision.

The value of self-assessment (the process of examining and making decisions about your own hierarchy of values and goals) is especially important in this process of analyzing the desirability of possible career paths involving graduate education. Sometimes a job requiring advanced education seems to hold real promise but is disappointing in salary potential or numbers of opportunities available. Certainly, it is better to research this information before embarking on a program of graduate studies. It may not change your mind about your decision, but by becoming better informed about your choice, you become better prepared for your future.

Have You Talked with People in Your Field to Explore What You Might Be Doing after Graduate School?

In pursuing your undergraduate degree, you will have come into contact with many individuals trained in the field you are considering. You might also have the opportunity to attend professional conferences, workshops, seminars, and job fairs where you can expand your network of contacts. Talk to them all! Find out about their individual career paths, discuss your own plans and hopes, and get their feedback on the reality of your expectations, and heed their advice about your prospects. Each will have a unique tale to tell, and each will bring a different perspective on the current marketplace for the credentials you are seeking. Talking to enough people will make you an expert on what's out there.

Are You Excited by the Idea of Studying the Particular Field You Have in Mind?

This question may be the most important one of all. If you are going to spend several years in advanced study, perhaps engendering some debt or postponing some life-style decisions for an advanced degree, you simply ought to enjoy what you're doing. Examine your work in the discipline so far. Has it been fun? Have you found yourself exploring various paths of thought? Do you read in your area for fun? Do you enjoy talking about it, thinking about it, and sharing it with others? Advanced degrees often are the beginning of a lifetime's involvement with a particular subject. Choose carefully a field that will hold your interest and your enthusiasm.

It is fairly obvious by now that we think you should give some careful thought to your decision and take some action. If nothing else, do the following:

❑ Talk and question (remember to listen!)

❑ Reality-test

❑ Soul-search by yourself or with a person you trust

Finding the Right Program for You: Some Considerations

There are several important factors in coming to a sound decision about the right graduate program for you. You'll want to begin by locating institutions that offer appropriate programs, examining each of these programs and their requirements, undertaking the application process by obtaining catalogs and application materials, visiting campuses if possible, arranging for letters of recommendation, writing your application statement, and finally following up on your applications.

Locate Institutions with Appropriate Programs

Once you decide on a particular advanced degree, it's important to develop a list of schools offering such a degree program. Perhaps the best source of graduate program information are Peterson's *Guides to Graduate Study*. Use these guides to build your list. In addition, you may want to consult the College Board's *Index of Majors and Graduate Degrees,* which will help you find graduate programs offering the degree you seek. It is indexed by academic major and then categorized by state.

Now, this may be a considerable list. You may want to narrow the choices down further by a number of criteria: tuition, availability of financial aid, public versus private institutions, U.S. versus international institutions, size of student body, size of faculty, application fee (this varies by school; most fall within the $10–$75 range), and geographic location. This is only a partial list; you will have your own important considerations. Perhaps you are an avid scuba diver and you find it unrealistic to think you could pursue graduate study for a number of years without being able to ocean dive from time to time. Good! That's a decision and it's honest. Now, how far from the ocean is too far, and what schools meet your other needs? In any case, and according to your own criteria, begin to build a reasonable list of graduate schools that you are willing to spend the time investigating.

Examine the Degree Programs and Their Requirements

Once you've determined the criteria by which you want to develop a list of graduate schools, you can begin to examine the degree program requirements, faculty composition, and institutional research orientation. Again, using a resource such as Peterson's *Guides to Graduate Study* can reveal an amazingly rich level of material by which to judge your possible selections.

In addition to degree programs and degree requirements, entries will include information about application fees, entrance test requirements, tuition, percentage of applicants accepted, numbers of applicants receiving financial aid, gender breakdown of students, numbers of full- and part-time faculty, and often gender breakdown of faculty as well. Numbers graduating in each program and research orientations of departments are also included in some entries. There is information on graduate housing, student services, and library, research, and computer facilities. A contact person, phone number, and address are also standard pieces of information in these listings. In addition to the standard entries, some schools pay an additional fee to place full-page, more detailed program descriptions. The location of such a display ad, if present, would be indicated at the end of the standard entry.

It can be helpful to draw up a chart and enter relevant information about each school you are considering in order to have a ready reference on points of information that are important to you.

Undertake the Application Process

The Catalog. Once you've decided on a selection of schools, send for catalogs and applications. It is important to note here that these materials might take many weeks to arrive. Consequently, if you need the materials quickly, it might be best to telephone and explain your situation to see whether the process can be speeded up for you. Also, check a local college or university library, which might have current and complete college catalogs in a microfiche collection. These microfiche copies can provide you with helpful information while you wait for your own copy of the graduate school catalog or bulletin to arrive.

When you receive your catalogs, give them a careful reading and make notes of issues you might want to discuss on the telephone or in a personal interview, if that's possible. Does the course selection have the depth you had hoped for?

....

If you are interested in graduate work in management, for example, in addition to classic courses in management theory and organizational behavior, consider the availability of colloquiums, directed research opportunities, and specialized seminars.

....

What is the ratio of faculty to the required number of courses for your degree? How often will you encounter the same faculty member as an instructor?

If, for example, your program offers a practicum or off-campus experience, who arranges this? Does the graduate school select a site and place you there, or is it your responsibility? What are the professional affiliations of the faculty? Does the program merit any outside professional endorsement or accreditation?

Critically evaluate the catalogs of each of the programs you are considering. List any questions you have and ask current or former teachers and colleagues for their impressions as well.

The Application.   Preview each application thoroughly to determine what you need to provide in the way of letters of recommendation, transcripts from undergraduate schools or any previous graduate work, and personal essays that may be required. Make a notation for each application of what you need to complete that document.

Additionally, you'll want to determine entrance testing requirements for each institution and immediately arrange to complete your test registration. For example, the Graduate Record Exam (GRE) and the Graduate Management Admission Test (GMAT) each have 3–4 weeks between the last registration date and the test date. Your local college career office should be able to provide you with test registration booklets, sample test materials, information on test sites and dates, and independent test review materials that might be available commercially.

Visit the Campus If Possible

If time and finances allow, a visit, interview, and tour can help make your decision easier. You can develop a sense of the student body, meet some of the faculty, and hear up-to-date information on resources and the curriculum. You will have a brief opportunity to "try out" the surroundings to see if they fit your needs. After all, it will be home for a while. If a visit is not possible but you have questions, don't hesitate to call and speak with the dean of the graduate school. Most are more than happy to talk to candidates and want them to have the answers they seek. Graduate school admission is a very personal and individual process.

Arrange for Letters of Recommendation

This is also the time to begin to assemble a group of individuals who will support your candidacy as a graduate student by writing letters of recommendation or completing recommendation forms. Some schools will ask you to provide letters of recommendation to be included with your application or sent directly to the school by the recommender. Other graduate programs will provide a recommendation form that must be completed by the recommender. These graduate school forms vary greatly in the amount of space provided for a written recommendation. So that you can use letters as you need to, ask your recommenders to address their letters "To Whom It May Concern," unless one of your recommenders has a particular connection to one of your graduate schools or knows an official at the school.

Choose recommenders who can speak authoritatively about the criteria important to selection officials at your graduate school. In other words, choose recommenders who can write about your grasp of the literature in your field of study, your ability to write and speak effectively, your class performance, and your demonstrated interest in the field outside of class. Other characteristics that graduate schools are interested in assessing include your emotional maturity, leadership ability, breadth of general knowledge, intellectual ability, motivation, perseverance, and ability to engage in independent inquiry.

When requesting recommendations, it's especially helpful to put the request in writing. Explain your graduate school intentions and express some of your thoughts about graduate school and your appreciation for their support. Don't be shy about "prompting" your recommenders with some suggestions of what you would appreciate being included in their comments. Most recommenders will find this direction helpful and will want to produce a statement of support that you can both stand behind. Consequently, if your interaction with one recommender was especially focused on research projects, he or she might be best able to speak of those skills and your critical thinking ability. Another recommender may have good comments to make about your public presentation skills.

Give your recommenders plenty of lead time in which to complete your recommendation, and set a date by which they should respond. If they fail to meet your deadline, be prepared to make a polite call or visit to inquire if they need more information or if there is anything you can do to move the process along.

Whether or not you are providing a graduate school form or asking for an original letter to be mailed, be sure to provide an envelope and postage if the recommender must mail the form or letter directly to the graduate school.

Each recommendation you request should provide a different piece of information about you for the selection committee. It might be pleasant for letters of recommendation to say that you are a fine, upstanding individual, but a selection committee for graduate school will require specific information. Each recommender has had a unique relationship with you, and their letters should reflect that. Think of each letter as helping to build a more complete portrait of you as a potential graduate student.

Write Your Application Statement

··

For the business major, the application and personal essay should be a welcome opportunity to express your deep interest in pursuing graduate study. Your understanding of the challenges ahead, your commitment to the work involved, and your expressed self-awareness will weigh heavily in the decision process of the graduate school admissions committee.

··

An excellent source to help in thinking about writing this essay is *How to Write a Winning Personal Statement for Graduate and Professional School* by Richard J. Stelzer. It has been written from the perspective of what graduate school selection committees are looking for when they read these essays. It provides helpful tips to keep your essay targeted on the kinds of issues and criteria that are important to selection committees and that provide them with the kind of information they can best utilize in making their decision.

Follow Up on Your Applications

After you have finished each application and mailed it along with your transcript requests and letters of recommendation, be sure to follow up on the progress of your file. For example, call the graduate school administrative staff to see whether your transcripts have arrived. If the school required your recommenders to fill out a specific recommendation form that had to be mailed directly to the school, you will want to ensure that they have all arrived in good time for the processing of your application. It is your responsibility to make certain that all required information is received by the institution.

Researching Financial Aid Sources, Scholarships, and Fellowships

Financial aid information is available from each school, so be sure to request it when you call for a catalog and application materials. There will be several lengthy forms to complete, and these will vary by school, type of school (public versus private), and state. Be sure to note the deadline dates for these important forms.

There are many excellent resources available to help you explore all of your financial aid options. Visit your college career office or local public library to find out about the range of materials available. Two excellent resources include Peterson's *Grants for Graduate Students* and the Foundation Center's *Foundation Grants to Individuals*. These types of resources generally contain information that can be accessed by indexes including field of study, specific eligibility requirements, administering agency, and geographic focus.

Evaluating Acceptances

If you apply to and are accepted at more than one school, it is time to return to your initial research and self-assessment to evaluate your options and select the program that will best help you achieve the goals you set for pursuing graduate study. You'll want to choose a program that will allow you to complete your studies in a timely and cost-effective way. This may be a good time to get additional feedback from professors and career professionals who are familiar with your interests and plans. Ultimately, the decision is yours, so be sure you get answers to all the questions you can think of.

Some Notes about Rejection

Each graduate school is searching for applicants who appear to have the qualifications necessary to succeed in its program. Applications are evaluated on a combination of undergraduate grade point average, strength of letters of recommendation, standardized test scores, and personal statements written for the application.

A carelessly completed application is one reason many applicants are denied admission to a graduate program. To avoid this type of needless rejection, be sure to carefully and completely answer all appropriate questions on the application form, focus your personal statement given the instructions provided, and submit your materials well in advance of the deadline. Remember that your test scores and recommendations are considered a part of your application, so they must also be received by the deadline.

If you are rejected by a school that especially interests you, you may want to contact the dean of graduate studies to discuss the strengths and weaknesses of your application. Information provided by the dean will be useful in reapplying to the program or applying to other, similar programs.

PART TWO

THE CAREER PATHS

CHAPTER NINE

INTRODUCTION TO THE BUSINESS CAREER PATHS

The chapters that follow are viable options for business undergraduate degree candidates. These career paths have been selected, investigated, and written with an eye to a candid appraisal of the job market for business majors with limited experience and an appreciation that no job is forever. Whatever employment decision you choose to make after college, think about acquiring specific skills *quickly* to ensure not only that you *stay* valuable to the job market but also that you can *move* from job to job because the skills you have obtained work well in many different employment settings.

SALES

Not only is sales a logical place to begin this book, it is also a solid beginning to many careers. Sales justifiably claims to be the "world's oldest profession" because sales are so crucial to commerce. Sales generates the kind of income that sustains all the other important activities of a business; including research and development, product testing, consumer research, packaging, etc.

The sales force is a vital link between the consumer of a product and the manufacturer of that product. The consumer might be the faculty at an institution of higher learning, building service workers in a hospital, the purchasing agent for a manufacturing plant, or the proverbial person on the street. Sales representatives "represent" the organization, speak for the organization, and are the personification of the organization for most customers.

When you work in sales, you acquire skills that you will use for the rest of your working career. Of course, you will learn a great deal about people and how to best communicate with various folks. But, the most valuable people skill you'll learn in sales will surprise you. Listening. It's not accurate, however, to think that sales has a special corner on teaching you how to make presentations. Every career path in the book will help you improve your interpersonal skills. Sales may just do it faster and with more intensity.

Sales will teach you about products, how they are manufactured, packaged, shipped, distributed, and presented to the final consumer. You'll learn to analyze the features and aspects of a product, to realize the multiple uses and dimensions possible for various goods and services. These are skills you will be able to apply to any future employment situation you find yourself in. When you can break a product or a service down into multiple aspects, you discover new ways to market and advertise that product or service to new and different segments of the buying public. Sales offers significant opportunities for developing creative thinking skills.

Sales also teaches the value of everyone in an organization. This understanding will serve you well in future leadership or management roles. For example, you will learn to appreciate the telephone receptionists who are able to convey to your customer the professionalism of your firm through the efficiency and dispatch of their call handling. The shipping clerk who stays that extra minute to get a package ready for early departure the next morning has a direct influence on how you—the salesperson—are treated on your next call to that firm that received the order so promptly. The accounts department whose bills are on time and easy for customers to understand, even the janitorial staff that maintains the home office as a place that reflects your customer's good choice; the sales staff soon learn the value of each member of the organization to their success.

Sales is first among the paths because it is also the easiest career to access. Of course, employment in the top sales firms like those listed in *100 Best Companies to Sell For* are very competitive. Nevertheless, the reality is that as a new graduate, sales jobs are everywhere. Sales recruiters are the most common tables at job fairs, in campus recruiting offices, and in newspapers advertisements.

Exactly who that "ideal" sales candidate might be remains a mystery. Even to those doing the hiring. And if you were to put a number of professional sales recruiters together in a room to discuss what constitutes a "strong" candidate—get ready to hear a heated debate!

Energy, curiosity, creativity, and an ability to connect with people in an authentic way are generally accepted as essential ingredients for a salesperson. Beyond that, things get hazy. You see, sales can be inside, where customers come to you, outside, where you travel to your customers, or telemarketing, where everything is done by phone. So sales holds phenomenal potential for all types of individuals, including those who might think themselves too "shy" for a sales job. Additionally, sales can accommodate individuals with physical disabilities with less difficulty than many other professions.

The ease of entry is deceptive because the turnover is high. Sales is hard work. But for the new graduate who wants a job and is willing to work hard, sales provides wonderful rewards: the highest incomes; oftentimes the nicest package of benefits, including vehicles; expense accounts; and very challenging assignments. No matter where you go after sales, you are likely to take away a legacy of polished interpersonal skills, problem-solving abilities, an appreciation of the team concept in a work setting, and a deeper and richer understanding of market concepts.

RETAILING

Retailing comes next on the career pathway because of its dominance on the landscape. It is perhaps that sector of the economy that you have been most aware of and become most appreciative of as a consumer. The inside story is as exciting as a dramatic window display. Retailing is vital, dynamic, filled with risk and opportunity.

Though retailing has traditionally not placed a high value on education *per se,* its executive suites are heavily populated with business graduates. They arrived there, not by virtue of their diplomas but by having assembled solid track records of success on the selling floor and through a succession of department assignments, using an understanding and appreciation of the market they are trying to service, managing the risk factors of the decisions they make, and thoughtfully analyzing and reviewing sales performance for future decision making.

In retailing, the spotlight is on you the individual. Though many retailing organizations are justifiably termed conglomerates, even the biggest are structured as many smaller businesses, and individuals in retailing at any level have opportunities to take charge. Taking charge means making decisions and handling the consequences of those decisions. Retailing is not for the faint of heart.

It's ironic that this book may be your first serious introduction to retailing, which is often sadly neglected in business curricula. Ironic because it is a career path that will exercise almost every academic course you've taken in your college studies. Retailing is the pulse of the nation, and to do retailing best, you need to have high levels of general information. All those liberal arts courses you frequently wondered why you had to take will come in very handy in a retailing career when you are asked to provide items for sale to all kinds of people, from sports enthusiasts to dieters to three-year-old girls to retirees. You'll be grateful for your philosophy, sociology, psychology, and other general education courses, including foreign language training.

Retailing may be about providing people with goods and services they need, but the skill in retailing comes in anticipating these needs in the quantities and at the price levels that will secure the most profit for your organization. Retailing is the art and science of predicting human behavior in a shopping situation, and you cannot do that successfully without mixing with the public.

Nobody stands on ceremony in retailing. Of the jobs listed in this book, retailing puts the least emphasis on hierarchy of work. Everyone in retailing pitches in and does what needs to be done to get stock unpacked, and get it on the floor, displayed, and marked so consumers can buy it. This is how aspiring retail executives learn what customers do, how they act and react to the selling situation. You can't make good retailing decisions from an office high above the selling floor. You need to get down behind a counter, roll up your sleeves, and talk to the customers, and then watch what they do.

No matter what happens in your career history after retailing, you gain an economist's view of market forces, for retailing is remarkably influenced by politics, weather, interest rates, and many other factors, large and small, that together give you the whole picture of how the economy works.

You learn in retailing how to put together a package that appeals to the public, price it, advertise it, merchandise it, and sell it. The ability to synthesize these elements can be utilized directly in countless other job situations, as a practitioner designing a trade show for manufacturers in the building trade or as an analyst serving on a consulting team advising a troubled business.

Most importantly, retailing teaches you how to make decisions. Retailing is about careful analysis, decision making involving risk, and data collection systems to provide the right kind of feedback necessary for future decision making. Whether you're in charge of a small section of the floor of a department store, a branch, or an entire building, retailing gives you enormous responsibility early in your career.

H EALTHCARE

Healthcare in the United States is currently in the throes of great change. The volatility and growth of the healthcare industry makes it a perfect time for you as a business graduate to enter the field. Because it *is* a specialized and technical field, you may not have considered it. One of the goals of this book is to give you strategies to transform your credentials from a general business degree to specific marketable talents and techniques. Getting in on the ground floor of healthcare will accomplish that.

Moreover, healthcare's changing climate will provide more opportunities than other paths in this book for job advancement, for as the industry shifts, realigns, consolidates, expands, and contracts, you will be given increased responsibility and increased opportunities to ride that growth while at the same time enhancing your own career.

Why are *you* attractive to healthcare? Watch the nightly news and read your local paper. You cannot avoid the constant barrage of news stories about the increasing conflict between the need to contain escalating health costs and still maintain patient care and focus. Until the healthcare industry began to undergo dramatic changes, the business side of healthcare was accomplished and maintained by homegrown professionals. Now that the industry is under such economic stress, they have realized the advantages of a solid business background and are willing to train business people in the unique culture and vocabulary of the health world.

This is an industry that needs new systems, new ways of doing things, new kinds of jobs, and new methods of handling people and completing paperwork. One of the reasons why this is an exciting field to enter after graduating is that what you'll learn is usable in many other non-medical settings. What healthcare is about is handling large numbers of people in a highly individualistic way, people who need expensive products delivered in the most cost-conscious and efficient manner. The applicability of that to the hospitality industry, travel and tourism, hotels, and other similar service industries is obvious and is just another reason to look seriously at healthcare.

You'll need a strong systems orientation in this industry, so your quantitative skills need to be good. But even more important is the need to couple your analytical ability with a deeply sensitive and compassionate understanding of the nature of your business and the various reasons people seek healthcare. This sensitivity is evident in waiting rooms built with booths and partitions designed for a measure of privacy for an emotional or anxious time. Having no partitions might make for a larger, but less caring, facility. It's this constant juggling between fiscal reality and human considerations that makes this field so fulfilling as a career entity.

Of the five career paths in this volume, healthcare is the most volatile right now, and careers in healthcare are the most subject to the kinds of shifts and changes this book is designed to help you with. Entering healthcare in patient administration, fiscal management, facility support, or any other area, you need to stay cognizant of what skills you are acquiring and could acquire. Though you may not take your medical terminology to another job, you will certainly use any computer software skills, systems design and analysis, strategic planning, and evaluative skills.

These talents are of inestimable value to any employer who is interested in staying competitive. It's the talent of bringing the "big picture" to bear on a particular operational entity, doing a needs assessment, and prescribing changes, if necessary. It's a talent you'll use all of your working life, and you can acquire that in the changing field of the healthcare industry.

Nonprofit Organizations

Nonprofits will be the biggest surprise for the business major and, in a way, that's a sad comment. There are wonderful careers for business majors in the nonprofit world, and there's no connection between the words "profit" and "rewarding lifestyle." Moreover, nonprofits welcome the business major in a way for-profits do not, for the business major is still relatively rare as an applicant in the nonprofit world.

Nonprofit organizations have not been a big part of the business curriculum. One of the biggest reasons for that is that nonprofits do not make as big a marketing splash as their for-profit cousins. Their advertising is seldom as colorful, as sexy, as eye-catching, or as expensive. Most have a lower profile in the business world.

Of course the nonprofits do market themselves, because most nonprofits need the public support and contributions that marketing brings them. However, the nature of the marketing as well as the nature of their financial statements tends to be more conventional, less controversial, and not as dramatic an illustration for the business textbook or classroom that a professor might choose.

Sadly, business educators seem to value business practices only when profit is involved, and yet, from a business standpoint, managing and sustaining a nonprofit corporation using public support, donations, corporate gifts, and federal grants requires infinitely more resources, inventiveness, cost consciousness, and sheer business acumen than many more wasteful for-profit organizations. And for a good cause!

In nonprofits, the cause or mission of the organization replaces the for-profit motivation of the dollar. Whether it's the homeless population or Bosnian refugees, infant nutrition in the Sahara or medical services for Eastern Europe, forestry conservation or animal rights, nonprofits are *about* something other than money. They have a goal, and if you believe in that goal (and you must, if you're going to do a good job and enjoy your work), then every day you are going to be able to use your business education in a dramatically uplifting and ennobling way.

If you've had a classic business education, you may be conditioned to wonder "What do I give up for this job?" The answer is *you need give up nothing.* Nonprofit career professionals have good incomes that are increasingly competitive, and, in the senior leadership positions of organizations, entirely competitive. Nonprofits understand the need to provide incomes and benefits that will enable workers to stay committed to the organization and its goals. They know lower turnover of staff improves the quality of the organization and its ability to achieve its aims.

Of all the career paths listed in this book, the world of nonprofits may present the longest and most consistently enriching path, for not only will nonprofits reward your longevity of employment with increased responsibility and the material rewards that accompany that, but as Jeremy Rifkin, the nonprofit activist and writer suggests, nonprofits are the sector of the economy that may best weather the vicissitudes of a changing world and may be the last sector of the economy to be diminished.

Are the jobs in nonprofit different in any way from those in for-profit organizations? No. Any type of position in for-profit organizations can also be found within the nonprofit sector, including every other career path discussed in this book. Nonprofits need accountants, managers, salespeople, administrators, computer specialists, marketers, advertising specialists, public relations agents, and publicity managers. The list is endless. Sure, budgets are often tighter, so you'll very likely learn better cost control management and gain an appreciation for the possibilities of reaching goals without expansive budgets. Working in a zero-based budget model is, obviously, excellent training, no matter where you career takes you. It teaches you to make the most of what you have and to be judicious when you have more.

Nonprofits are not usually thought of as glamorous, but your work in nonprofits could take place in some of the most interesting cities in the United States or the world. You could find a job in Washington, D.C. or in Kuala Lampur. You could work at a desk in New York City or on a boat in the Adriatic. Additionally, the nonprofit culture is one of pluralism, for nonprofits tend to be less concerned with homogenization and standardization. Nonprofit organizations welcome many kinds of people with many different talents.

A Strategy for the MBA

The final career path tempts you with a different option: graduate school, but with a twist. The MBA is a different kind of graduate degree, because for many career business professionals, an MBA *is* the terminal degree. The Ph.D. may be the final degree for academicians and theorists, but for working professionals, the MBA is the degree of choice.

For an employer, the MBA brings an expectation of experience and expertise. Men and women with MBAs are expected to be worth their often considerably higher salaries for they have experience and specialized skills that can be put right to work. That sounds reasonable, right? So what's the problem?

The problem is that an MBA program can be a place new business undergraduates decide to hide until the job market gets better. They often think, "Not only will I avoid a tough job market, but I'll arrive back on the scene more valuable than ever." This is erroneous on a number of counts. Not only does the MBA imply experience to potential employers, but the MBA programs themselves are usually geared to experienced, older, working professionals, leaving the younger inexperienced MBA graduate with a credential on paper but nothing to back it up. Inexperienced MBAs often end up with jobs that neither require a graduate degree nor make it, financially, worth your efforts to obtain the degree.

The chapter on the MBA degree discusses how you can gain valuable analytical skills as a financial analyst or research associate and *then* return to graduate school for your MBA. You gain wonderful experience that will leave you fully prepared for the rigors of the very best MBA programs. After completing your MBA, you are ready to reenter the market with the enhancement of your new degree and business experience that is valuable in its own right.

The idea of thinking about even a traditional move such as graduate school in this carefully considered way is the same strategy that underlies each of the five chapters that make up the career paths in *Great Jobs for Business Majors.* You want to make a productive, fulfilling life for yourself. You want a return on the investment you've made in your undergraduate education. Most importantly, you want to be able to weather the storms of an increasingly uncertain economy by building a resume of talents that will allow you employment flexibility for the rest of your working life.

CHAPTER TEN

PATH 1: SALES

INTRODUCTION

MEMORANDUM

From: Your Career Advisor

To: The Reader

Subject: Sales Careers

Suggestion: Take another long, hard look at sales
                   careers.

Rationale: In a business world where conditions
                   change rapidly, one element remains
                   constant: the need for skilled and talented
                   representatives of an organization to
                   connect with customers to build new
                   markets for products and services. That
                   could be you!

Advantages: A ready hiring market that allows you
                   access to employment immediately upon
                   graduation. The opportunity to acquire
                   specific product information and become
                   an expert in your field. Countless

continued

---

continued

opportunities to learn and improve inter-personal skills that will remain valuable assets throughout your working life.

Disadvantages: Not many. There is a strong emphasis on individual decision making, time-management skills, and self-direction. Increasingly, professional salespeople are required to be technically astute in order to manage a sophisticated technology needed for customer contact and service provision. A need to be more of a listener than a talker, a problem solver, not a solution dictator, and a consultant, not a high pressured order taker.

Return on Investment: Significant! A sales career will transform even the most broad-based of business majors into a real specialist in business affairs. You'll understand marketplace economics, consumer behavior, and organizational systems in a way never possible in the classroom. You'll also gain immeasurably in your ability to interact with individuals and groups in every type of setting. Sales is a jumpstart to a career in which recognition comes faster than in almost any other employment sector.

Take another look at sales!

Sales: Setting the Record Straight

There's no question—sales is misunderstood as a career option. Sales certainly has had its share of image problems. In literature (*Death of a Salesman*), film (*Tin Men*), and in real life, we have encountered salespeople whose persona resembles caricatures of the fictional snake oil purveyor. The reality is far, far different for the college graduate. As a practicing career counselor, I see two sides to the question, "Is sales a career for me?" Students have one opinion of sales, generally not very positive. Employers have another view of sales, and that is that it is not only positive, but exciting, challenging, and highly attractive. Well, since many of these employers were college students themselves not too long ago, you figure it out!

Teaching and counseling at a small public college, I am no longer surprised that, with the exception of business majors, few college graduates view a sales job as attractive. Even among business majors, there is some reluctance about sales as a career, and many students have concerns about compensation, measures of performance, ethical issues surrounding product quality, and accuracy of sales information.

But I also have the opportunity to meet and talk with professional salespeople throughout the year. I meet them when they visit my campus to recruit, when I attend job fairs and professional conferences, and when I make site visits to employers. Some of these sales professionals are new college graduates themselves, others are mid-career veterans, and yet others are senior staff who have long years of experience. They represent a full spectrum of experience in the field. It's fascinating to hear them speak enthusiastically of the many personal and professional rewards that careers in sales have brought them. Without exception, they speak of the professional challenges of larger accounts, important presentations to management, exciting travel opportunities, superb professional development opportunities, and satisfying financial rewards. Most often, they speak of wonderful, interesting colleagues and business friends.

Sales: The Insider's Surprising View

Most interesting is how they think of themselves. As a group, they are poised, professional, and comfortable in social situations. They would tell you, often as not, that a career in sales is the reason. Individually, they range from extroverted toastmasters to quieter, more scholarly types. Some are comfortable with large groups, others prefer one-on-one. Many think of their jobs as educational and informative, not persuasive and certainly not hard-sell. They are deeply respectful of the people that comprise their market and do not see them as easily manipulated.

Ask any successful salesperson, "What is the most important skill you have?" You might expect the answer would be "personal power," or "persuasiveness," maybe "the ability to overcome objections" or "product knowledge." While all these attributes of a salesperson have their place, the skill most successful salespeople say they value above all is the *ability to listen*.

Sales: Selling Through Problem Solving

Contrary to public opinion, the objective of sales—certainly sales as practiced by professionals with a college degree and working for a reputable firm—is not to *make* somebody buy your product.

An IBM salesperson describes it this way:

> I see myself as a problem solver. I try to get inside and understand my customers' work, their needs, and their problems. I listen. After I've had an opportunity to think about it, I'll prescribe solutions to their problems. Those solutions will include my company's products, but sometimes I will recommend a competitor's product if that is better suited to the job. I'm in this job for the long haul and my belief is each time I sell only what the customers need, I build trust. The more trust I build, the less "selling" I have to do. If I continue to get good at what I do, I may never have to "sell" again.

Sales: A Crucial Role for Both You and the Company

Beginning your career in sales offers considerable advantages, both professional and personal, as a career path. *Great Jobs for Business Majors* begins with the sales career path for the very simple fact that, for most businesses, the sales function is the only aspect of the business *generating* income.

To illustrate this, take an example you are all familiar with—your own college. All those buildings, all that equipment, faculty and staff salaries, food and supplies are supported largely by tuition. Tuition comes to the college with each accepted applicant and the admissions office is charged with recruiting and selecting those applicants. Recently, demographics have been such that with the number of college-age students down, competition has become quite fierce for eligible students. School overhead just doesn't disappear. The admissions office role of selling the school to applicants is crucial to a college's success and prosperity.

In a business, everyone else is using up the income that sales has generated. In fact, some organizations go so far in emphasizing the importance of the sales force that they draw their organizational charts with sales at the top and the chief executive officer at the bottom.

What is it about the sales role that is crucial for the business major to know? Sales and sales professionals are crucial to an organization's longevity. Organizations that employ sales staff have an important or even vital sales function. You will have a difficult time aspiring to top management positions in a business where sales are a top priority if you have not experienced the sales role yourself. It would be difficult, if not impossible to maintain credibility in establishing salary guidelines for sales personnel, to develop new promotional pieces to be used by the sales force, or to appreciate the sales impact of a product's features and attributes unless you have been there yourself.

Sales: The Job Specifications

Let's identify some of the activities engaged in by salespeople. Of course, sales professionals are as varied as the women and men who take on those functions. How they do their job is highly individual; with top sales professionals, you'll often see a singular professional style that is not only highly idiosyncratic but also indulged and approved of by top management. Glancing over this list, you can immediately understand that this job is far more complex and sophisticated than popular myth would have it:

- Identifying and contacting prospective customers

- Anticipating needs and maintaining good relations with existing customer base

- Designing and delivering sales presentations

- Keeping records/activity reports/sales performance records

- Tracking sales orders/delivery schedules and other details

- Handling complaints/returns when received

- Keeping an eye on the competition and reporting activity

- Learning about new products and mastering marketing strategies

This short list of duties emphasizes communications, as you would expect, but there are many other skills and attributes that are suggested by this list.

Let's identify and examine some of these other important skills and attributes close up. Each is followed by a pertinent excerpt from a recently advertised sales job (set in boldface type).

Product Knowledge. It is generally held that there are two kinds of "power" a salesperson has in the sales exchange. One kind of power is *referent power*— the perceived interpersonal connection between the parties in the sales exchange (discussed below). The other kind of power is the salesperson's knowledge of the product being presented. Experts tell us that even if we don't personally care for particular salespeople, we appreciate those who obviously have an in-depth knowledge of their product.

This expert product knowledge comes about in a number of ways. You may be attracted to the position because you already know something about the product or field. Your employer will provide training. You will learn from sales colleagues about their successful techniques for communicating a product's attributes to the market. And you will learn from your customers, who will indicate those features and satisfactions they derive from your product. Though your product knowledge may be specific, your growing understanding of how to communicate a product's many features and advantages to a customer is a skill you will take with you. **"Some background in healthcare or the life sciences would be advantageous."**

Promotability. I know of one large banking corporation that requires all new executive hires to spend some time on the teller line. For those joining the firm with new MBA degrees, working as a teller might seem to be not the best use of their talents. The senior management of this bank, however, long ago learned that unless their lending officers, portfolio managers, and administrators had contact with the average customer, they would never understand the basic business of the bank.

In any organization that has a sales force, to begin work there is to understand the organization in a very concrete, specific way. In the sales force, you learn how the organization is perceived by the consumer. This is true whether you are an admissions representative for a college or selling industrial boilers. Customer contact and your understanding and appreciation of the demands of a sales job will be the foundation and source of your credibility and authority as you advance in your career. **"This position will serve as training for future outside sales and marketing opportunities."**

Customer Knowledge and Contact. Sales is about meeting people—lots of people. Each of these persons has a different need and appreciation for your product. Most of the time you encounter your clients on the job. Since you have initiated the meeting, you will also encounter a variety of receptions, from a warm welcome to a glacial stare. It's going to be up to you and your sales skills to make these moments work. One way you'll learn to do this is by appreciating exactly what each customer wants. Is it service? Perhaps it's product quality. It might be dependability. Sometimes it's the lowest price available. When customers are busy, you soon learn to judge each as an individual, find out what that customer needs and get down to business! **"Develop and cultivate contacts with the healthcare industry, senior community, and participating physician's groups to enhance this new product's presence in the marketplace."**

Communication Skills. A professional saleswoman I know is known for her buoyant, cheerful personality. It's not an act. She is genuinely a positive, happy person who displays incredible energy and vitality. People like her, and her customers enjoy and anticipate her bright, cheery disposition. But she has her thoughtful days, like we all do. She has learned that if she's in a reflective mood, people ask "What's wrong? What's the matter?" Body language, including facial expression, becomes very important. Professional salespeople need to be very aware of how they're coming across, at all times.

Clients won't believe you're interested in them if you're looking at your watch or tapping your foot while they speak. Eye contact, your full attention, and the appropriate sounds and movements of affirmation and understanding convey the message "I'm listening to you!" Salespeople understand that communication is a complex business.

Sales is the art *and* science of communication. The communication is often about important issues such as product features, delivery dates, prices, conditions of sales, financing, etc. A miscommunication can result in far more costly problems than just a lost sale. It's important that both parties understand each other. Professional salespeople become adept at ensuring that their messages are correctly received and "decoded."

We've mentioned the importance of listening. Answering the client's concerns is also important. Ensuring that the client understands you can be accomplished through questioning, reframing and restating what you've said, and by writing things down. Who said salespeople were just great talkers? Salespeople need to be excellent writers, speakers, listeners, and nonverbal communicators! **"Business degree and excellent writing and communication skills required."**

Personal Attributes.   Of course, talking to someone who is currently in sales or who has had sales experience is one of the best ways to begin to appreciate the career path and your suitability for it. Whenever I talk to someone who is currently in sales or has enjoyed a sales job in their work history, they invariably speak of the personal skills that they gained from sales work. What are these personal gains and why are they so important? I've identified some of the most critical skills below and quoted from sales job announcements that refer to these skills as a hiring criteria:

- ❑ **Poise.**   Meeting new people, ease in all social situations, and the ability to chat and make friends with a variety of people all develop unconscious poise and confidence in sales professionals. It stays with them throughout their careers, no matter where that may be. Many sales professionals refer to this as the great gift of a start in sales. **"The candidate must possess the ability to relate to engineers, end users, and contractors."**

- ❑ **Ability to Handle Stress.**   Sales situations—any situations involving people and negotiations—will involve stress as well. A sales career teaches the kinds of planning and strategies to anticipate and avoid stress and the social skills to define and minimize the tension of stress producing situations. **"Enjoy working in a fast-paced, dynamic environment. . ."**

- ❑ **Time Management.**   Most sales positions demand exceptional time management. Learning which clients to call on during which times, deciding when to do your paperwork, determining how to best use drive and fly time, and strategizing your week, your month, and your year for best effect all develop excellent time management skills. Many senior executives, when asked how they can be so productive, respond, "I began in sales and learned to use my time effectively." **"Requires excellent communication and time management skills. . ."**

❏ **Decision Making.**   Whether you're out on the road alone, in negotiations with a client, competing for a major account against a worthy adversary, or discovering new markets or sales opportunities, there will be a need to make decisions. A sales job puts a strong emphasis on the individual and that's why the hiring process is often lengthy and complex. Management knows you will frequently be called upon to think for yourself and the good of the firm. You'll have your successes and your mistakes. Hopefully, you'll be supported from above in each instance and will learn from both. Your job in sales will continue to demand good decision-making skills, many times on the spot. **"Are you an aggressive sales professional who knows how to think on your feet?"**

DEFINITION OF THE CAREER PATH

There are as many different types of sales positions as there are individuals to fill them. Each job holds the potential for both personal and professional growth, to varying degrees. Each job also places different demands on the job holder in terms of work productivity, self-management, travel, professional relationships, and product knowledge.

Great Jobs for Business Majors emphasizes the changes occurring in the world of business and the need for the worker to be ready to "reposition" for a job change or an employer change. To be in the best position to accomplish these likely-to-be required moves during your work career, you'll need to pay attention to your skill acquisition. Hold each job up against your own list of criteria:

❏ Does this sales job give me skills I can take with me to a new position within the same organization or, if necessary, to a new job outside my organization?

❏ If I have to move from this position, how easily can I document my achievements?

❏ Does this position offer me opportunities to learn new skills, new techniques, the use of new business tools?

❏ How does this position allow me to "connect" with the larger organizational structure and how often will I make those connections?

Let's begin the discussion on career paths for sales professionals by looking at some of the variety of jobs being advertised at the time this book was being written:

Wisconsin Sales Territories Available: An accelerated program designed to give participants a thorough foundation in consumer goods sales and sales management in preparation for a career in field marketing management. Due to the decentralized nature of the alcoholic beverage industry, career assignments with this firm are as much involved with developing marketing strategy as they are in sales execution. Successful candidates will be mature, aggressive, results-oriented self-starters who possess both a strong sales personality and have demonstrated above-average leadership aptitude. A strong interest in a sales management career is a prerequisite for success with this firm. Our recruiting program is focused on graduating baccalaureate candidates in Business.

This is certainly an aggressive advertisement because it emphasizes management and marketing grooming functions outside of sales. It suggest candidates for the sales position being advertised will need to be potential management material. It seems to subscribe to the old-fashioned theory of a sales personality being born, not made. Nevertheless, this job ad for an outside sales position emphasizes education and training to a significant degree. It also clearly emphasizes that hiring decisions will be based on potential for promotability to field management. The college business degree requirement is also consistent with these expectations of high standards. A demanding position with lots of exposure to top management and very likely excellent compensation.

College/Military Dormitory Furniture Sales: Customers nationwide for our hardwood furniture designed to meet specifications for these settings. This position requires you to work as part of a five-member team to plan and implement a marketing approach, use all media to communicate with customers, represent the company at trade shows, help independent reps to increase sales in their territories, and execute bid documents for institutional purchasing departments.

This is a combination inside sales (working from within your organization), outside sales (visiting clients at their places of business), and marketing position that involves a team approach to very large purchases of institutional furniture. These necessitate highly consultative sales presentations with modifications of product frequently required. Each sale is critical and may take significant time to consummate; client relations are critical. This position also offers opportunities to work in a team, to gain experience in advertising and other media, to plan and execute presentations at trade shows, and to learn the specifics of institutional buying—all highly *portable* skills.

Inside Sales and Service Representative: Handle PC software orders from our customers on the telephone. You will process orders on our AS/400 system and use PCs for other daily operations. You will need a BS in Business or equivalent, and at least one year of prior customer service or inside sales experience and excellent communication skills, systems/PC familiarity, and strong desire to deliver excellent service.

An inside, technical sales job requiring significant product knowledge and superb communication skills. What often can be achieved easily face-to-face requires far different types of skills to succeed when the contact is by phone.

A Word About Product Classifications

There's a difference between selling furniture and insurance. It's not very different from the distinction between high quality, gourmet take-out food and dinner in an elegant restaurant. Tables or take-out are both concrete, real products that can be judged on the composition of their ingredients, quality of the workmanship, raw materials, and skill in preparation. Using easily established criteria, the *tangible* products can be judged independently of the organization producing them.

Insurance and fine dining both have elements that are less easy to assess; words such as the security, safety, stability of the corporation or, on the other hand, elegance, atmosphere, and class of the restaurant are *intangible* and very much in the eye of the beholder. They are far more difficult to assign value to, for their importance varies with the customer and the customer's needs.

The selling of tangibles versus intangibles puts different demands on the salesperson and affects the dynamics of the sales presentation and even the nature and type of client and client interaction. Selling a tangible product allows the interaction to focus on product suitability and product specifications (color, design, performance). The transaction tends to be crisper and more succinct. Buyer and seller interaction is focused on the product and its features. Tangibles are bought by a wide range of consumers, from the least sophisticated and educated to professionals.

Intangible sales involve a more complex dynamic between the salesperson and the buyer. More credibility and trust needs to be engendered and all sorts of subtle cues come into play (appearance, vocabulary, demeanor of the salesperson). The focus is on the interaction with a salesperson as much as on the product. For this reason the selection of salespeople for intangible product classes is more sophisticated and complex and they need to be more creative and verbal.

WORKING CONDITIONS

Sales jobs are plentiful, but as this chapter indicates, they vary widely in quality, professionalism, training provided, opportunities to interact with colleagues, compensation, and growth potential. When you are a new grad out on the market for a sales job, there's a temptation to look at all the sales jobs available, rationalize away any concerns you might have, and take the first one offered you.

Most of the window dressing for your first job as a college graduate can be very attractive and distracting. A month of classroom training at the home office with all living arrangements provided, a company car that can be employed for personal use as well, the best salary you've ever imagined, beautiful business cards, a handsome leather briefcase—the list goes on and on. It's hard to look beyond these very tangible proofs of your successful employment and judge this new job by any other measure.

There are, however, three aspects of most sales jobs that are so dominant that they serve to define the nature of the employment experience, and the reader would be well advised to consider his or her suitability for a sales position against these criterion. Go back to Chapter One, Self Assessment, and review what you learned about your personal traits, values, and skills. Measure what you've learned about yourself against the following three critical aspects of sales positions:

- ❑ **Degree of Sociability.** Most people remark on how easily sales professionals talk to just about anybody. It's quite easy to explain. Despite the fact that their jobs emphasize connecting with people, most sales professionals work alone and their contact with others is fairly brief and intermittent. They spend quite a bit of time on their own and would tell you that you need to be comfortable with yourself to be good at sales.

  Some sales jobs involve teams; others are inside sales jobs where you are surrounded by the same coworkers each day whom you can get to know and build relationships with. Think clearly about your own past experience and how well you can handle the degree of sociability or the demands of being alone presented by the sales jobs you are considering.

❑ **Nature of the Client Contact.**   In most sales jobs, the actual "selling" of a product is not as challenging as connecting with the client. There are basically two ways to see a client: an invitation through some sort of pre-screening or pre-sales work that has the client requesting your visit, or the cold call, when you call on a client who may not yet be aware of your product or service but whom you believe might be a good prospect for it.

Whether being invited or inviting yourself is more appealing or more challenging to you has much to do with your personality. Your tolerance of risk, your ability to handle new situations, and your ease in making acquaintances will be good barometers of which situation would be best for you over the course of a career.

❑ **Productivity/Competitiveness.**   Sales is often repetitive. It's not a career where you can sit at home and rest on your laurels. For many in this profession, a success only motivates them to further achievement. This competitive drive may not be directed at others. In some organizations, sales staff are not aware of other's track records in the field. It may simply be a competition with yourself. Because sales always involves seeking new markets and new clients for products and services, that competitive spirit is essential.

This competitive drive can be hard to maintain if you are selling intangibles. For example, if you are working for a major pharmaceutical manufacturer talking to physicians about drug therapies and encouraging them to try your products, you cannot legally "sell" anything. You simply can stress advantages of your product(s) and encourage the physician to prescribe the drug(s) when indicated. Thus, it can be difficult to measure success when selling such intangibles. You might wonder at the end of the day "What have I accomplished?" Do you need to see an order sheet all filled out? Each of us has different needs for feeling successful and a carefully chosen sales job can meet that need.

TRAINING AND QUALIFICATIONS

People who hire for sales positions know best how difficult it is to predict who will do well in this profession. Most of you have little prior experience on which to judge your suitability and you have a sneaking suspicion that your sales technique classes in college may not have been as challenging as the "real thing."

Hiring professionals know all this. But they also know the demands of the marketplace and the sophistication and educational background of people you'll be meeting. They know that the increasing demands of sales automation require an ability to master the computer and to manage one's own time and workflow. They have found a college degree to be the best training ground for many of the demands of today's professional sales consultant.

Though you may have some natural ability for sales, you will need further training in sales skills. In addition, you will want to be provided with a structured opportunity to learn about the products and services you'll be selling. The best sales positions offer the greatest amounts of formal training. However, the training is not always provided *before* you begin selling. Some firms have their new sales recruits attend formal sales schools, complete with dormitories, exams, and classroom presentations before you meet the public. Other organizations have found training to be more worthwhile following a brief period of actual field sales, perhaps three to six months. The philosophy behind this decision is that some exposure to the demanding role of the sales professional will help you to appreciate the training and be more aggressive in your studies. Both philosophies have merit.

Be wary of those positions that ask you to fund yourself until you are paid, provide your own transportation, or offer no formal training. This kind of employment structure places no responsibility on the hiring organization. Consequently, rapid turnover (common in these jobs) is not very damaging since the organization has spent little money on each salesperson. A firm that invests in your training has invested in you and wants you to succeed. Here's a strong statement about training from a recent advertisement for a national wine salesperson:

Type of Training: Both classroom and on-the-job. Program participants will typically spend between one and two years as a Sales Representative calling on high-volume retail stores and a similar period as a first-level Sales Manager in charge of four to eight Sales Representatives. Simultaneous classroom training will be provided during both stages of development to equip participants with the necessary theoretical and conceptual foundation in sales and sales management.

---

*E*ARNINGS

Sales offers the entry-level graduate the highest possible earnings available with a college business degree, with only a few exceptions for some technical majors. High earnings are attractive to many students who graduate with some debt burden and a strong motivation to begin to live on their own and make a life for themself.

A recent survey by the Dartnell Corporation reports that today's salesperson earns about $30,000 in an entry-level job. Intermediate-level sales professionals average about $40,000 and senior sales positions can easily exceed $53,000. An additional 30 percent of these incomes is given out in benefits.

Positions in selling pay either a salary, a commission, or a combination of the two. As an entry-level salesperson, you will probably be more attracted to a salaried selling position. It seems less risky and seemingly puts less responsibility on you to produce than a commission system does. Straight-salary plans work best for employers when it is difficult for management to determine which person on the staff actually made the sale or when the product involved has a broad, cyclical sales pattern, which would leave the sales staff with virtually no income during the slow periods if commissions were involved. Of course, straight salary plans reward slackers.

Sales professionals who have gained skills and confidence in their abilities are often more attracted to commission plans. Commission plans offer them unlimited income if they are successful. Straight commission gives the greatest incentive to salespeople while maintaining a predictable sales cost in relation to sales volume. Two factors working against straight commissions are: 1) high turnover and burnout of sales staff and 2) a sales process tainted by the need of sales personnel to *move* product to pad the salesperson's paycheck regardless of a customer's true need for the product/service.

Consider compensation plans carefully, regardless of your financial needs. It can be very disheartening to leave a position because of a disagreement over the pay arrangements when a little forethought might have anticipated problems.

Combination plans exist with fixed salaries and incentive features added on. This builds continuity in the sales force, yet allows superior sales staff to shine, and it encourages everyone to develop more business.

The bouquet of roses of each pay scheme has its own thorns. A straight-salary job cannot reward superior achievement, and that may grow to be a frustration if you are exceptionally successful in your position. If you expect to be the best you can be, shouldn't your paycheck reflect that? With a straight-salary job, you and the poorest performer take home the same paycheck!

Commission rewards ability and performance and that can be attractive to the confident sales pro. However, be sure you understand what the minimum performance levels are, how much you need to do to earn your commission, and how feasible those goals may be. What is the waiting period, following a successful sale, before you receive your compensation? Occasionally, when commission salespeople are "too" successful, an organization will redivide their territory and add sales staff. The philosophy behind that move is that if one individual can do so well, there may be even more opportunity if additional sales staff are employed. However, for the successful salesperson, this only means less territory and much harder work to realize the same income as before.

Commission is not as risky as most graduates think. If (and this "if" is important) the organization that hires you is spending money and time on your training, they do not want to see you fail and are taking steps to ensure you succeed. Their compensation plans are based on experience borne of what past salespeople can do and what incentives they needed to do it. There is no success if salespeople drop out because they can't make any money. The organization would suffer and, ultimately, fail.

Benefits Are Important, Too

Take some time to review a book like *The 100 Best Companies to Sell For* and develop a sense of the benefit packages offered by the best organizations. It will help give you a standard by which to judge your own package. Benefits are income when they apply to your educational progress, your medical or dental bills, or your need for a vehicle and insurance. A good benefit package is estimated at a third of your income, so if you are salaried at $30,000, your benefits can cost your employer another $10,000, depending upon your usage.

Some typical benefit items include:

- ❑ Medical/dental
- ❑ Life insurance
- ❑ Disability insurance
- ❑ Travel allowance
- ❑ Company car
- ❑ Profit sharing
- ❑ Stock purchase plan
- ❑ Child care
- ❑ Retirement plan
- ❑ Savings/investment plan
- ❑ Tuition assistance
- ❑ Relocation assistance
- ❑ Memberships (fitness clubs, etc.)

CAREER OUTLOOK

Whatever volatility our economy is feeling these days, sales jobs remain critical to a firm that needs to move its product on to the next stage in the channel of distribution. Everyone in that channel, from the originator of the product to the retail merchant, is seeking someone to buy what they themselves have just bought. The longer any channel member holds the product, the more risk they engender of perishability, fire, theft, obsolescence, loss of market value, encroachment by competitors, or failure to realize a profit.

Salespeople are critical in organizations of this kind for they generate that vital activity of moving the product on, making the profit, and reducing the risk of holding that product too long. Salespeople are not only the largest occupational group in the United States but the one with the largest projected number of new jobs in the coming decade. It's quite amazing to think about the sales process occurring for an infinite number of products to an infinite number of market segments of consumers. Somewhere in that sales cosmos is a market and product you would enjoy.

A Word About the "Marketing Contract"

College graduates like yourself are sometimes amazed at the vast array of products that are bought and sold in the marketplace, many of which you've never heard of, others seemingly objectionable and distasteful to anyone. Who buys this stuff? The answer is quite simple.

The marketing contract says that if the public demands a product, channels will exist to distribute that product and purveyors will appear who will stock and sell that product. That explains not only all the different carbonated beverages in a supermarket aisle but also the booming trade in pornography or drugs. Products do not stay "in the market" if there is no demand. As salespeople, you will find—if you do any kind of research or exploration—that there is an incredible array of goods and services, tangible and intangible, available on the marketplace, and one of these will demand your particular talents and skills. Go out and find it!

STRATEGY FOR FINDING THE JOBS

Your Job Search Approach May Be Your Ticket to a Job!

There's something interesting about the hiring of sales personnel that's different from the hiring of other kinds of professionals. With accountants, analysts, purchasing agents, or administrative support, the employer looks for professionalism in the resume and cover letter but is more interested in finding out what the job candidate knows, what his or her experience has been, and whether the candidate seems adequately prepared for the job under consideration.

In the sales personnel market, every aspect of the coming together of the candidate and potential employer is a clue to the candidate's potential in a sales job. What better exercise in persuasiveness is there than the job search? Can you think of any other activity that puts as much emphasis on the kind and quality of one's communication as the job search and the interview itself? A job search is by and large a sales exercise, and if you wish to become a sales professional, an employer has every right to expect to see the beginnings of brilliance in how you go about seeking your job! Consider:

The Significance of the Resume and Cover Letter

All sales jobs involve some degree of written communication. In fact, it's probably a fair corollary that the more important or senior the sales position, the more it will involve written proposals, presentations, and projects. Early signs of a salesperson's professionalism might be the resume and cover letter. Do they:

- ❏ Get to the point?

- ❏ Interest and excite the reader?

- ❏ Look attractive and distinctive?

- ❏ Display the hallmarks of attention to detail/accuracy?

It is no exaggeration to say that many resume/cover letter readers have every right to expect that if you cannot put together a *perfect* sales package for yourself, you won't be able to do it for them, either.

When executives have only a day to devote to interviewing and they must reduce a pile of 200 resumes and cover letter to 8 to 10 candidates, the first ones to go in the wastebasket are those that have typographical errors, or look confusing or "tricky" with too many typefaces or overly fancy graphics. "Gee, the candidate must not have proofed this work. Poor attention to detail. I wouldn't want something like that going out under our letterhead." And out it goes!

The Unique Importance of the Interview for Sales

For a sales position, the key to being hired is the interview, for it is the most obvious early demonstration of your communication facility at presenting a product (yourself) and ability to make a winning case for your employment. Even acknowledging your newness at interviewing and the anxiety of most new college grads during interviews, most recruiters will still want and expect to see some nascent indications that you have what it takes. If you're shy and retiring or fail to demonstrate your skills, you'll disappoint your interviewer. If you are overly confident, a braggart, or loud and pushy, you'll turn your interviewer off.

Try and *balance* the interview as best you can. Try to give as much information as you get, and answer questions with as much information as you can. If the interviewer ends up doing all the talking, they learn nothing about you, and if you do all the talking, you miss a great opportunity to learn more about the organization.

Sales is about communication, but sometimes that communication is not just about the product or service you are selling. Interviewers, accordingly, will want to know what you're reading, your opinion on current events, and your views on national legislative issues. Salespeople need to be well read and have high levels of general information, for they will need to draw on that each day as they communicate with a diverse range of customers.

Chapter Five of this book contains good information on how to prepare for an interview. For the sales job candidate, there are additional considerations for both the telephone and person-to-person interview.

The Telephone Interview for Sales.   When sales work involves the telephone or when a firm needs to screen a large number of applicants, the telephone interview as a first-stage interview technique is helpful and inexpensive for employers. Some important tips for sales candidates in the phone interview include:

❑ Arrange to take the interview where you will not be disturbed and where background noise will be at a minimum. You don't want to miss any information, nor do you want the interviewer to be distracted by background noise.

❑ Have a large writing surface near the phone and try to note as much of the information being given as possible. It'll come in handy later. Don't be shy about asking to have important details repeated or to ensure you have a proper name correctly.

❑ Speak very clearly and distinctly into the mouthpiece. Don't let your responses go on and on. When you've finished a response, it should be clear to the listener.

❑ Most of all, try as best you can to let your voice express its natural warmth. Be yourself and be as natural and as relaxed as a job interview situation allows. Using your facial muscles to smile when thinking about a question or expressing pleasure is a technique many successful phone speakers find helpful in conveying emotions through the voice.

The Personal Interview for Sales.   The key word here is "appearance." Your first impression is largely determined by how you look. Your interviewers know the impression you make on them is basically the impression you'll be making on the organization's clients and potential customers. Many, many salespeople are selected in large part for their personal appearance. It's called *referent power,* and it is the ability of the client or customer to relate to the salesperson as someone of their standing, background, or education.

1. Make the most of what you've got! We all can't look like supermodels, but we can certainly arrive at the interview making the most of what we *do* have. When buying suits for the interview process, seek help to ensure clothes fit in a becoming way and that patterns and colors are appropriate for you and your body type. For women who choose to wear makeup, consult with makeup professionals in a major department store or salon for appropriate colors and techniques for business wear. For both men and women, hairstyles in sales positions are often dramatically different from the styles you have been accustomed to in college. Check out business magazines or professional sales journals for cues as to how the practicing professional wears his or her hair. Then select a style that looks right for you!

2. Don't make a fashion statement. An article on dressing for job success in the *New York Times* (April 2, 1995) urges college graduates to err on the side of conservatism in the early stages of the interview process. In sales, you want the customer's reactions to be focused on your product, not on your personal appearance. Think of dressing professionally, not in a distracting manner.

3. Now, forget how you look and focus on connecting! If you've taken sufficient care with your appearance, you can focus on what are, actually, the more important issues. The interview is a time to convey your intelligence, your perceptiveness, your verbal dexterity, your listening skills, and your warmth and sense of humor—whatever personal qualities that make you the unique individual you are.

POSSIBLE EMPLOYERS

Sales Jobs Are Everywhere: How Do You Find the One for You?

It's true! Sales jobs (of every type and description) seem to be everywhere. In fact, many other kinds of job seekers complain that sales jobs are all they ever see. Each sales job describes itself differently and each job description seems to focus on a different aspect of the position. For some it's customer contact, for others it's product knowledge, and yet others emphasize productivity or profit margin. How do you judge what's best for you?

Make a list of what you want in a sales position. We all want different things, so list your requirements. Perhaps financial security is Number 1 on your list. Then you need to be on the lookout for those sales jobs that offer a salary and avoid commission status. Perhaps you want to further your education and want additional training. Seek out those sales positions advertising training programs or emphasizing high quality professional development for its sales force. Other priorities might be travel, activity level, productivity, income production, calling on established clients, or making cold calls on prospective clients. Whatever it is, you need to draw up your own working list of elements you're seeking in a sales position so you can adequately judge and compare the market offerings.

Begin with the best and establish your own criteria. Start with a reference work such as *The 100 Best Companies to Sell For* and learn the particulars of the sales job from the crème de la crème of sales organizations. This book will give you valuable insight into:

❑ Entry-level salaries for sales

❑ Senior-level salaries for sales

❑ Products and services offered by each company

❑ Benefits (including bonuses, perks, etc.)

❑ Corporate culture and style

❑ Training—which firms stress formal training programs and which emphasize on-the-job experience

❑ An in-depth discussion of the firm and the role of sales in the organization

❑ Criteria used in selecting sales candidates

Now that you have drawn up a list of your criteria and you have read about and understand the criteria of the best in the business, you want to begin the process of applying for the jobs that seem to meet your needs.

Sales jobs are widely advertised and recruited because hiring firms often have to talk with and screen a number of candidates before they find one that fits their needs. You will have to do the same in your search. For that reason, the job search for sales is a busy one with lots of resume mailing, telephone interviewing, job lead follow-up, and cold-calling before you "connect" with that perfect job. Some of the best places to look are:

Your career office. Your college career office will not only contain numerous subscriptions to job posting newsletters offering entry-level sales jobs, but is also on the mailing list of many employers who look on college campuses to fill sales jobs, especially in the spring. Your career office can direct you to resources that you might otherwise never discover. For example, *Sports Market Place 1996* contains thousands of sales positions in sporting equipment and sports-related products and services. Visible Ink's *Marketing and Sales Career Directory* is another rich source of employers seeking sales candidates.

Large metropolitan newspapers. These are excellent sources for sales jobs, especially Sunday editions. Check them out every week.

Job fairs. Job fairs come in all varieties, specializing in many kinds of jobs. The sales job fair is one of the most common type. These provide a good way to distribute your resume, meet lots of employers, practice your stand-up interviewing skills, and check out the competition.

Alumni networks. Informal or formal networks amongst your college alumni are a fine way to tap into the hidden job market. You'll need to be just as on-your-toes as you are in the job search, but alumni contacts can give you the inside track to unadvertised job openings.

Possible Job Titles

The sales industry itself works very hard to improve the professional standing of its salespeople and move them out from under any stigmatizing labels or job titles that might inhibit their abilities to do their jobs. So you'll see several titles listed below that don't even contain the word "sales." Get used to that in seeking out sales positions. It may be your first signal that the hiring organization has paid particular attention to the role of their sales force.

Account executive	Product line manager
Account representative	Product manager
Area director	Regional manager
Area manager	Sales director
District manager	Sales manager
Major account representative	Salesperson
Market representative	Sales representative
National sales manager	Sales specialist
Outside sales representative	Service representative

Related Occupations

The skills you've acquired in sales tend to be rather universally esteemed: listening, speaking, public presentation, decision making, time management, product specification knowledge, and an ability to "connect" with people authentically and quickly. Sales professionals are easily transitioned to a wide variety of occupations. A sampling would have to include the following:

Advertising	Product management
Career counseling	Promotions
Chambers of commerce	Public relations
Communications	Real estate
Consulting	Trade fair design
Manufacturer's representative	Training and development
Marketing management	Travel agent

PROFESSIONAL ASSOCIATIONS

American Marketing Association
250 South Wacker Drive, Suite 200
Chicago, IL 60606
Members/Purpose: Professional society of marketing and marketing research executives, sales and promotion managers, advertising specialists, academics, and others interested in marketing.
Publications: *American Marketing Association—Proceedings, International Membership Directory, Journal of Health Care Marketing.*

Association of Incentive Marketing
1620 Route 22
Union, NJ 07083
Members/Purpose: Conducts education and information programs to improve the effectiveness of incentive merchandising through the influence of the professional incentive executive.
Publications: *Incentive Casebook: How Marketers Motivate, Association of Incentive Marketing—Incentive Report, Association of Incentive Marketing-Membership Directory.*

Association of Sales Administration Managers
P.O. Box 1356
Lawrence Harbor, NJ 08879
Members/Purpose: Seeks to resolve problems with production, distribution, sales services, employment, and internal financial functions.

Bureau of Salesmen's National Associations
1819 Peachier Road, NE, Suite 210
Atlanta, GA 30309
Members/Purpose: Salesmen of wholesale women's, men's, and children's apparel and accessories, shoes, toys, and western wear and equipment.
Publications: *Bureau News.*

Direct Selling Association
1666 K Street, N.W., Suite 1010
Washington, DC 20006
Members/Purpose: Manufacturers and distributors selling consumer products door-to-door, by appointment, and through home-party plans.
Training: Offers specialized education.
Publications: *Direct Selling World Directory, International Bulletin, Membership Directory, News from Neil, Who's Who in Direct Selling.*

Hotel Sales and Marketing Association International
1300 L Street, N.W., Suite 800
Washington, DC 20005
Members/Purpose: An international organization devoted entirely to education of executives employed by hotels, resorts, and motor inns.
Training: Conducts seminars, clinics, and workshops.
Publications: Directory, annual. *Marketing Review,* quarterly. *Update,* 8/year.

Life Communicators Association (LCA)
Bullock Drive PH.5 Markham
Ontario, Canada, L3R 0G1
Members/Purpose: Encourages the interchange of experience and ideas. Advertising, sales promotion, public relations, and company communications specialists of life insurance companies.
Training: Conducts workshops to aid in educational development of junior members.
Publications: *Life Communications,* Membership roster.

National Association of Professional Saleswomen
P.O. Box 2606
Novato, CA 94948
Members/Purpose: Women actively involved in or interested in professional sales and marketing careers.
Publications: *Successful Saleswoman.*

National Association of Publishers Reps
200 East 15th Street, Suite A
New York, NY 10003
Members/Purpose: Independent publisher's representatives selling advertising space for more than one publisher of consumer, industrial, and trade publications.
Publications: *Bulletin, Roster of Members.*

National Network of Women in Sales
710 East Ogden, Suite 113
Naperville, IL 60563
Members/Purpose: Women who are in a sales or related career or seeking to enter the field. To further the careers of professional saleswomen by providing support and sharing expertise and experience.
Training: Conducts monthly programs and seminars; offers counseling on resume writing, interview techniques, and career development.
Publications: *Contacts, Network News, Directory.*

National Society of Pharmaceutical Sales Trainers
5 Homestead Lane
Avon, CT 06001
Members/Purpose: Seeks to improve professionalism within the field by raising standards of development and training programs; encourages members' self-development by facilitating information exchange.
Training: Conducts workshops annually.
Publications: *Newspost,* roster.

National Society of Sales Training Executives
203 East 3rd Street, Suite 201
Sanford, FL 32771
Members/Purpose: Corporate managers and directors of sales and marketing training and human resources development.
Training: Conducts educational conferences and sales training clinics.
Publications: *Sales and Marketing Training.*

Pi Sigma Epsilon
155 East Capital Drive
Hartland, WI 53029
Members/Purpose: Professional fraternity—marketing, sales management, and selling.
Publications: *Convention Update, Dotted Lines, Headquarters Bulletin, Journal of Personal Selling and Sales Management.*

Promotion Marketing Association of America (PMAA)
257 Park Avenue South, 11th Floor
New York, NY 10010
Members/Purpose: Promotion service companies, sales incentive organizations, and companies using promotional programs. Supplier members are manufacturers of premium merchandise, consultants, and advertising agencies.
Training: Sponsors seminars.
Publications: *Outlook, PMAA Membership Directory, Promotion Marketing Abstract.*

Radio Advertising Bureau (RAB)
304 Park Avenue South, 7th Floor
New York, NY 10010
Members/Purpose: Membership includes radio stations, radio networks, station sales representatives, and allied industry services, such as producers, research firms, schools, and consultants. Exhorts advertisers and agencies to promote the sale of radio time as an advertising medium.
Publications: *RAB Instant Background: Profiles of 50 Businesses.*

Sales Association of the Paper Industry

260 Madison Avenue
P.O. Box 7673
Garden City, NY 11530–7673
Members/Purpose: Sales, marketing, advertising, and sales promotion personnel for primary producers of pulp, paper, and paperboard.
Training: Sponsors seminars and meetings with speakers on special subjects.
Publications: *Bulletin, Directory of Members.*

Sales and Marketing Executives of Greater New York

13 East 37th Street, 8th Floor
New York, NY 10016
Members/Purpose: National organization of company executives interested in improvement of marketing and sales management techniques. Purpose is to develop and disseminate improved marketing and sales.
Training: Sponsors monthly seminars.
Publications: *Roster Issue, Sales Executive.*

Sales and Marketing Executives International (SMEI)

Statler Office Tower, No. 977
Cleveland, OH 44135
Members/Purpose: Seeks to make overseas markets more accessible by interchange of selling information and marketing techniques with executives in other countries.
Training: Sponsors seminars, conducts career education programs, offers Graduate School of Sales Management and Marketing at Syracuse University, NY.
Publications: *Marketing Times, SMEI Leadership Directory.*

Society for Marketing and Professional Services

99 Canal Center Plaza, Suite 250
Alexandria, VA 22314
Members/Purpose: Employees of architectural, engineering, planning, interior design, landscape architectural, and construction management firms who are responsible for the new business development of their companies.
Training: Provides specialized education through regional seminars held two to three times a year.
Publications: Membership roster, *SMPS Marketer.*

Specialty Advertising Association International (SAAI)

3125 Skyway Circle N.
Irving, TX 15038–3526

Members/Purpose: Promotes industry contacts in 30 countries. Suppliers, distributors, and direct selling houses of specialty advertising including calendars, imprinted specialties, and executive gifts.

Training: Holds executive development and sales training seminars.

Publications: *Specialty Advertising Association International—Membership Directory and Reference Guide, Specialty Advertising Business.*

Women in Advertising and Marketing

4200 Wisconsin Avenue, N.W., Suite 106–238
Washington, DC 20016

Members/Purpose: Professional women in advertising and marketing. Serves as network to keep members abreast of developments in advertising and marketing.

Publications: Membership directory, newsletter.

Women in Sales Association

8 Madison Avenue
Valhalla, NY 10595

Members/Purpose: Promotes professional development of women in sales. Provides opportunity to establish business contacts, and to share information and ideas.

Training: Conducts work sessions on topics; sponsors career guidance workshops.

Publications: Membership directory, *Sales Leader.*

Women's Direct Response Group–New York Chapter (WDRG)

224 7th Street
Garden City, NY 11530

Members/Purpose: Seeks to advance the interests and influence of women in the direct response industry; provide for communication and career education; assist in the development of personal career objectives; and serve as professional network to develop business contracts and foster mutual goals.

Training: Sponsors monthly seminar, workshops, and summer internship program.

Publications: *Women's Direct Response Group—Membership Roster, Women's Direct Response Group—Newsletter.*

CHAPTER ELEVEN

PATH 2: RETAILING

etailing is the sale of selected merchandise directly to the consumer. Though this definition of retailing might be satisfactory for a business exam, in actuality retailing defies description! Retailing is an exciting career with enough change and excitement to keep you fascinated and on your toes for the life of your career. But retailing can also be a doorway, through which you can enter the worlds of fashion, sales, product management, or training and development. The majority of today's top managers in these fields began their careers in training programs offered by the retailers that were their very first employers after graduation.

Dramatic changes are taking place in the world of retailing. Let's examine a few examples of this marketing revolution and what those changes mean for the business major looking for a dynamic and fast-paced career opportunity.

> Motion picture and television companies, seeking incremental income and enhanced brand image, are increasingly opening branded-merchandise stores. Warner Bros. has 111 stores and plans to open 45 more. Disney operates 339 specialty stores and plans to increase that number to 600. Viacom's MTV plans to develop a themed restaurant chain that will offer virtual reality technology and merchandise, in addition to food.

We have at least two critical clues here to the importance of retailing in the American marketplace. Major corporations such as Warner Bros. and Disney realize that for reaching the public, retailing is a worthwhile investment in capital expenditure, training and development, and hiring of expertise. Organizations are beginning to see retailing as the important "missing link" in their presentation of a complete array of goods and services. In today's competitive arena, many business enterprises appear to want more direct contact with the consumer.

MTV is already an influential network, with a sharply defined target market. But it has obviously assessed that market and determined the profitability of retail restaurants as a means to both further the bond of their current viewers and introduce potential viewers to the television network through a meal!

You can see from the example above that it isn't enough to just know your product. The career-minded retail professional must stay abreast of demographic trends (such as population shifts and changing lifestyles). Retailing often is on the cutting edge of technology. Retail stores were the first to use fashion/music videos on continuous loop on the sales floor to stimulate customer awareness and interest in apparel products. These tapes were early forerunners of music videos. Retailers are the first to sell in cyberspace and will be the first to use virtual reality to let shoppers "try on" clothes or experience home furnishings or outdoor equipment, and so on.

Manufacturers, hoping to differentiate their brands from private-label brands, are increasingly opening their own retail outlets. Footwear maker Dr. Martens, for example, has opened a department store in London's Covent Garden district. The store, in addition to selling boots and shoes, sells branded gift items and provides services. The company hopes to create a lifestyle brand.

The concept of *forward integration,* manufacturers controlling the retailing of their own products, is an increasingly common phenomenon. It is another dramatic signal to business majors that retail is not only important, but getting bigger and bigger. The idea has obvious merit. If manufacturers really care about their shoes or clothes or ski equipment, what could be better than creating their own stores, with a complete line of their products and retail salespersons specially trained by them to display and educate the public in a way not possible with retail employees who must learn about and sell a huge array of products.

Wal-Mart Stores will open an environmentally friendly "eco-store." The store, which will carry Wal-Mart's standard merchandise assortment, has beams made of wood instead of steel, skylights that provide natural light and chlorofluorocarbon-free air-conditioning system. The store has a recycling theme and an on-site recycling center. Analysts predict that other retailers will adopt such concepts.

The idea of stores responding so dramatically to the public's concern with the environment is but one example of the changes that constantly alter the face of retailing in today's marketplace. Retailing is the pulse of the public. If you want to know what the American public values, where their interests lie, how they play or dress, what they read, eat, or buy, just visit a store! And as the public's interests change, often overnight, retailing is the first to respond.

> Retail stores and shopping malls are facing a variety of competition, ranging from superstores to video shopping, and are countering by introducing entertaining into their retail plans. The Mall of America contracted with Knotts Berry Farm to provide a central amusement core in this, the largest mall in the United States. Some malls are also offering more refined amenities such as museums, schools, and even churches.

Retailing is no place for the amateur or for the faint of heart. It's a world that demands you take a risk, for only the strong survive. One reason why the business graduate is a welcome candidate for jobs in the retail sector is the constant, unrelenting competition demanding a variety of skills, decision-making ability, and solid business education.

> The number of earth stores, retailers selling environmentally friendly products, in the United States has grown from virtually zero in 1990 to about 200 in 1993, according to *Green Marketing Alert* editor Carl Frankel. Retailers such as Earth Mercantile, Earth General, Restore the Earth Store, Terre Verde, and Eco–Wise can be found in most regions of the country. Frankel estimates that earth-store revenues reached about $28 million in 1992.

It could be environmentally related products; it could be angels, quilting materials, or mountain gear. The point here is the trend towards narrow focus and "boutique" concepts in retailing. No longer do you try to do everything for everybody. What people want now is someone targeting a narrow market with specific products that have an appeal to the aware consumer, be it coffee or clothing. But there's a lot of risk here. If you're just putting brown eggs in your basket to sell, you darn well better be sure that there's a strong, continuing market for brown eggs!

Was Retailing Missing from Your Business Curriculum?

A common reason for making poor career choices is one's lack of information about all the possibilities. Though retailing careers continue to appear on every published list of "Growth Careers for the Future," college students considering career selection consistently overlook the retail sector. Business majors may find their department offers a single course in retailing, but more than likely, retailing is discussed as part of the larger subject area of marketing or consumer behavior.

If retailing is so big now and continues to grow, why aren't business majors more exposed to it in college? One possible reason is that retailing is so varied and so dynamic that it presents real challenges to design one course, much less one chapter of a book, to do justice to such a broad topic. In retailing a person can work almost anywhere in the world, with any type of merchandise, for nearly anyone, including themselves. They can work with large corporations or they can work for any of hundreds of thousands of small merchants. Some people forge lasting and rewarding careers in local stores. Others learn the business within one organization and then branch out in business for themselves. The organizational structure of retailing, however, is such that even within a large corporate retailer, being your own boss and independently responsible for your unit is the way business is done.

Furthermore, many, many people are involved in the movement of goods from manufacturer to consumer, and the retail industry hires people with a wide range of talent, from shipping clerks to window designers. We opened this chapter with a definition of the *retail industry*—that sector of our economy that brings the consumer into direct contact with goods and services. The focus of this career path chapter, and the primary interest of most college graduates, is in the merchandising jobs—buyer, merchandise manager, and store manager.

Focus on Merchandising

Retailing is a term we are all familiar with. We use the term every day to describe the industry that sells us things. *Retailing* as a technical term, however, most accurately describes the movement of goods from their final point of presentation in the channel of distribution (the retail outlet) to the purchase by the consumer. *Merchandising* is a term used to describe all the buying and selling activities within a store or chain. Merchandise managers decide what to buy based on what will sell. These are immensely complicated decisions.

For example, you are a buyer for men's shirts for a large chain. You must, months in advance of the selling season, choose from among hundreds of fabric possibilities (all cotton, nylon, silk, and blends) weaves (oxford, cambric, poplin, point-on-point, twill), collar styles (button down, tab, many varieties of spread collar, and collarless), cuff styles (French, buttoned), and, of course, price points at which all these various shirt models will be sold. You make all these decisions, including final price, based on a thorough understanding of your market: the people that shop in your store and what they will buy.

This is one of the great areas of confusion about the area of retail merchandising. Many people feel suited to retail because they have "great taste" or "they love to shop." These reasons are not sufficient to get you hired in retail. People who succeed and rise to the top in retail are people who have the best sense of what their market will buy. They develop this strong sensitivity by mixing with the market *on the floor*. A good merchandiser stays in touch with the customers by working the floor, selling merchandise, hearing complaints and praise about the products, and watching and noting the gender, age, and buying considerations of the public.

It is these positions for which employers are most interested in the talents of the college business major. You've noticed how retailing examples are used over and over again in business texts to illustrate investment principles, risk management, the costs of carrying inventory, pricing strategies, and many other basic principles of sound business management. There's ample evidence that retailing is an important business activity, and yet you don't feel you know very much about is as a career choice. Why is that?

Three Reasons to Consider Retail

There are three principal reasons why business students don't have the opportunity to seriously consider retail careers upon graduation. First and foremost is that the subject of retailing is an art and science unto itself. It is serious, big business that incorporates healthy doses of psychology, human behavior, and intuition along with a high tolerance for taking risks. Though there are programs such as the Center for Retailing Studies at Texas A&M where retailing gets the attention it deserves, many business programs simply don't have the faculty expertise to do justice to the exciting, complex, frustrating, and constantly changing field of retail.

The second obvious reason many students fail to consider retail is that retail puts no special premium on the attainment of a college degree. Of course, if you entered the executive suite of our largest retailers, everyone you'd meet would have a college degree. So would most of the preeminent retail managers, sales managers, and buyers. But the emphasis in retail hiring is on decision making, leadership, previous retail exposure, and the ability to juggle an ever-changing workload in a fast-paced environment. In retailing, what you can do and who you are counts more than degree attainment. The following ad for a major national retail chain store manager makes this point:

Who Says You Can't Have It All?

Store Management: An interesting career . . . a welcome challenge . . . AND rewards. If you're ambitious and determined to make the most of your career, we want you to play an active role in our success and yours! As the nation's leading specialty retailer of imported home furnishings and related items, our store managers are involved in all aspects of our business. That's why we provide a comprehensive on-the-job manager development program to prepare you to take charge of a store, including P&L, visual merchandising and people management.

We seek managers with strong retail experience, (**college degree a plus**), proven leadership abilities, a commitment to customer satisfaction, and the drive to handle a diverse workload in a challenging, fast-paced environment. Candidates must be willing to relocate. Investigate a career that offers it all, including competitive compensation and benefits, and stock purchase/ 401(k) plans . . .

The third reason students don't take a more serious look at retailing as they graduate has to do with a misperception of retailing in the hierarchy of American jobs. Let's take a look at a typical college job fair. Business majors are going to be attracted to the professional sales, the large corporations, and the prestige and esteem of classic "management" positions. The retailers may also be at this job fair, but since students haven't had any in-depth exposure to retail careers in their major, all they're apt to see is store management and sales associate jobs. They don't consider the potential here.

The plain and simple reality is that almost any of the retailers present at that job fair will offer careers with more latitude, more fiscal responsibility, more decision-making authority, and more downright opportunities to take off (or crash and burn) than any of the narrowly-defined, terminal-in-a-cubicle positions that exist beyond the impressive facades of the corporate management positions. Retailing is about giving talented people an opportunity to chart their own course, within the retailer's concept, for as long as any particular concept remains profitable. Retailing *listens* to employees' reasoning and, if it finds it sound, will support their decisions to add product lines, expand selling space, branch out into new markets, or redefine their image.

DEFINITION OF THE CAREER PATH

One of the most disappointing realities of any new job for the college graduate is how mundane the first year of employment can be. Students return to visit me and recall how surprised and disheartened they were to find themselves in a supposedly great corporate job, on the management fast track, and yet chained to a desk with very routine, ordinary assignments while they learned the ropes. None of this is true for retailing.

This is the field where you can jump right in and start a career *if* you are people oriented, service oriented, and willing to take advantage of opportunities. Retail personnel are in the front lines of getting the product to the consumer. They are the final marketing intermediaries. Customer contact and customer service is the key to unlocking the consumer's interest in purchasing your product. Customer contact provides the answers to ordering and pricing mysteries. Customer service is an art and a science, made up of both analytical and communications skills. It is these distinctions that keeps your customers coming back.

The four most common entries into retailing for a college graduate are buyer, sales management, store management, and formal retail executive training program. We will examine each of them in turn.

Buyer/Merchandising Trainee

This is the so-called "glamour job" in retailing. Buyers are those individuals whose job it is to choose merchandise. Many people assume buyers are charging all over the globe in search of the most exotic chessboard, or perfect sweaters or inexpensive furniture. But that's hardly the reality.

Most buyers actually spend only a small percentage of their working year in the buying process. And, yes, for some shoes or leather articles, that buying might take place in Italy, but more than likely, most buying will occur at a buying exposition for small leather goods in a convention hall in Atlanta or Dallas.

As a trained buyer, you'll work under the supervision of a senior buyer. You'll need to learn to anticipate your customer's shopping needs several seasons before the merchandise is in the store. You will find yourself considering a variety of issues. Will men switch to a two-button suit? Will misses-sized women tolerate a shorter skirt length? How many of each size children's shoe to order? And so on. There are mountains of paperwork and sometimes daily reports of sales to analyze. And, if you haven't bought right, your mistakes stare back at you from store shelves!

You'll learn to negotiate with vendors on costs, delivery dates, and shared advertising budgets. You will work with store staff on merchandise displays and as you gain experience, you will take on more responsibility in each of these areas. Before too long, you will be in charge while your senior buyer is away. Some organizations will require that your training include a stint in store management so you may spend some time in a branch store. Promotion to buyer positions can take two to five years. Realize that movement to middle management is faster than in many other industries.

Sales Management Trainees

We have mentioned the art *and* science of retail. Sales management is an area where both are especially important. Sales management is the crucial job of providing everything necessary to sell the merchandise you have on the floor. The basic tools in your power kit are sales staff, maintenance of stock, displays, in-store promotional material, and the ambiance you can create with music and lighting.

Your career will begin under a sales department manager whose main responsibility is the supervision of a sales staff, the productivity and profitability of a department, and the physical configuration, including displays, signage, racks within that department. Sales managers and their assistants work closely with buyers and their duties sometimes overlap, especially in the areas of inventory control and turnover of merchandise.

You'll be learning the merchandise, working the floor, scheduling staff, arranging displays, anything and everything to keep your department running smoothly. This is a hands-on, roll-up-your-sleeves, dig in, and get involved kind of job.

Typical paths are trainee, assistant department manager, assistant store manager, store manager, and on to vice president. There is considerable movement of sales management staff from store to store, and relocation as part of a promotion is common for successful managers. Workloads may be heavy, but rewards of rapid advancement are there.

Store Management

The goal of the store manager, in any size operation, is to run the store at a profit. Store management involves the merchandising functions discussed above, with the addition of store operations (staffing, shipping, receiving), accounting, and advertising. In smaller stores or decentralized branches of larger chains, the store manager might handle all of these functions. The central office, however, often provides varying degrees of assistance with advertising layout, administrative forms, policy statements, and training. In a larger store, the store manager would have assistant managers handling each of these functions. Chain stores with centralized administrative functions would control all accounting and buying and probably supply all advertising set-ups, relieving individual store management of those functions.

Executive Training Programs

Your entry title in either of the general paths listed above would be termed a "trainee" position, and that is not just to emphasize that they are entry-level. Most retailers have developed very sophisticated and comprehensive Executive Training Programs in both the sales management and buyer categories which allow trainees to move through a number of carefully designed training seminars and related work assignments. Excellent classroom presentations by senior executives and practical, hands-on experience are a highly effective way to learn your job and, more importantly, to succeed in it!

WORKING CONDITIONS

This work is fast paced, at times exciting, with numerous opportunities to connect with the public and respond to its needs. It is a career that rewards your ability to sense and stay ahead of consumers' wants and needs. There are drawbacks, however, as with any job. Retailing often involves long hours and, at the beginning of your career, a not-very-exciting paycheck as well as some very mundane chores.

Be ready to accept some drudgery in your job. You'll need reserves of physical stamina. Even senior management, on occasions, have to plunge in and help shift stock, relocate racks, or change displays. In retailing there are no primo dons or prima donnas. Everyone pitches in and does what is necessary to move merchandise.

In addition to physical stamina, you'll have to be willing to tolerate risk. Retailing means playing the roulette wheel of trying to anticipate what the market will want six or nine months in the future—ordering all that merchandise in the size, colors, and quantities now for a future you can't entirely predict.

Everyone in this industry will agree on one thing: for those who love it, if you demonstrate your zeal and enthusiasm with competency, you can expect to be recognized early on and rewarded with promotions and bigger paychecks.

Job factors given below are among the most important when making a considered choice to pursue retailing as a career. As you read these, compare these jobs demands to the results of the self-assessment you did after reading Chapter One of this book.

Rapid Advancement. Ambitious people usually want positions that demonstrate their talent to advantage and then reward that talent with responsibilities and duties that will further stretch and develop their skills. Retailing offers these possibilities. Talent is immediately recognizable in the fast paced and highly responsive world of retailing.

Suppose one of your first assignments as a buyer trainee is to purchase the comforters for the bedding department. Hundreds of thousands of dollars worth of decisions involving fabric composition, stuffing contents, price range, crucial color and design choices, and, of course, various price lines and sizes. If you choose well, your stock moves off the shelf and daily sales reports trumpet your success to store executives. If not, you see your mistakes every time you visit the floor.

Action. Some people love to be busy, the busier the better. They cannot tolerate sitting at a desk all day, chatting around the water fountain, or catching up on business journals. They seek action and avoid the boring and repetitive. The answer is retailing. No day is like another, and the only constant is change. Each day has a different outcome as each customer through the door presents a different collection of needs to be satisfied. Merchandise arrives daily, customers need to be serviced, stock must be rearranged or freshened, and paperwork demands attention. Demands can be incessant. This is a business for the strong and energetic. The pace is fast, exciting, and fulfilling, but only if you enjoy the work. If you're not happy, you'll see it as chaotic, frantic, and frustrating!

Contact with People. Sometimes job applicants make the mistake of telling the interviewer "I'm a people person." What does that really mean? In retailing, a "people person" must be comfortable with all kinds of people from all walks of life and, increasingly, from many different parts of the world. You will have to want to understand their needs and enjoy making an effort to fulfill those needs.

Merchandise. To be the most effective you can be in retailing, you need to enjoy and appreciate what you sell. If you don't, how you display it, how you talk about it, and how you feature it in your store will betray your lack of interest. Retailing is about the goods that are sold, and there should be an enthusiasm on your part for that merchandise, whether it's snowblowers or fine bed linens. Retailers who love their merchandise convey that enthusiasm to their markets.

Mobility. Retailing careers offer unparalleled mobility. Retail opportunities exist worldwide and in every size and variety of emporium, so if you are anxious to live on the west coast or in the plains states, you can do it.

Entrepreneurship. This word has special meaning for retailers because, in a sense, every buyer, merchandise manager, or store owner is in business for themselves. Retail structure encourages you to think for yourself, make decisions, and run your operation as if it were your own business. Each department or operating unit in today's retail stores has its own printout of profit and loss. You will easily be able to demonstrate your entrepreneurial spirit.

But working within the retail establishment is also the best preparation for a career as an independent retailer. As a buyer, merchandise manager, or store manager, you'll be exposed to many of the issues, concerns, and decisions that you would have to make if you were running your own business.

Travel. If you're an auditor in the accounting industry, you expect to travel to clients and may stay for a week at a time. Sales representatives frequently travel and stay overnight. Retail positions, however, have very little associated travel, although most retailers get welcomed opportunities, on occasion, to travel to a trade show or product fair. Top buyers for large stores often travel to locate goods to sell, and some buyers travel to foreign markets frequently, but buying trips tend to be limited in time and restricted to particular times of the year.

Work. Everybody works, and there's no place to hide. The work may not be arduous, but it never ends. Everyone is expected to pitch in when needed, and those who don't are easily noticed.

Long Hours. Take a look around. Retailers are open holidays (even some of the most sacrosanct, such as Christmas), evenings, weekends, and late nights. Stores need to be staffed and maintained and managed. You'll be working many times when the rest of the world is out playing! Retailers soon learn that they work when others play or have holidays, and they have time off when everyone seems to be at work! Competition is intense in retail, and management often puts in long hours on and off the floor to stay abreast of the competition.

No glamour. Even when you obtain the coveted position of buyer, you'll be shocked to find your office is a cubbyhole tucked behind the dressing rooms on the fifth floor. Store floor space is for merchandise. Employees take what's not usable or left over. A very successful buyer for leather goods for a famous New York store once told my students, "If you think visiting Florence, Italy is glamorous, you ought to see me in July on the bed in my hotel room eating a tuna-fish sandwich and trying to decide how many of which gloves I should order for next winter!" Is that glamorous? I don't think so. Glamour is for the customers.

TRAINING AND QUALIFICATIONS

The environment of retailing is less one of glamour, travel, and clothes than one of computer printouts and statements of profit and loss. You need to have an entrepreneurial spirit of excitement about running your own million-dollar department and making solid, increasing profits because those are the factors that move retailers ahead. Of course, retailing has many attractive, exciting, and, yes, even some glamorous aspects, but to base your career decision on those expectations is to invite disappointment by misunderstanding the basic concepts of the retail trade.

Because computerized information can tell the retailer so much about what is required in terms of inventory, labor, and so on, students seriously considering retail careers need to consider mastering computer technology, including spreadsheet software and statistical packages, and have some exposure to database management. As our economy becomes increasingly technologically oriented, the candidate who can apply high-tech, information-based skills to a successful career in retailing has many advantages.

In addition to these technical skills, there is a need for analytical skills. Accounting and business organization courses give you the solid basic background you'll need to understand the language and culture of a business climate. Courses in marketing, general management, and economics will give you an even broader picture of the changing and very dynamic scope of retailing in our economy. The appearance of increasingly large merchandisers, whether they are department stores, warehouse showrooms, or grocery retailers, places demands on those candidates to understand the mechanics of "big" business.

Join marketing or retail clubs, if your college offers them, and participate actively. These groups may provide an opportunity to work with retail people outside of the college environment. That will help in your future dealings with people from a variety of backgrounds.

Internships or a co-op program, if your school has one, are ideal ways to help you ascertain your interest and suitability for the retail profession. Additionally, they help you to add valuable entries on your resume that will attract employers following graduation.

Part-time employment in any area of the retail sector will give you immense credibility as a manager who can truthfully say to rank and file workers, "I've done that."

Retailing is about people, not just machines, and it is this combination of the technological and human that demands the retailing candidate have some exposure to other cultures, anthropology, sociology, and psychology. This background will help in understanding your market, communicating with them, and assessing their needs and wants.

EARNINGS

The most recent salary survey conducted by the College Placement Council shows starting salaries increasing modestly at this point for general undergraduate business majors entering retailing, though increasing somewhat more strongly for those business students who have elected a retailing or merchandise management major. Earnings vary according to the size of the retail establishment. But remember: retailing is one of the few sectors of employment where there is a direct compensation for the volume and quality of the work accomplished. Thus, even without a graduate degree, you have opportunities to boost your pay through outstanding performance. The *Boston Globe,* in an article on job outlooks for 1995 graduates, quotes the Collegiate Employment Research Institute at Michigan State University as indicating starting salaries for college graduates with business majors entering retailing at $22,195, a 1.6 percent increase over 1993–94 salaries. The following are some very general guidelines:

General Merchandise Manager (GMM).   Usually these individuals have vice-president status and overall responsibility for a major division of a store. While not involved in actual buying, they coordinate buying and selling activities for departments within their divisions. They also plan sales promotions, determine quantity of merchandise to be stocked, and decide markups and markdowns. These positions report directly to the chief executive officer.

Divisional Merchandise Manager (DMM).   These positions report to the GMM and are responsible for one (or more) of the classifications of merchandise within the division. So, in a home supply store, it might be garden equipment, furniture, and lighting. In a department store, it might be Juniors coats, dresses, and sportswear. The DMM's first duty is to achieve the profit and sales goals set for the department by top management. With the help of the buyers under his or her supervision, the DMM keeps stock of merchandise, displays, replenishment, and sales movement.

Both GMMs and DMMs are college graduates in the large retail corporations of today and many have achieved these positions following years of floor work, stints as buyers, and the usual path of advancement to top management. Salaries vary widely and according to size of employer, volume of sales, and potential for bonus.

General Merchandise Manager	$60,000 to $200,000
Divisional Merchandise Manager	$50,000 to $120,000

Buyer.   These personnel seek out and purchase all the items stocked by a retail store, from can openers to diamonds. The argument over the degree of glamour in these jobs will never cease. Nevertheless, these positions do involve some travel and occasionally (depending upon the store and what is being purchased) foreign travel. Using past experience or market research as a guide they buy what they believe will sell in their stores. About 150,000 buyers work in retail stores around the country and most are located in major metropolitan areas. Generally, these positions require the breadth and quantitative exposure of a college degree, although the training comes from the store where they begin as assistant buyers or buyer trainees. Earnings vary as discussed, but buyers make $40,000 to $80,000.

Assistant Buyers/Buyer Trainees. While training is underway (at least 12 months to follow the yearly cycle) to become buyers, assistant buyers manage voluminous paperwork, process orders from vendors, check invoices on material received, and keep track of stock. The salary range for junior to senior assistant buyers is $20,000 to $50,000 depending upon store size, volume of traffic, and so on.

Department Managers. Department managers oversee the selling floor and stock areas. They ensure merchandise is properly ticketed, markdowns are taken, displays are well stocked, the selling area is in order, and sales staff coverage is adequate. Earnings between $15,000 to $50,000.

Sales Staff. Over three million people are employed in retail businesses altogether with the largest numbers of sales staff in department stores. Solid training programs often begin sales staff in areas requiring little customer assistance (housewares, notions, etc.) and build experience to those departments with "big ticket" and greater customer assistance, such as in furniture, designer labels, custom tailoring, or appliances. Salaries vary dramatically from hourly wages of minimum wage to as much as $50,000 a year.

CAREER OUTLOOK

According to the well-respected *Occupational Outlook Handbook* published by the U.S. Department of Labor's Bureau of Labor Statistics, as many as 877,000 new jobs in retail sales may be created through the year 2000.

Consolidation of buying activities because of mergers amongst organizations will reduce the demand for buyers through the year 2005 to a growth rate somewhat more slow than average for all occupations. Although the same industry conditions obtain for sales managers, the number of store outlets will keep this job category growing at an average rate.

The variety and scope of retailing today is obvious to us all. Disposable income is increasing among the middle and upper middle classes and people are constantly seeking retail outlets that offer the mix of goods they want. As the largest segment of our population—the "baby boomers"—reaches their peak earning years, demographics suggest an increasing demand for retailing services and the management staff to direct those initiatives.

Strategy for Finding the Jobs

Retailing holds many exciting possibilities for the business graduate. The jobs are creative, demanding, and well worth your investment in a college education. The future of retailing is full of surprises but is certain to include increased technology and innovative new ways to both reach and satisfy the consumer market.

The statistics given on earnings certainly make the profession a desirable one. And the projections of growth in the retail sector should lead you to the conviction that if you really want to enter retailing as a career and have the personal characteristics the industry is seeking, there is a job waiting for you.

Retailing is, however, an incredibly diverse field. Merchandise lines run the gamut from lingerie to lawnmowers, and there are "big" names in each field (Victoria's Secret/John Deere). Geographically, retailing is literally "all over the map" and you can find retail employment throughout the United States and the world. Once you're located somewhere, there is equally as much choice about job duties; buyer, merchandise manager, store or department manager, site development, advertising, finance . . . the list goes on and on.

With the following outline you can develop a successful strategy for finding the right job *for you* in the retail sector. If you 1) have enough time to do a thorough job search, 2) have access to all the options listed below, and 3) want to be sure you've covered all possibilities, then go through this plan step by step. Not only will you succeed in finding the jobs, but the process of implementing this search will also make you a better and more informed interview candidate and increase your chances of being selected because you will truly understand the world of retail. However, if time or your options are limited, then pick and choose amongst this list for what is most doable for you.

Shop Locally!

Essential Preparation

If you're a business major, your own school is apt to have plenty of ways for you to get your career search in high gear. Use them.

Marketing/Retail Clubs.   Business clubs that bring majors together for common interests are wonderful sources of information about a possible career in retailing. Try to meet each guest speaker that comes to campus to speak to the club on business issues. Let them know of your career plans and ask their advice. Serve on speaker committees and special career-related projects. If your club has an opportunity to attend a national convention, try to be part of your school team and use that opportunity to meet guests, gather information, and network.

Cooperative Education.   Your college may provide an opportunity for you to elect a work/study plan called co-op. If you can manage it (it may add anywhere from a semester to a full year to your degree), cooperative education is a proven way to access a career, learn the ropes, meet influential people in your field, and be exposed to the dimensions of your chosen career area while you earn some money for tuition.

Internships.   The single most effective way to improve your ability to move from graduation to a job is through an internship. Internships are generally non-paid or low-paid training positions in your chosen field that give you broad exposure to a variety of tasks and management role models. They can last from a few weeks to a semester and sometimes longer. Internships can often be used for college credit towards your degree. Many successful interns have been offered positions at their internship sponsoring organization upon graduation. Many more credit their job success to their internship. *Internships 1996,* a Peterson publication, lists some superb retail internship opportunities.

Alumni Career Connections.   Either the career office or alumni office on your campus can put you in touch with former graduates of your college who are now working in the retail job market. These alumni connections can be very helpful, offering informational interviews, background on the firms that employ them, and general insights into the retail job market. Depending upon the sophistication of your school's alumni database, they may be able to actually isolate who's working as a buyer, a merchandiser, or store manager. Remember, when contacting these individuals for career guidance, that you are representing your college *and* every other student who may someday want to use this valuable referral service. Be prepared with a list of questions for your alumni contact and use their time wisely. You'll make a good friend and have increased insight into your chosen career field. Many alumni will invite you (distances permitting) for a visit to their place of business and may offer to assist with your resume or job search strategy.

Campus Job Postings.   The binders that contain some of the hundreds of job advertisements that come through the mail to your career office on campus can inform you of many excellent retail entry-level jobs. These may be duplications of the advertising copy that was placed into a newspaper classified want-ad section or it may be a special recruitment mailing to a local college for qualified applicants. These job postings are easy to flip through and, because they change frequently (new ones arrive weekly), should make this kind of "catalog shopping" a weekly activity!

On-Campus Recruiting. The employers from the retail sector who visit your campus are giving you a strong indication of their interest in your school's students. Sign up for every recruitment interview with a retailer that you possibly can. On-campus interviewing can and does lead to actual job offers. It's excellent interview practice, as well. Most importantly, you will begin to develop a sense of what each employer is offering and start to make distinctions about what you feel is the best "fit" for you in a retail career offering. Unlike the job fairs, these are private interviews, one-on-one with a senior representative from the retail organization. Even better, it's held on campus in familiar surroundings, which should prove helpful to you in controlling those interview jitters. Your campus career office probably maintains files on all the recruiting firms to allow you to be thoroughly prepared for your interview.

Shop Around!

Job Fairs

Job fairs are valuable job search tools for the student seeking a retail career opening. *First,* they are very efficient. How else would you be able to meet and talk with so many possible job contacts *in one day? Second,* retailers use them! Rosters of employers at past job fairs indicate retailers are traditionally very well represented. Retailers enjoy job fairs because it allows them to meet and see a number of highly qualified business majors. *Third,* the job fair process of walking up to an employment representative, greeting him or her, and giving a one-minute "infomercial" about who you are and what you might have to offer the organization is a perfect example of the specific kind of people skills retailers seek out.

If a recruiter at a job fair is interested in you, he or she may ask you to submit a formal application or you may be invited to one of the employer's *open houses* or an actual interview. They may extend this invitation at the job fair or by telephone or letter at a later date. Strong student job candidates who take full advantage of job fair opportunities are consistently amazed at both the number of responses and how much later after the fair some of them arrive.

"Careers '96," the nation's Number 1 college recruitment conference, always offers a premier gathering of some of the country's top retailers at its annual job fairs for college seniors each spring in Puerto Rico, New York, Atlanta, Washington, D.C., and Chicago. Your career office at college will have application forms for this prescreened job fair as well as a folder of forthcoming job fairs in your area that will be featuring jobs in retail. Some of these fairs are free, some have a modest fee. Take advantage of all of them for they vastly improve the efficiency of your job search.

Shop by Mail!

The Classic Cover Letter/Resume Campaign

Get to your nearest college library and dig out some of the excellent reference books listed in the bibliography that accompanies *Great Jobs for Business Majors*. Books such as *The Corporate Address Book* and *The 100 Best Companies to Work for in America* or *The Encyclopedia of Business Information Sources* might be a good beginning. Start to list all of the retailers you might enjoy working for and send them your resume with an interesting, informative cover letter as suggested in Chapter Two of this book. Be ready to follow up your letter with a phone call and see if you can arrange an interview. Don't be concerned if the retailer's headquarters are far away from your campus. They may have an executive attending a conference in a nearby city who could interview you, or a senior buyer at a trade show might have time to meet and talk with you and report back to the home office about the impression you made.

No Obligation to Buy!

The Option of "Temping"

In the Winter/Spring 1995 edition of *Managing Your Career, The College Edition of the National Business Employment Weekly*, published by the *Wall Street Journal*, Maureen Rorech makes a strong case for the possible benefits of "temping." The benefits to the employer are well known; no benefits, no commitment, and the ability to expand or shrink the work force according to demand without severance costs or legal problems.

For you, the advantages are a chance to "look inside" the kind of organization you might eventually call home. You'll be paid for your work, of course, but more importantly, you'll meet people, network, add a relevant job to your resume, and perhaps be able to access the organization's internal posting system. A 1992 survey by Ms. Rorech's firm indicated more college graduates were hired through temping than through on-campus recruiting.

Temping has changed. Once a source of clerical and light industrial workers, now temping provides any level of professional or managerial expertise needed.

SOME SPECIAL INTERVIEW TIPS
FOR TALKING WITH RETAILERS

Eventually you are going to be called upon to sit down and interview for your position. Chapters Five and Six of this book contain all the information you need in order to prepare a solid interview. Polish and performance will come with experience. However, there are three special considerations you'll want to be aware of in talking to professionals in the world of retail:

1. Be prepared to talk trends!　Each issue of *Fortune* magazine has a column entitled "Selling" devoted to tracking current trends in population, changing lifestyles, and buying patterns that form the seeds of any present and emerging strategies and technologies for selling in the retail sector. Here's a job ad for a control buyer for a major off-price women's dress store that mentions "trends" twice in this simple job description. It's all the clue you need to know that a discussion of women's fashion trends is going to surface in your interview.

> **Control Buyer:** Based on merchandise selected, as well as historic and current fashion trends, you will plan and buy a category for our stores. This will include monitoring merchandise levels and rebuying based on customer demands and trends. This challenging and visible position will also track and expedite vendor deliveries.

2. Understand consumer behavior.　Your business curriculum probably included some marketing courses, including consumer behavior. Just as important are courses in the liberal arts, such as psychology, sociology, anthropology, and philosophy. They help you as a potential retail employee to understand better and, consequently, interact more effectively with the consumer. This advertisement for a very up-scale British retailer of clothing and small home furnishings is obviously concerned with their employees' ability to relate to and communicate effectively with their clientele:

> **Shop Manager:** In the retail industry, we are known for quality, superior English fashions and home furnishings. We seek an enthusiastic, aggressive Shop Manager to join us. All candidates must have excellent customer service standards and be creative and poised problem solvers.

3. Are you ready to analyze?   Good retailers take accounting and business organization courses for the language and understanding of the structure of business. Here's a job that centers around analysis but requires superb "people" skills as well.

> **Merchandise Analyst:** You will be responsible for maximizing customer satisfaction and company profits by providing and replenishing each store with the proper quantity mix and presentation of merchandise. By reviewing store performance and analyzing store history, trends, and planned promotional activities, you will develop and adjust store ranks by class, category, and style. Maintaining close contact with merchants, stores, and logistics staff is also key responsibility. Candidates should have strong analytical skills.

POSSIBLE EMPLOYERS

Any retailer would be pleased to add to their employment ranks a freshly minted college graduate interested in a career in merchandising. That doesn't mean, however, you should be interested in them! This book has made a strong case for using your employment to add portable skills to your resume—skills that are not industry specific but that you can move with you from job to job. One of the best ways to ensure you are adding those skills is by selecting those employment sites with high quality management, a respect for the college education, and possible training options. The following retailers provide these.

Bruce Wallace, Recruiter
Bob's Stores
160 Corporate Court
Meriden, CT 06450

   Bob's is the original casual clothing and footwear superstore and a subsidiary of Melville Corporation, the parent company of CVS, Marshalls, Thom McAn, Linens 'n Things, and other successful businesses. Bob's recruits management trainees for additional new stores. They are primarily interested in business, management, and marketing majors. Management trainees take part in a 12-week training program that rotates through all areas of their stores.

Linda Goodale, College Relations Manager
JC Penney Company, Inc.
P.O. Box 10001
Dallas, TX 75301–8115

JC Penney is one of the nation's top retailers and enjoys a leadership position in the fashion industry. JC Penney hires more college graduates than any other retailer.

College Relations
Office Depot, Inc.
P.O. Box 5085
Boca Raton, FL 33431–0885

The Number 1 retail office-products company with more than 400 stores in the United States and Canada, they offer formal management training, ongoing leadership skills development, a superb benefits package, and excellent advancement opportunities.

Manager of College Relations
Saks Fifth Avenue
611 5th Avenue
New York, NY 10022

Currently operating in 45 locations across the nation with sales of more than $1 billion annually, Saks is committed to training top buyers and managers through their Executive Training Program, based in New York. Two distinct paths are available in the buyer program (store management path or merchandise management path), both offering comprehensive training and eligibility for an assistant buyer position.

Bob Wery
Sears Merchandise Group
333 Beverly Road
D/707–4—E2-101B
Hoffman Estates, IL 60179

Sears has a long history as a successful and innovative retailer. It is one of the largest retailers in the world, based on merchandise sales and service, employing more than 350,000 associates. Among its strengths are a loyal customer base, powerful network of retail stores, highly focused product lines, national service and delivery organizations, and credit operations. Sears provides a challenging work environment and recognizes individual and team contributions.

Terri Smalley
Talbots, Human Resources
175 Beal Street
Hingham, MA 02043

An upscale women's chain of more than 350 stores, Talbots values individual challenge, ability, and effort with programs in finance, marketing, merchandising, and advertising/catalog in a fast-paced retail environment.

Human Resources
Toys "R" US *or*
Kids "R" Us
461 From Road
Paramus, NJ 07652

These two stores (which hire separately, so send separate resumes to each store's human resource staff) have made children's toys and fashion an over $9 billion dollar business with more than 40,000 employees. They value fast learners and creative thinkers who are still kids at heart and see life as a world of possibilities.

Michael DeFrank Jr.
Venture Stores, Inc.
2001 East Terra Lane
O'Fallon, MO 63366

Venture Stores is an upscale discount retailer that has been in operation since 1970. Headquartered in St. Louis, Missouri, Venture operates 113 stores throughout the Midwest and Southwest. They have major markets in Illinois, Indiana, Kansas, Missouri, Oklahoma, and Texas. Currently, sales are in excess of $1.9 billion. Venture offers a wide selection of both hardline and softline merchandise, with an emphasis on brand names, value pricing, and genuine customer service.

POSSIBLE JOB TITLES

Assistant buyer	Merchandise manager
Buyer	Sales associate
Buyer trainee	Store manager
Department manager	

Related Occupations

Comparison shopper	Retail sales workers
Insurance agent	Services sales representative
Manufacturer's representatives	Traffic managers
Procurement services managers	Wholesale sales representative

Professional Associations

American Marketing Association
250 South Wacker Drive, Suite 200
Chicago, IL 60606
Members/Purpose: Professional society of marketing and marketing research executives, sales and promotion managers, advertising specialists, and others interested in marketing.
Publications: *American Marketing Association—Proceedings, International Membership Directory, Journal of Health Care Marketing.*

American Money Management Association
4620 FM 1960 West, Suite 550
Houston, TX 77069
Members/Purpose: Corporations, credit unions, associations, savings and loans, and banks. Provides money management, financial planning, and insurance services.

ARMS—The Association of Retail Marketing Services
3 Caro Court
Red Bank, NJ 07701
Members/Purpose: Devoted to the promotional needs of the retail industry. Recommends incentive promotion at the retail level.
Publications: *ARMS-Membership Directory, Directory of Top 50 Wholesale Grocers.*

Food Business Forum
3800 Moore Place
Alexandria, VA 22305
Members/Purpose: Fosters cooperation between chain store organizations and the suppliers. Serves as liaison between members. Assists in the exchange of trainees among members firms.
Publications: *Euro Food Focus,* membership directory.

Institute of Store Planners

25 North Broadway

Tarrytown, NY 10591

Members/Purpose: Persons active in store planning and design; visual merchandisers, students and educators; contractors and suppliers to the industry. Dedicated to the professional growth of members while providing service to the public through improvement of the retail environment.

Publications: *Directory of Store Planners and Consultants, ISP International News,* newsletter.

International Mass Retail Association (IMRA)

1901 Pennsylvania Avenue N.W., 10th Floor

Washington, DC 20006

Members/Purpose: Purpose is to conduct research and educational programs on every phase of self-service general merchandising retailing.

Training: Conduct seminars and workshops.

Publications: *IMRA Membership Directory and Exposition Guide, Operating Results of Mass Retail Stores, Perquisites in Mass Retailing, Shrinkage Study, State Legislative Service.*

Museum Store Association

1 Cherry Center

501 South Cherry Street, No. 460

Denver, CO 80222

Members/Purpose: Sales departments in museums, including museums of fine arts, history, ethnology, and science. Encourages dialogue and assistance among members.

Publications: Membership list, *Museum Store, Product News.*

National Association of Buying Services

39 South Milwaukee Avenue

Wheeling, IL 60090

Members/Purpose: Serves as clearinghouse for the exchange of information and ideas relating to buying services. Acts as centralized distribution source for promotion of national products.

National Association of Men's Sportswear Buyers

500 5th Avenue, Suite 1425

New York, NY 10110

Members/Purpose: Sponsors trade shows for buyers of clothes for men's wear stores. Conducts media interviews to discuss men's wear and educational programs.

Publications: Newsletter, also distributes fashion videotapes.

National Retail Federation (NRF)

325 7th Street N.W., Suite 100

Washington, DC 20004

Members/Purpose: Department, chain, mass merchandise, and specialty stores retailing men's, women's, and children's apparel and home furnishings.

Training: Conducts conferences and workshops. Provides recruitment and training.

Publications: *Retail Control, STORES Magazine.*

Office Products Dealers Alliance

Business Products Industry Association

301 North Fairfax Street

Alexandria, VA 22314

Members/Purpose: Objectives are to serve as a resource for branch store dealers, to help increase professionalism, and to develop ways to combat competition. Seeks to explore areas of interest for retail dealers, including merchandising and product representation, advertising, store financing, personnel development and training, and strategic business planning.

Publications: *Dealer Operating Profile.*

Retail Advertising and Marketing Association (RAMA)

333 North Michigan Avenue, Suite 3000

Chicago, IL 60601

Members/Purpose: Persons in retail sales promotion and advertising and persons serving retailers in promotional capacities.

Publications: *RAC Digest, Who's Who in Retail Advertising.*

CHAPTER TWELVE

PATH 3: HEALTHCARE

One of the first hints that the healthcare field may prove agreeable to you as a new business graduate is the terminology currently of importance in this field: physician's *corporation, managed* care, health *maintenance* organization. Healthcare is big business, no question. More significant, however, is the fact that it is a business that is under heavy scrutiny to do a good job. The government watches healthcare, physicians have a vested interest, vendors and suppliers have every reason to pay careful attention, and the public, most of all, pays close attention to even the smallest change in healthcare provisions.

Why? The reasons are largely economic in every instance. Healthcare costs are steadily increasing, and as those costs increase, the employers and individuals who pay for healthcare complain. Here's an example appearing in the press as *Great Jobs in Business* is being written. We are all quite familiar with natural childbirthing techniques. Natural childbirth is best defined as childbirth with prepared parents who have received education about the birthing process and who hope to experience the birth with a minimum of anesthetics or other drugs. (Having fewer drugs makes for a healthier baby and a faster recovery for the mother.)

Years ago, women stayed in the hospital for lengthy confinements. They delivered their babies under heavier anesthetics which required more recuperation time. They also stayed in the hospital to learn about baby care from medical professionals. At this time, hospital costs were not as dramatic as they are now. But things have changed.

Hospital stays began to shorten considerably. Parents became better educated about childcare, mothers were using very little medication, and we realized long hospital stays were increasingly costly and not a good use of medical staff. Others could teach parents about new-baby care more efficiently and more cheaply outside the hospital.

Business Sensitivity to Medical Issues

Now, however, the controversy in the medical and popular press is that stays for childbirth have shortened too much. Hospital stays have now become as short as two or three days and many women are having uncomplicated deliveries and being discharged after one night's stay or, in the most extreme cases, after as little as 12 hours! Insurance companies reward brief stays to encourage reduced costs. The U.S. Centers for Disease Control and Prevention reports that hospital stays for vaginal births have dropped from an average of 3.9 days in 1970 to 2.1 in 1992, and for Caesarean births, from 7.8 to 4 days.

Legislators in Massachusetts, New Jersey, and Maryland have actually passed laws regulating hospital stays for childbirth and many other states are contemplating such legislation. What's going on here?

Business and Medicine: Uneasy Partners

What's going on is a battle between healthcare professionals and cost containment interests (hospital administrators, employers, governmental agencies such as Medicaid and Medicare) and the employers who provide that insurance. Healthcare professionals want to provide patients with the very best healthcare they can. Increasingly, the cost of providing that care has escalated as larger and larger monetary judgments are made against healthcare providers for mistakes, omissions, or in some cases, malpractice. A significant increase in healthcare costs is attributable to the threat of litigation.

Insurers and health-care cost-containment professionals want costs to stay as low as possible and all have different reasons. Some want to make a profit on their policies; others want low costs to keep care affordable to as much of the public as possible.

This is obviously a situation that cries out for good business skills and management that is sensitive to the public's healthcare and financial needs. Doctors and nurses provide quality healthcare, administrators manage paperwork, and insurers watch bills, but who is looking at the overall system? The important adjuncts of the treatment process are patient screening, long wait lines for services, presence or lack of amenities such as food services, shopping, and convenient parking at healthcare providers. How successful can a doctor/patient interaction be if the patient wasn't able to find a parking space or feels they've paid too much for it, or the patient has waited in line for an hour only to be confronted with paperwork they cannot understand?

DEFINITION OF THE CAREER PATH

Because there are so many available job sites, each with th
ditions, let's begin by looking at a number of healthcare positions _
a recent graduate with a business degree. A good start might be with a position that emphasizes some of those skills and attributes we associate with the
business degree. The following position is located within a major health maintenance organization (HMO) in the greater Boston area:

Assistant Home Care Contract Administrator: Responsibilities
include negotiation and administration of contracts for home care
services. Under direction of the Administrator, you will develop reim-
bursement agreements, ensure contract compliance, administer contracts, and perform cost and utilization analysis. Requirements include:
- BA/BS in Business or a healthcare field
- Proficiency in Lotus 1–2–3/Excel
- Willingness to participate in training/workshops to acquire clinical/
  technical background in infusion therapy, DME, and respiratory
  services.

Here's a marvelous entry-level opportunity that will really groom you in
the field of contract administration, specifically in the field of respiratory therapy. It will draw upon your computer skills, your economics classes, your
business law course, and many others. This is the kind of exciting position
that transforms a generalist business major into a skilled professional.

This next position is also for an HMO, another large and well-known entity
with a reputation for excellent management. This position has a quantitative side,
too, but with an emphasis on sales and promotion as well.

Account Manager: Oversee the day-to-day operational aspects of
medical benefit plan administration for major existing accounts;
providing ongoing guidance to major accounts with respect to
projecting and planning for future medical benefit needs; working
with underwriting, communications, and enrollment departments to
initiate and complete annual renewals; and providing education
regarding plan guidelines and benefits.

continued

ontinued
To be considered, you must have a bachelor's degree in business or equivalent and 1–3 years of related experience in a sales or service capacity. Strong communication and presentations skills are essential. Knowledge of self-funded and managed-care health benefits preferred. Extensive local travel will be involved.

The following position is more suited to the graduate who enjoyed marketing courses or consumer behavior. This advertisement is for a position in a small to mid-sized hospital:

Manager, Media Relations & Special Events: If you have excellent writing, interviewing, media relations, editing, and supervisory skills this might be the right position for you. Individual will be responsible for project management in Media Relations and special events as well as developing community outreach programs such as lecture series, public forums, etc. Position requires a Bachelor's degree in Business, Marketing, Journalism, Health Care, or a related field.

Granted, the subject matter of your copywriting may be issues such as how to prevent osteoporosis or common skiing injuries and how to avoid them. The language and level of sophistication is for a general audience and you will have professionals available to check the accuracy of the text. The craft and technique of media relations and special events remains the same. This is an exciting position on its own, but one that could propel you to a larger medical facility or health maintenance organization, to magazines or other media specializing in health issues, or into the commercial world.

This next position is really pure sales and marketing in a healthcare setting. A newly opened, short-term care facility needs to build its clientele (patients) and this position will create the business they need:

Admission Marketing Director: Full-time position available for energetic, enthusiastic person with a minimum of one year sales/marketing experience, preferably in a managed health care environment. Position includes marketing of a newly developed short-term rehabilitation unit. Extremely competitive benefits package. Salary commensurate with experience. . . .

One item you've probably noticed in these job listings is the requirement for a business degree *or* healthcare background. There are a couple of reasons for this lack of insistence. First, the field is a relatively new one and it would be foolish to demand what the job market cannot provide. Healthcare degrees are still in short supply and many of those graduating from healthcare programs are more interested in clinical (patient contact) positions, not administration or management.

The second reason for some equivocation in degree or experience requirements is that the industry itself is not sure which expertise is most critical, the management or the medical! Right now, in similar jobs all over the country, there are professionals from both backgrounds doing excellent work.

We've mentioned that healthcare graduates are not yet available in large enough numbers to staff the growing personnel demands of the healthcare industry, and those who are graduating may very well want more patient contact. That may be true of you as well! If you're exploring the healthcare field as a business graduate, part of that interest may stem from an interest in people and their well-being, so you may want some contact with the patient population. You can! Let's look at a couple of recently advertised positions that would offer some of that patient contact. Here's a hospital-based position:

Executive Directors: Will be the senior manager in our adult day-care center and is responsible for all aspects of a center's operation: meeting census and payer mix objectives; providing outcome-based care according to company standards; continuously improving center efficiency and achieving profitability targets. At least 50% of the ED's time will be spend on marketing and sales. He or she must have the following qualifications:
- Some previous management experience
- BA degree
- Willingness and ability to sell service to community
- High energy, enthusiasm, warmth, and compassion

To do this job well, you'll need to know your market. You'll need to appreciate what motivates individuals to place parents or relatives in adult day-care and you'll want to mix with the clients to learn their stories and their complaints and satisfactions with the care they're receiving. Though the patient population here is, by and large, healthier, you will encounter clients with eating difficulties, hearing loss, poor vision, and perhaps symptoms of presenility, dementia, or early stages of Alzheimer's disease.

Another word about medical terms. Reading these advertisements, you may be interested in the jobs but concerned that you don't understand all the medical jargon and terminology. Actually, even medical professionals struggle with the lingo outside their areas of expertise. You've encountered a number of terms in the ads listed above; respiratory therapy, continuous quality improvement, census, payer mix, DME, rehabilitation, and so on. Don't be dismayed. Every field of work has its own vocabulary. The terminology of the stock market is equally confusing to the uninitiated. What do you do?

Consult a dictionary! *Black's Medical Dictionary, Stedman's Medical Dictionary,* or the *Merriam Webster Medical Desk Dictionary* (all listed in the bibliography and generally available in larger reference libraries) are a few examples of the many resources available to you. Certainly, you'll want to investigate and understand any terminology in the job ad itself and, once on the job, begin a regular self-tutorial to learn the vocabulary of your new environment.

Let's look at one final job posting with patient contact:

> **Assistant Manager, Admission, Discharge and Transfer Services (healthcare):** Second in command for the preadmitting, admitting, transfer, and discharge processes of the XYZ Healthcare System. The qualified candidate will have some administrative experience, strong information system knowledge, a Bachelor's degree in Business, MBA preferred.

How patients enter, are processed, and discharged from a facility is not just a cost issue, but a patient care issue. Repeat business in situations where clients can select their provider may be in large part influenced by how smoothly they felt the administrative process was managed. On the patient care side, an agitated, anxious patient who has been waiting too long, is overly confused by paperwork, or whose admission records are missing, is harder to treat and takes longer to respond to treatment. The individual with this job can have a positive and direct effect on a patient's well-being!

WORKING CONDITIONS

We've looked at a variety of job types and environments. But, despite the variety, there are still some generalizations we can make about working conditions that can guide you in your job search.

Behind the Scenes

The administrative, quantitative, computer-oriented, and analysis jobs are going to be located, in most cases, in the offices and administrative suites that lie behind the scenes of patient care. While some of these kinds of offices may be located in a section of a healthcare facility, many are not; they are situated in office buildings indistinguishable from neighboring buildings. Billing services for a radiological corporation of physicians may not even be located in the same town as the medical office. So even though you are in healthcare, you are not necessarily at a work site where healthcare is being delivered. That may or may not be your preference.

On the Front Lines

There are, however, numerous jobs sited at hospitals, adult day-care facilities, nursing homes, rehabilitation centers, health maintenance clinics, and other similar type locations that receive a constant flow of patients and their families. In some of the jobs we have listed, some contact with the patients is important to do the best job possible. If you're a patient care administrator, not only will you do a better job by getting out and talking to patients about their treatment, but you'll also recognize errors sooner.

Know Your Environment

In the healthcare field, the better you know the clientele, the patients, and their families, the better you can do your job. One of the major complaints about non-medical personnel in the healthcare field is that they don't have a sense of appreciation for the individual patient and focus overly much on the paperwork, forgetting the human element. Let that criticism be a warning of how you might be perceived with a business degree and not a health background. You'll need to be concerned about patient welfare and let people know that you are. Take action steps to keep yourself informed of these issues by reading professional journals, newspapers, and watching the local news for coverage of healthcare issues.

Because healthcare is undergoing dramatic changes, both in new developments and in its structure, you're going to experience a lot of change in your job. New employees will arrive at your organization to fill new jobs, new forms will appear to meet new needs, new ways of doing things, new products, new techniques, and a constant flow of information. If change is difficult for you on the job, you may find a career in healthcare a challenge to your peace of mind.

On the other hand, the work day is relatively structured and most administrative staff have very regular hours. Office spaces are generally attractive. Because you're in healthcare, where the well-being of the individuals is paramount, it's recognized that workplace aesthetics and working conditions make a major contribution to an employee's sense of well-being. Of course, as a salaried worker, you'll probably find there are many times when your day doesn't begin or end with any regularity.

Workplace Risk Issues

There is a myth among the uninitiated that if you work in healthcare and work in a hospital, you're going to get sick, catch some disease, or generally be more susceptible to infection. *Absolutely not!* There is no documented evidence that working in a healthcare facility in any way increases one's average rate of illness or infection.

TRAINING AND QUALIFICATIONS

You're Hired for Your Business Education

As an undergraduate business major, you probably don't have any medical background, other than your own experience as a patient in the medical community (which may be valuable!). You might have had some college or high school courses in physiology or chemistry, but nothing medical or health related. That's okay. Your entry into the world of healthcare will not depend upon that. You're being hired essentially for your business degree.

Remember what you've read about the volatility of the healthcare field. One of the major ingredients in the constant redefinition of healthcare delivery is the increasing pressure that exists between the field of medicine and the realm of medical cost containment. Professionals hired on the business side of the equation are well advised to know their stuff! Whether you're looking at sales, finance, systems management, accounting, administration, or facilities management, be prepared to demonstrate, display, and talk about your business education. The prize (a great job) will go to the candidate who knows what she's talking about.

Begin a Healthcare Study Program

Your initial attractiveness to the healthcare employer will be your potential to cut costs and improve the delivery of patient care delivery. Your competition will be those earning healthcare degrees or even those with master's degrees in public health or hospital administration. If you can demonstrate good management skills, a strong goal orientation, and an appreciation of the dynamics of the healthcare industry, you'll find the focused generalist (hopefully, you!) is still a competitive bidder for many entry-level jobs.

While your entry into the field will not depend upon your grasp of the healthcare industry, *your successful career progress will.* Your healthcare career will be a sophisticated and complex combination of patient awareness, medical expertise, and economics. You will be learning about each as you progress. More than any other path described in this book, the healthcare career path demands that you constantly educate yourself, both on and off the job. On the job, avail yourself of the expertise of those individuals who are more experienced than yourself and have them teach you all they can about the profession. Ask for and take advantage of every professional development opportunity your employer makes available to you. Outside of your working hours, keep up with television and press coverage of healthcare issues, and read professional journals and magazines to increase your store of information on every aspect of your profession, from disease entities to patient service provisions.

Once you've secured your position and begun your own training program, both formally and informally, your ability to hold your job and to advance in your field will be directly related to your grasp of those larger issues you've been reading about. Eventually in all management jobs, you'll be called upon to concentrate on the more conceptual aspects of your job; i.e., planning and implementing new systems and procedures. This means letting others have responsibility for many of the technical skills and procedures you may have enjoyed and done well. You won't be ready for that change if you haven't taken time to educate yourself along the way in the bigger issues of your industry.

EARNINGS

You can reasonably expect that in an industry growing as fast as healthcare the earning power of skilled workers will be correspondingly high and growing. While managerial types in healthcare (those with business backgrounds) are currently very highly paid, the volatile nature of the industry and the increasing rate of takeovers, mergers, and consolidations of services make earnings very difficult to predict.

While the demographics discussed below would indicate that as the number of people needing healthcare rises, the value placed on that care and the people who provide it should rise, the correspondingly great pressure from government and private industry to reduce costs may have a dampening effect. There are already situations in state-run healthcare facilities where skilled workers are paid less than bus drivers. These discrepancies are being increasingly challenged in the courts under the doctrine of job comparability, which has thus far not received any legal sanction but remains an arguing point in contract negotiations.

Some of the best information about starting salaries in healthcare is available from the Collegiate Employment Research Institute at Michigan State University. Here are some entry-level salaries for undergraduate business degrees pursuing careers in healthcare that correspond to some of the job postings reviewed earlier in the chapter:

Human resource management	$23,187
General administration	$23,950
Media/public relations	$21,870
Sales	$24,782
Financial Administration	$26,838
Information systems mgmt.	$32,762

CAREER OUTLOOK

Even with the many challenges the industry presents as it seeks to contain costs and provide good care, the career outlook for jobs in the healthcare industry is superb. The U.S. Bureau of Labor Statistics predicts that the health services industry will add 3.9 million jobs by 2005—17 percent of total employment growth!

There may only be a small segment of job types among those jobs that you are interested in, but even a small percentage would mean thousands of jobs. Labor Department figures indicate positions for administrators in healthcare will increase by more than 50 percent by the year 2005. In fact, half of the 30 fastest-growing occupations the Bureau projects are professional and technical healthcare jobs. Almost every occupation in healthcare will have higher than average growth through the 1990s, including the highly paid managerial positions. Among these 30 occupations, in addition to those that would be attractive to someone with an undergraduate degree in business, there are some that do not require college degrees (home health aides, secretaries, etc.) and some requiring advanced degrees (psychologists, psychometrists, etc.).

What has fueled that growth? A number of specific trends, including:

Demographics. An aging population is aging with better health and more activity than ever before and more income to spend on health maintenance. Those over 75 years old, requiring the most medical assistance, will increase by 35 percent over the next two decades. In 1980, the United States achieved the distinction for the first time in history of having slightly more than half its citizenry past the age of 30. Birth rates and fertility rates remain rather low but median age continues to climb and remains the single most impactful demographic component of the healthcare revolution. A continuously aging society will cause many changes in our future, but the one that concerns us here is the expanded workforce in the healthcare field.

Technology. Examples of new technology include: reading x-rays long distance, lengthening shortened limbs with external fixation devices, and patient-administered analgesics at bedside. As technology proliferates, more services are created and more care opportunities evolve.

Changing finances.   Talk to anyone you know who is on a medical coverage plan, and they will tell you they have experienced changes: changes in providers, changes in administration, and especially, changes in cost and who bears that cost. With hospitals forced to deal with cuts in government support, and with the new types of healthcare organizations (HMOs and PPOs) growing across the country, management and accounting skills are more highly valued than ever before. We can expect continuing changes in the mix of public and private financing of our healthcare system.

Home healthcare.   As hospital stays decrease, technology increases, and a patient's confidence in his or her ability to self-manage care continues, the possibilities for what can be done in the patient's home grow.

STRATEGY FOR FINDING THE JOBS

Because your business program has probably not exposed you to the healthcare field in any significant way, much of your job search will involve discovering an entire new sector of our economy. If you are like others who have sought employment in the healthcare field, you'll find the field very fertile ground for the newly minted business degree student.

I recommend you obtain a good guide to healthcare employers, such as Peterson's *Job Opps '95 Health Care.* This book is readily available to borrow from many college libraries, college career centers, and larger city libraries. It is also available at a modest cost in larger bookstores.

It's a solid resource for two reasons. First, it lists thousands of healthcare employers (indexed geographically and alphabetically), and tells you what they do, how many people work for them, and what expertise they may be looking for in new hires. It should expand your horizons about what is possible. For example, perhaps you have some experience in information systems. You probably already realize you can apply at hospitals, larger nursing homes, HMOs and the traditional sites. Reading through this guide, you will begin to recognize other employment opportunities, such as eyecare firms, hospital equipment manufacturers, and pharmaceutical manufacturers.

Expanding your list of possible job sites should be very helpful to you. Each type of employer has its own work environment, its own "climate." Some may suit you more than others. Also, as an entry-level employee with a general business background, you need the flexibility of lots of places to look for entry-level positions in a specialist world such as healthcare.

The second reason I recommend this guide is that it contains an index by hiring needs. Of course, that will help you to locate employers based upon your own talents and career objectives. But it helps in other ways as well. If you are interested in finance, you'll find a long list of employers who generally seek those skills. But, if your job search is localized to a specific geographic area, you can still get some excellent ideas from this book about the *kinds* of healthcare employers that seek finance skills. Use that information to generalize your search to your own geographic area.

For example, under "Finance" there are several listings for State Health and Human Services departments. You might never have thought of those agencies in your own search. While the listings in Peterson's are for federal positions, it's a good bet that your state agency has similar needs. Call them and make an appointment to go in and talk to their human resource department about their hiring expectations for college graduates with interests in finance.

Don't overlook any area of the market:

Assisted living services	Medical management firms
BioMedical firms	Medical records management
Dental companies	Medical software firms
Health maintenance	Medical systems
organizations	Mental health agencies
Hospitals	Pharmaceutical manufacturers
Instrumentation manufacturers	Physician services
Insurance companies	Rehabilitation centers
Laboratories	Senior citizen's homes
Life sciences companies	Therapy associates

In examining sectors of the market, look for job opportunities that fit your expertise. Healthcare is no different than other areas of employment; it maintains all the essential functions of any business including marketing, sales, administration, finance, accounting, public relations, and all the other traditional business functions.

Because healthcare is growing so rapidly, you'll encounter many new and smaller firms that are growing rapidly. These firms have leaner staffs and make more use of cross-training. Staff members need to be very flexible and may change jobs frequently as the organization grows. You might want to consider a strategy of affiliating with a smaller, rapidly growing healthcare firm. Work hard, learn all you can, and you could find you're riding along with that growth in your own professional advancement.

Here's an eight-step checklist of items to consider in seeking out the best job for you:

1. Check-out Prospective Employers.   Everyone in the career field is always suggesting you research the company you are considering. How do you do that? Do you have time to learn to be an employment researcher? Probably not. Start by asking a good reference librarian what you might be able to find out about a company. They'll suggest everything from stock ratings and Better Business Bureau complaint histories to articles in periodicals. If you can visit the office, park your car outside and observe who comes and goes. What's the building like? Is it attractive and well maintained? How do employees act and dress? Stroll into the lobby (don't worry, nobody will remember you!), look around, ask the receptionist about the firm, and pick up any promotional literature you might find displayed. An on-site visit can be very revealing.

2. Display Your Communication Skills.   Your resume, cover letter, thank-you note after an interview, and your manner on the telephone and during an interview are all examples of how you communicate and how you'll do as a communicator for an employer. You'll be judged on that as much as anything. Ensure your written communications are perfect and practice your interviewing skills. Get on the telephone with a friend who will act as the employer in a phone conversation to critique your telemarketing skills. You'll be glad you did.

3. Do You Know a Foreign Language?   It may be too late now to begin a college program, but Spanish ability would be a real plus in many healthcare organizations. Certainly, foreign travel and a sensitivity to other cultures is a valuable experience and one you'll want to talk about, if you can.

4. Prove You Are Results Oriented.   Healthcare is under the gun and everyone is working hard to produce good results that are economically viable and sensitive to patient and physician needs. In your resume and during your interview, you want to communicate to the best of your ability that you are a results-oriented person.

5. Add to Your Experience.   Going into a field such as healthcare with a language all its own and a different focus than the kinds of business entities you've studied in college will put some heavy demands on you to grow and add to your experience—quickly. Before that happens, take advantage of your own rich college experience and sample some of the wonderful guest speakers, seminars, and conferences that occur on your campus. Raising your general information level makes you a more valuable employee. You are aware of more issues and can relate more easily to other people through shared ideas and an enhanced appreciation for differing viewpoints. Each learning opportunity of this kind adds to your value to an employer.

6. Network.   Chapter Four of this book described the mechanics of networking. In the healthcare field particularly, there are many shared relationships. Professionals in the field share many of the same concerns as healthcare both grows and changes. You'll meet many fine people during your job search. Regardless of the outcome of those meetings, maintain those relationships and stay interested in those individuals, for they may prove helpful in furthering your job search or in performing your job once you land one.

7. Set Your Job Goals.   Healthcare is a busy field. The business section of a major Boston, Massachusetts daily recently featured healthcare-industry business maneuvers in four of the five front-page stories. With newsworthy changes occurring daily, healthcare is not an industry where employees will have free time to help you figure out what you want in a job or career. Learn about the industry, learn about the jobs they do, and make your own decisions about where you might best fit in. Change your mind as much as you want and as circumstances and information alter your ideas about career paths. But have a plan.

8. Raise Your Level of General Information.   Healthcare is its own field, with its own concerns and issues. You can't change that, but *you* can change. You can adapt and grow and develop new skills, new talents, and new ways to use your education. By far the best technique to improve your chances of getting hired is to stay abreast of the issues currently facing healthcare in this country today. Current issues such as length of hospital stay, litigation, medical malpractice and mis-dosing of prescriptions, new advances in radiology, pain, genetics, and countless other issues that will tune you in to the concerns, vocabulary, and players in the healthcare game. You'll be guaranteed to draw on this information again and again. Make reading the daily paper a habit!

COMMON JOB SOURCES

Of the 3.9 million jobs predicted by the year 2005 by the U.S. Bureau of Labor Statistics, 1.3 million of these jobs are anticipated to be in hospitals, 900,000 in physician's offices, and 700,000 in nursing and personal-care facilities.

Listed below are just a sampling of the variety of resources available to the healthcare job seeker. Begin with these and then move on in your own exploration with the assistance of your career office or reference librarian.

Periodicals with classifieds

Federal Jobs Digest
Box 594, Department D30, NY 10546.

Published biweekly. Up to 30,000 federal job vacancies listed per issue. The federal government employs more than 100,000 healthcare workers. Approximately 15,000 healthcare job vacancies are projected yearly in the federal government due to retirements. This publication provides comprehensive federal careers articles with each issue.

Hospitals (American Hospital Association)
737 North Michigan Avenue, Chicago, IL 60611.

Published bimonthly, it has classifieds for a broad spectrum of healthcare occupations.

National Business Employment Weekly
P.O. Box 9100, Springfield, MA 01101.

A comprehensive monthly jobs feature titled "Healthcare," published on the third Friday of each month, provides hundreds of national job ads.

Directories

AHA Guide to the Health Care Field
American Hospital Association, P.O. Box 92683, Chicago, IL.

Published annually, this is a comprehensive guide to the healthcare field. It includes information on member hospitals, healthcare systems, organizations, and other valuable information. (Also available on computer disks.)

American Association of Homes for the Aging
1129 20th Street, NW, Suite 400, Washington, DC 20036.

Published annually, it lists more than 3,400 member homes and facilities plus 800 suppliers, and individual and associate members.

Blue Book Digest of HMOs
National Association of Employers on Health Care Action, P.O. Box 220, Key Biscayne, FL 33149.

Published annually.

Medical and Health Information Directory
Gale Research Company, Book Tower, Detroit, MI 48226.

Available at larger libraries, this compendium of resources lists medical associations, federal government agencies, medical schools, grant-award sources, healthcare delivery agencies, journals, newsletters, and miscellaneous data.

Possible Job Titles

Account manager	Documentation coordinators
Admission marketing director	Executive director
Billing coordinators	Home-care contract
Billing supervisor	administrator
Business manager	Manager, media relations
Collection representative	Manager, special events
Director of services	

Note: *Allied healthcare personnel* is a classification of employee you are bound to come across again and again in your job search. Pharmacists, physical therapists, respiratory therapists, X-ray technicians, medical technologists, and occupational therapists are but some examples of the trained, certified, and in many cases, licensed professions that are included under the rubric *allied health.*

Related Occupations

The issue of related careers is a fascinating subject unto itself. If you've been a surgeon for 10 years and decide you no longer want to practice medicine, what can you do? The answer does not lie in the surgical skills, but in the investigative aspect of surgery, in diagnosis and designing solutions to complex problems, and working actively with patients to solve those problems. Counseling, research, and teaching are all skills of the surgeon, but to emphasize those too greatly is to undermine the very dynamic, physical, and realistic part of the surgeon's job that takes place in the operating room.

Leading an outward-bound program or running a halfway house for troubled adolescents would bring to bear both the diagnosis, counseling, and active participation that a surgeon brings to his or her work. In other words, our jobs are often *content bound.* To do good work, we have to amass information, vocabulary, skills, and facts very specifically relegated to the content of our jobs. This information very seldom "moves" to other areas of employment, and in the healthcare field that may be more true than some other sectors of the economy.

If you look at the healthcare industry as a concept of large numbers of people being serviced in a sensitive, caring, and highly individualistic way, then you can begin to see the relevance of a career in healthcare to a career in hotel/restaurant management, which shares many of the same issues. The hospitality industry, in general, hires many individuals who have had careers in some aspect of the healthcare field. The following list of possible employers should be thought of only as a starting point:

Banking/financial services	Mental health services
Community/social work	Museums
Educational institutions	Public relations
Food services	Resorts
Hotel industry	Restaurant management

Professional Associations

One of the preeminent sources of information on careers in healthcare is The Summit on Manpower, a consortium of 18 professional healthcare groups (including the American Hospital Association).

The Summit on Manpower
1825 K Street, N.W., Suite 210
Washington, DC 20006

Other helpful associations are listed below, including addresses, any associated training/development, and publications. Make use of these organizations; they are there to foster their professions and have a vested interest in raising the quality of employment candidates.

American College of Healthcare Executives
840 North Lake Shore Drive, Suite 1103W
Chicago, IL 60611
Members/Purpose: Works to keep members abreast of current and future trends, issues, and developments, shape productive and effective organizational strategies and professional performance.
Training: Conducts research programs. Holds educational seminars and training programs on healthcare management.
Publications: Directory, *Frontiers of Health Services Management.*

American Medical Association (AMA)
515 North State Street
Chicago, IL 60610
Members/Purpose: County medical societies and physicians. Disseminates scientific information to members and the public. Informs members of significant medical and health legislation at state and national levels and represents the profession before Congress and governmental agencies. Provides practice counseling for management problems, and keeps membership informed on health and medical legislation.

Publications: *Journal of the American Medical Association (JAMA), American Journal of Diseases of Children, American Medical News, Archives of Dermatology, Archives of General Psychiatry, Archives of Internal Medicine.*

American Public Health Association
1015 15th Street, N.W., Suite 300
Washington, DC 20005
Members/Purpose: Seeks to protect and promote personal, mental, and environmental health.
Publications: *American Journal of Public Health, The Nation's Health, Salubritas.*

American School Health Association
7263 State Route 43
P.O. Box 708
Kent, OH 44240
Members/Purpose: Promotes comprehensive and constructive school health programs including the teaching of health, health services, and promotion of a healthful school environment.
Publications: *ASHA Newsletter, Journal of School Health.*

American Society for Healthcare Education and Training of the American Hospital Association
840 North Lake Shore Drive
Chicago, IL 60611
Members/Purpose: Purposes are: to foster professional development of members, to demonstrate the value of comprehensive education as a management strategy, to promote continuing education among all healthcare personnel, to develop coordination among organizations involved in the education of healthcare personnel, to formulate information and evaluation programs, and to recommend action on national issues relating to healthcare education.
Training: Conducts educational programs.
Publications: *Healthier Education Dateline, Hospitals, Journal of Healthcare Education and Training.*

American Society for Health Care Marketing and Public Relations
c/o American Hospital Association
840 North Lake Shore Drive
Chicago, IL 60611
Members/Purpose: Persons employed or active in hospitals, hospital councils or associations, hospital-related schools, and healthcare organizations responsible for marketing and public relations.
Publications: *Directory of Hospital Marketing, Planning and Public Relations Consultants.*

Association of Academic Health Centers

1400 16th Street N.W., Suite 410
Washington, DC 20036
Members/Purpose: Chief administrative officers of university-based health centers in the United States. Interdisciplinary in focus, with a primary interest in total health manpower education.
Training: Education programs.
Publications: Directory, general meetings.

National Association of Health Care Career Schools

10963 St. Charles Rock Road
St. Ann, MO 63704
Members/Purpose: Objectives are: to promote the interests and general welfare of health career training schools and their students, and to conduct and promote research for the advancement of the educational offerings of such schools.
Publications: Bulletin.

National Association for Healthcare Recruitment

P.O. Box 5769
Akron, OH 44372
Members/Purpose: Promotes sound principles of professional healthcare recruitment. Provides financial assistance and consultation services.
Training: Conducts regional seminars, symposia, and workshops.
Publications: *Annual Recruitment Survey, Who's Who in Recruitment Resources.*

National Rural Health Association (NRHA)

1 West Armour Boulevard, Suite 301
Kansas City, MO 64111
Members/Purpose: Purpose is to create a better understanding of healthcare problems unique to rural areas, utilize a collective approach in finding positive solutions, articulate and represent the healthcare needs of rural America, and supply current information to rural healthcare programs throughout the country.
Training: Offers continuing education credits for medical, dental, nursing, and management courses.
Publications: *Journal of Rural Health, Rural Health Care.*

International Academy of Healthcare Professionals

70 Glen Cove Road, Suite 209
Roslyn Heights, NY 11577
Members/Purpose: Provides for educational exchange among members. Recognizes outstanding achievement in healthcare field. Offers research and educational materials to Third World healthcare institutions.
Training: Provides educational exchange among members.
Publications: Fact sheets and up-to-date news sheets.

International Society for Healthcare Executives
2810 Mary Avenue
St. Louis, MO 63144
Members/Purpose: To advance the delivery of healthcare by improving administration. Seeks to help its members succeed in the healthcare field.
Training: Sponsors research and development activities and educational programs.
Publications: *Executive Update, Healthcare Management.*

CHAPTER THIRTEEN

PATH 4: NONPROFITS

There's no argument. Today's job seeker faces serious problems! Not only are the number of available jobs dwindling, but the types of jobs that remain are very different from the entry-level positions available to college graduates only a few years ago. Just as our per-capita economic picture seems to be evolving into a case of the "haves" and "have nots," the labor force seems to be mimicking this same trend. We have a leaner core of "elite" workers staffing large operations and a diminishing mass labor market being replaced by workerless factories or virtual companies. Accompanying these shifts is a burgeoning class of service workers absorbing previously displaced skilled workers in an economic transformation as dramatic as the shift from an agricultural base to the machine age. The college graduate today is likely to find the corporate waiting room filled with middle-aged professionals fighting for the same entry-level jobs.

The Changing Picture of Work

We are, perhaps, witnessing the beginnings of the redefinition of work in our society. Not just a redefinition of how we define *work,* but of the place and status work holds in our value system. Work has always been the fulcrum of American culture and one of the defining forces in how we see ourselves and others. In any initial conversation between two adult Americans, the question "What do you do?" arises within minutes. Now as we look around, we see human labor being eliminated from the workforce in exponentially increasing numbers. Major U.S. corporations, now cutting two million positions annually, were once the prized catch of any business graduate. Today they are seen as far more risky employment sites than small to mid-sized firms. The picture is definitely changing, and as you leave college to enter the job market, an awareness of these changes will inform your job search strategy.

Automation is increasing apace. Electronic bar codes and scanners increase the efficiency of each checkout person and reduce the overall need for staff. Fast-food drive-up windows replace human order-takers with touch-sensitive screens, and electronic home shopping is in an infancy that should worry many store retailers. Though off to a controversial start, the attempt to force the public to use ATMs for most common bank transactions by having them pay a service fee to use a teller is simply the first wave of an increasingly displaced workforce. Displaced workers place increased pressure on those jobs that remain and competition becomes more intense.

Nonprofit Deserves Your Attention

You've read the papers, you've watched the prime-time news shows, and you know all too well the job market looks very unpromising. Your own personal life may have already been touched by these workplace changes. You may know someone who has had direct experience with organizations that have "leaned down" or consolidated, or merged with other organizations and, in the process, have eliminated what the British refer to as "redundant" workers. What can you do to best prepare yourself for employment upon graduation?

This book is a guide to five alternatives. Each chapter advocates its own strategic assault on the battlefield of employment. Chapter Ten, Sales, advocates going for that sector of employment that needs lots of people and pays well, but cautions new employees to pick and choose carefully and take some good skills with them when they leave. Chapter Eleven, Retailing, suggests you analyze growth patterns in the retail sector, which is growing fast and furiously and needs management help, especially for those with strong entrepreneurial tendencies and a good tolerance for risk.

Doing the Opposite of Everyone Else

This chapter advocates a "contrary" strategy in your job search. "Contrarianism" is doing what others are *not* doing—focusing where the attention *isn't*. Think of a magician. If you want to figure out what the magician's secret is, don't look to the hand that is drawing your attention. Look at the other hand! While nonprofits may not have been much in evidence during your business education, you may, nevertheless, have heard of the contrarian strategy. Investors use it successfully to find a profitable niche, buying stocks in categories away from where current attention is focused. Focusing on nonprofits in your job search will definitely put you in the minority of job seekers. Let others cling to the older, traditional job search techniques while you explore vast new uncharted opportunities for the business major in a world of enterprise that, at first glance, might seen inimical to your education and outlook.

The Rationale

Surprised? Whether you're contemplating a business major or just about to graduate from college with one, nonprofit business has probably not been one of your chosen options. And yet, for many reasons, especially for the business major, the world of nonprofits deserves your attention. Here are three reasons right up front to grab your attention:

❏ **There are jobs in the nonprofit sector**
❏ Business majors are valued in nonprofit enterprises
❏ The work culture is "life friendly"

Who Are the Nonprofits?

Let's begin by defining nonprofits. An easy definition is that it comprises one of the three main sectors of our economy: government, private business, and nonprofit or independents. One of three main sectors of the economy and yet seldom addressed in your business education or probably in the advice you've encountered so far in your job search.

What constitutes a nonprofit organization? The obvious first difference is a legal one. Organizations legally termed nonprofit declare that money they receive, or earn, returns to the organization to further its mission and promote its activities and services. It is not returned to investors or owners. Profits, or excess of capital over expenses, may accrue, but they are returned to the activities of the organization.

In legal terms of business incorporation, the nonprofit category (501–c) that designates a nonprofit organization as exempt from taxes by our government covers educational, religious, charitable, scientific, and literary organizations, civic leagues, social welfare organizations, and local employee organizations. If you closely follow the press, you will have noticed a growing number of legal cases challenging the supposed tax-exempt status of many organizations in these areas. This happens as national, state, and local governmental bodies—increasingly hard-pressed for operating expenses—carefully examine the tax exempt privileges of those organizations under their purview.

Nonprofits are taking on more and more of the strategies and techniques of the competitive profit sector in order to stay viable. Nonprofits, like any other business enterprise, compete for the public's attention, funds, and goodwill as vigorously as any profit corporation. After all, there's only so much disposable income to go around. If the nonprofit cares about what they do, they try as hard as the next organization to grab your attention and your financial support. They use all the same business tools and techniques you have studied in college.

Nonprofits Value Business Education

An excellent example of the increasing adoption of strict business-like management patterns by nonprofits comes from an article in the July/August 1995 edition of *Community Jobs* by Peter C. Brinkerhoff, president of Corporate Alternatives, an Illinois firm specializing in nonprofit organizations. He lists the following attributes of successful nonprofits:

1. A viable mission

2. A businesslike board of directors

3. A strong, well-educated staff

4. A tight set of controls

5. A bias for marketing

6. A vision of where you are going

7. Be financially empowered

8. Be social entrepreneurs

9. Respond rapidly to change

This list should sound very familiar to you and should serve as a strong argument for the readiness and willingness of the nonprofit sector to appreciate and value what you have to offer in terms of education and expertise.

Nonprofits Have Your Kind of Job

Even more importantly, however, they offer the kinds of positions, challenges, and projects that a business major would enjoy. There is research and development, marketing, portfolio management, risk analysis, production management, sales, marketing, advertising, training and development—every imaginable facet of the business curricula has its hands-on application in the world of nonprofit.

The Big Difference in Nonprofits

Another and far more significant difference in the day-to-day world of work are those underlying principles that animate and motivate the organizations themselves and the people that staff them. Devon Cottrell Smith, in her book *Great Careers: The Fourth of July Guide to Careers, Internships, and Volunteer Opportunities in the Nonprofit Sector,* outlines twelve principles that motivate the creation and continuation of nonprofit organizations:

Vision. Inspired Action based on a vision of the Good. *Self Motivating.*

Harmony.   Balanced feelings; accord; shared responsibilities; cooperation. *Cooperating.*

Power.   Providing resources; the authority to act. *Established.*

Purification.   Seeking out hidden problems to effect transformation. *Transforming.*

Truth.   Knowledge of the incontrovertible. *Educating.*

Law.   Principles on which shared ethics are based. *Leading.*

Love.   Fidelity to the principle of benevolence. *Sharing.*

Foundation.   Forms that support the function of institutions. *Structuring.*

Wisdom.   Expressing intelligence in life. *Creating.*

Virtue.   Evolving life through practical adherence to ideas. *Refining.*

Compassion.   Serving others, providing for basic life needs. *Serving.*

Sustainment.   Preservation of the social, conceptual, and artistic institutions of society. *Protecting.*

The Great Need for Nonprofits

Now, take these principles listed above and apply them to some of the pressing issues of today, such as:

- ❑ AIDS research
- ❑ African drought patterns
- ❑ Preserving natural resources
- ❑ Containing pollution
- ❑ Fostering the arts
- ❑ Organizing people for group strength
- ❑ Harmonizing extremes of wealth and poverty
- ❑ Attending to homelessness and hunger
- ❑ Encouraging diversity and tolerance

You can begin to see very clearly why organizations with these principles and these missions need the finest in business management techniques. Sadly, the concerns of many nonprofits are not uppermost in the minds of people. Some of that indifference accounts for the little time spent on nonprofit organizations in business schools. The goals of nonprofits are critical to our viability as a planet, however. To stay competitive, many of these organizations have realized that concepts such as Total Quality Management (TQM), strategic planning, work flow management, business communications, database information systems, and so on, are critical. Business majors interested in the goals of the nonprofits provide the essential cutting-edge skills these organizations need to survive.

A third big difference is organizational "culture." Most nonprofits do their work in a "life friendly" work culture. Some of this rejection of workaholism has to do with not being profit-focused and some with the caring, nurturing focus of many of the organizational missions themselves. Some evidence of this is in the heavy emphasis on professional training and development, allowing time off for college courses, workshops, community volunteering, and sabbaticals. Nonprofits recognize the value of workers recharging, meeting new people, and acquiring new skills.

DEFINITION OF THE CAREER PATH

There are many wonderful opportunities for the business major in the nonprofit sector. There are so many career pathways, in fact, that starting down one is apt to open up vistas of ever-widening opportunity. Nonprofits will surprise and delight the business major with the variety and number of job opportunities available.

Most nonprofit organizations share certain common departments, however. The following list will give you an idea of the duties and responsibilities of those departments and positions and the qualifications needed for them. Within each department there are numerous career paths possible as you grow in experience and training. Each of these areas has been illustrated with excerpts from a recent advertisement for that job, so you can see and read for yourself how employers express their needs in these areas.

Executive Director

Duties.   This position is called many things: dean, managing director, hospital administrator, chief executive officer, and so on. Responsibilities include directing the overall program and administrative activities of the organization and the effective use of financial and human resources. In smaller nonprofits, the executive director and a small support staff may be the only full-time employees. In larger organizations, the executive director's office is comprised of an extensive staff, all with different responsibilities.

Qualifications.   Executive directors today often have an MBA or MPA (Masters in Public Administration). However, there are still people rising to executive director positions who have come up "through the ranks" with an undergraduate business degree and the winning combination of drive, enthusiasm, and dedication.

Here's how a recent advertisement stated the qualifications required for the director of an international program:

Undergraduate degree; advanced degree a plus; educational background in international issues is desirable; high degree of sensitivity to national and cultural differences; budget development and management; ability to read and analyze budget information and generate narrative reports; Microsoft Word, Windows, Excel; must be able to travel extensively to locations throughout the world. Salary: $40s to mid-50s.

Development Office

Duties.   This is the department that raises money to support the organization's day-to-day as well as long-term needs for paying staff salaries and financing new initiatives, programs, or even facilities. The shrinking tradition of philanthropy in this country, the slow erosion of government support, and the increasing contention for what is left of our discretionary income make the role of this department both a central and challenging one. The more successful this department is, the more growth the organization can accomplish.

Qualifications.   A business major will find much of the activity of this office familiar. There is a strong sales orientation, and much time and effort is spent on marketing the organization to potential supporters. Direct mail campaigns and database technology are valuable tools, as is creativity in developing marketing concepts, promotions, and premiums (gifts). Most of this job is learned as you go, but basic requirements include: organizational ability, concern for the world and people, and the willingness to make a commitment. Skills in writing and research are often useful, and the personal qualities of confidence, articulateness, initiative, and curiosity are helpful.

The following excerpt from a job ad for an Assistant Director of Development is typical:

> Strong listening and counseling skills; ability to work with forms, paperwork, and computers; ability to relate to and accept diverse population; initiative and flexibility.

Programming

Duties. Responsibilities include directing the program activities, including grantwriting and special projects. They establish policies and procedures for their programs. This is the office that actually delivers the service of the non-profit. The range of service providers is as varied as the organizations are: nurses, doctors, lawyers, teachers, counselors, social workers, librarians, organizers, and many more. This is the role that is at the core of the nonprofit; it brings both heartwarming rewards and frustrating challenges and obstacles.

Qualifications. From absolutely no qualifications to the most advanced degrees available, the range of demands for these service providers vary across the spectrum of criteria. The ad below is for an entry-level position:

> **Programming Assistant Duties:** This position offers an opportunity for a creative, detail-oriented student to work with our Program Director, assisting in the development, marketing, and facilitation of multicultural workshops. Duties include researching and assembling packets in preparation for workshops; monitoring program registrations for our Saturday workshop series; managing contracts and vouchers for sub-contracts and consultants; marketing; public relations.

Membership Services

Duties. This role is not present in every nonprofit, obviously. Social service agencies, hospitals, animal shelters, and some schools have created special classes of "friends" and provide activities and roles for them to fulfill in support of the organization. Many of these groups have a dual function: building solidarity and fund-raising. Other organizations, such as public radio and TV, the Girl and Boy Scouts, and environmental and conservation organizations, could not exist without the existence of "members." Getting new members and keeping them involved is a full-time and very crucial job.

Qualifications. Abilities in building relationships, organizing and providing meaningful projects for volunteers, and writing and communicating for newsletters, bulletins, pledge drives, and more, are all important.

> **Museum Membership Office:** Seeking degreed individual with excellent computer skills for full-time position. *Must* be responsive, able to handle confidential information, energetic, and capable of working in a busy environment. Oversee database management, mailings, respond to requests for information, liaison with software firm, mailing house, printer, supply company, etc.

Publications

Duties. Most nonprofits produce annual reports at the least, and many have elaborate publication schedules of brochures, histories, reports, handbooks, newspapers, and glossy magazines. To perform this publications work, staff that includes editors, art directors, advertising managers, circulation supervisors, and mailing specialists are required.

Qualifications. The quality and professionalism of publications can often make or break a nonprofit's ability to raise funds and garner support among the various publics to which it tries to appeal. Consequently, in this department, high standards of quality control, meticulous attention to detail, an eye for color, symmetry, and balance, and superior writing and editing skills are crucial. The following job announcement for a brochure production assistant is a classic example of the qualifications the nonprofit marketplace would demand for this kind of position. This position, by the way, would be an excellent entry-level job in the publications arena.

> **Production Assistant:** Communications, journalism, public relations or marketing degree or major. Understand computer word processing (WP 5.1). Have the ability to work independently and be reliable. Being adept at PageMaker would be ideal.

Public Relations

Duties. Good public relations attracts new members, raises the public's awareness, brings in additional funding, and makes existing members (and employees!)

proud and enthusiastic about the organization. Thoughtful letters to the editor of newspapers, excellent relations with the media, special events for the community, and a continuing stream of press releases, announcements, brochures, photographs, speakers, and stories help to keep the organization in the public's eye in a positive and affirming way.

Qualifications.   This department overlaps in both function and staff demands with development and/or membership and the qualifications for those departments stand up well to the demands of this job. This ad is a fair breakdown of the job duties:

Marketing/Public Relations: Lead the museum in building and advancing attendance, relations with the community and media. The core of this job is to generate, analyze, and transform into successful marketing initiatives information about the museum's several audiences, and possess the communications skills to shape and persuasively convey the museum's message to its many constituencies. Supervise admissions and museum reception personnel. Mid to upper 20s.

Administration

Duties.   Accounting, personnel, finance, data processing, property management, maintenance, security, clerical, and secretarial functions all fall under the jurisdiction of this department. The department directs the internal administrative activities of the organization, including personnel and office administration. It establishes policies and procedures to manage support activities. In some nonprofits, it may also oversee financial activities.

Qualifications.   Because many of these more traditional business jobs *support* the functions of the nonprofit professionals and are not as directly involved with the mission and goals of the organization, qualifications, hiring practices, and salary and benefits may be very competitive with comparable jobs outside the nonprofit sector. The following very demanding list of job qualifications for an administrative assistant for a major conservation organization in the Washington, D.C. area contrasts sharply with the "softer" and more individualistic job announcements given in this section:

Required: Related undergraduate degree and at least two years of administrative office experience or equivalent combination of education and experience. Excellent telephone and writing skills, including proofreading. Proficiency with WordPerfect/Windows, Lotus/Windows, & Harvard Graphics or other graphics using IBM platform. Excellent organizational skill and attention to detail. Ability to juggle multiple projects simultaneously. Experience in a marketing environment helpful.

Working Conditions

How will working in a nonprofit differ from working somewhere else? You'll sense a different atmosphere because the operative motivation is different. In business, the goal is "gain," i.e., money. There's certainly nothing wrong with that, and if the business or service is supplying people with something everyone wants or needs, financial profit is the direct and expected result of a well managed enterprise. Without that profit, the commercial firm cannot continue to provide what the public wants. If you had a favorite restaurant, think how disappointed you'd be to hear they had closed because they hadn't charged diners enough to sustain their continued existence.

The Focus

In nonprofits, the emphasis is on the cause, not the reward mechanism. People in nonprofits tend to have bigger, more idealistic goals and see the work they do as part of a larger movement of good for society and the world as a whole.

The implications of this difference in focus are far ranging. There's less "What's in it for me" in workers' attitudes, less competitiveness in the office, and more emphasis on the big picture, not the bottom line. Some generalizations about staff extending themselves, being kinder to each other, and being more aware of the global implications of political, economic, and governmental machinery would probably not be very far off the mark.

There is an ample body of literature, films, and television dramas about workers and executives getting fed up with jobs that revolve around producing, selling, or convincing people to buy a never-ending stream of products. While nonprofits have their own share of frustrations, the goals and missions seldom are the cause of boredom or tedium on the part of workers.

The People

And who are these people you'll be working alongside? Well, they are creative, resourceful, funny, aware of the human condition, accepting, admiring of business talent, and appreciative of its application to their work. They share a commitment to their organizational goals, and, generally, that commitment overrides such issues as who has a corner office or does a potted plant come with a promotion. They are highly collaborative and team oriented and have a sense of fun and adventure about the important work that they do. Most of all, they are versatile and self-effacing, willing to give others credit, and don't stand on ceremony about whose job is whose.

The Nature of the Work and Its Rewards

This is important work, done in a spirit of cooperation, even fun. There is generally a lower stress level, because many of the superficial aspects of for-profit firms are missing—fancy clothes, expensive cars, and all the other accoutrements of a profit-based workplace. Nonprofits do sometimes complain about the quality and condition of their workplaces and technology, but they are also resourceful and enterprising in accomplishing their goals. Many people in nonprofits speak of a more relaxed pace and less pressure. They feel more flexibility to do many more jobs and hold greater amounts of responsibility than they might in a larger, more structured corporate world.

The Money Issue

For some, the salaries in nonprofits may be a drawback. For others, that may be less of a concern. Entry-level business majors can see the nonprofit sector as a place to enter the job market, especially if they identify with the mission and goals of the organization. Nonprofits are excellent schools for the kinds of skills and talents that are used in profit businesses as well.

However, concerns other than pay may prove more troublesome further down the road.

Decision-Making Differences

Nonprofits make decisions in a less arbitrary way than profit systems. Whereas your boss in a profit enterprise may simply say, "Do it this way," in nonprofits, decisions are often reached by consensus or committee and therefore take more time, even for comparatively small issues. This decision-making system has its merits and is easy to get used to because everyone has a voice. Switching to a profit firm later in your career may be a rude awakening for someone used to participative decision making.

Style Differences

Management style is more relaxed and less formal. While the opportunities for business majors in nonprofits are a direct result of nonprofits' need to adapt to more traditional management styles, this remains an issue that most experts feel is weak in nonprofits. Nonprofits traditionally have been very day-to-day in their orientation, with not much emphasis on long-range strategic planning.

TRAINING AND QUALIFICATIONS

Your college education is important to nonprofits, but even more important may be your interest in some particular segment of the nonprofit sector and any past experience in that area. This kind of experience substantiates your stated goals and ensures those hiring you that you understand and have a realistic picture of the work you're getting into. If you haven't yet graduated, consider spending a summer in an internship or devoting extra hours during the school year to volunteer work. This may even be worth your while after graduation if you can manage it.

For example, community service jobs are highly diverse, from medical services and social work to the organization of neighborhood efforts to defeat crime or drug traffic. Large housing services in cities have staffs that do nothing but manage property and lend money for construction. Your college degree may get you in the door, but to leave the interview with people still interested in you, you'll need to educate yourself to understand what they do and be able to express a well-reasoned explanation for not only why you want to join them but where you see yourself fitting in.

The arts are one of the major subgroups of nonprofit employers. Here you'll find you're up against the infamous "You need experience, but I can't give it to you." *Catch–22.* Entry-level jobs in arts organizations are tough to get and there is great competition. You may have to begin in a lower-level job to gain entry and work your way up in the organization through internal promotions. Or, you might approach the arts organization with a resume that relates your experience in another area to your interest in the arts. For example, if you've done fund-raising or special event planning, you might begin by knocking on the doors of the development offices of nonprofit theatres, symphony orchestras, or art galleries.

The environmental subgroup is so popular that hiring demands there are very competitive, requiring not only technical expertise but an understanding of specific environmental issues at a sophisticated level and the ability to advocate for change. If you are interested in the environment and lack a specialty degree, start locally as an intern or volunteer while in school and then begin your job search with state or regional groups.

Museums and other preservationist organizations look for a college education, some practical experience, and an understanding on the part of the applicant that these organizations have all kinds of work: membership services, security, curatorship, display and mounting, preservation and curating, marketing, sales, and public relations. Many of those are appropriate for a business major, and if you have a background in art, there are more possibilities.

A simple menu of the most basic requirements for business jobs in the nonprofit sector would include:

❑ A solid business college education

❑ A sincere commitment to the nonprofit cause

❑ An ability to define and enumerate your relevant skills and experience

❑ The flexibility to use your skills and experience in new ways

$\mathcal{E}$ARNINGS

Approximately half of current operating expenditures in nonprofit are spent on employee compensation. Most recent data indicate that wages and salaries in the sector are at 74 percent that of average wages and salaries of all other sectors of the economy in 1990, an increase from 73 percent in 1989, slight, but an increase nevertheless.

There's a curious dichotomy about salaries in the nonprofit sector that you should be aware of. On the one hand, nonprofits realize that to be successful and to attract the talent they need (that includes you!), they have to offer competitive salaries and benefits. On the other hand, many staff are attracted to the organization largely because of its goals and orientation and derive some "psychic" income in that way. For some employers, this is rationalization enough to set salary levels somewhat lower than is competitive. Both situations occur with mind-boggling regularity in the nonprofit sector. It varies from one organization to the next. Let's compare two similar position descriptions for similar organizations in our nation's capitol, taken from *Community Jobs,* that illustrate the Jekyll and Hyde situation of compensation. Both of these jobs in similar sized and funded organizations are for "program coordinators," a common nonprofit job title that refers to individuals who develop and coordinate education, advocacy, and organization plans for an organization. They attend meetings, publish newsletters, and attempt to build an activist base of volunteers to accomplish goals. It's an important job but can come with very different levels of rewards:

Job A	Job B
Program Coordinator: Proven organizing skills with national organization, excellent writing and editing ability. Team builder. **$25,000 salary.**	Program Coordinator: Proven leadership ability and supervisory skills, and the ability to motivate others and achieve goals. **Low to mid-30s.**

The full descriptions show these two positions to very similar in scope and demands and yet the possibility of a $10,000 difference in salary, in the same city, exists. This is a frequent situation in nonprofits and something you need to stay aware of.

While a "big fat check" may not be what working for a not-for-profit organization is about, on the other hand, you need to be realistic about your financial needs—now, and into the future. Salaries are an important and frequently discussed issue for all who choose to work in nonprofits.

Relationship to Budget

At the end of this section I have listed some general reference works on salary data in the nonprofit sector. There isn't very much information out there and one of the ways I have become proficient at estimating salary levels is by regularly and closely reading job ads for nonprofit sector employment. It remains my most valuable primary source of compensation information.

However, another very logical way to come to an understanding of possible salary levels is to *work down* from the chief executive salary to your level of management. A 1993 survey by *Board and Administrator* (Aspen Publishers, Frederick, Maryland) (Table 13.1) provides the following information on average executive director salaries compared to budget size. But individual chief executive salaries vary dramatically, depending upon the experiential history of the incumbent. *Board and Administrator* cites a $20,000 difference between an incumbent with more than fifteen years of nonprofit employment history at a senior level and one with less than five years experience. Obviously, one would expect these differentials for experience would translate to lower levels, as well (Table 13.2).

Table 13.1

Average Nonprofit Executive Director Salary
Compared to Budget Size

Budget Size	Salary
Less than $500,000	$32,823
$500,001-1,000,000	$42,446
$1,000,001-1,500,000	$47,266
$1,500,001-2,000,000	$50,038
$2,000,001-2,500,000	$55,861
$2,500,001-3,000,000	$55,617
$3,000,0001-4,000,000	$61,518
$4,000,0001-5,000,000	$62,918
$5,000,001-6,000,000	$69,117
More than $6,000,000	$74,881

1993 Aspen Publishers, Inc. All figures are shown in US $

Table 13.2

Annual Budget, and Salaries (in Thousands of $)

Position	Less than 1M	1M-4.9M	5M-9.9M	10M-49.9M	Above 50M
CEO/Executive Director	59.8	85.6	115.0	182.7	204.5
Deputy CEO/Director	37.2	71.1	86.8	127.7	132.7
Top Administrative Position	30.3	40.9	59.2	100.2	110.5
Top Financial Position/Controller	35.1	44.9	71.3	95.9	115.6
*Executive Assistant	30.9	34.3	32.0	50.3	58.8
*Top Editorial/Publication Director	29.8	37.7	37.7	74.3	72.9
*Top Public Relations Position		39.1	46.0	83.9	80.5
*Top Marketing Position		57.1	54.7	94.5	103.7
*Top Membership Position	41.0	37.6	37.6	73.3	81.1
Directors of Management					
Information Systems	33.1	37.3	37.3	69.6	78.2
Top Development Position	43.8	46.1	64.6	99.4	111.2
*Top Fundraising/Grant Position	42.5	45.7	52.8	69.7	56.3

*Indicates a position for which the corresponding salaries do not follow a direct relationship with the increased annual budgets.

Salaries given in italics highlight salaries which apply to the combined budget categories under which they appear.

Source: Coopers & Lybrand

Other Forms of Compensation

Benefits are one way to add to an employee's package of compensation without as direct an outlay of funds as simple salary. Nonprofits are competitive in regard to benefits with their private sector counterparts, as reported in *Board and Administrator's* survey that divides nonprofits into small budgets (less than $500,000) and large (budgets of 6 million dollars and more). Note: these benefits are as reported for executive directors.

Percentage of Nonprofits Offering Selected Benefits		
	Small budget	**Large budget**
Health insurance	74%	96%
Life insurance	49%	87%
Retirement	42%	90%
Dental	33%	63%
Disability insurance	32%	60%
Education assistance	21%	43%

RESOURCES ON NONPROFIT COMPENSATION

Board and Administrator:
1994 Report on Nonprofit Executive Director Compensation
Aspen Publishers, Inc.
7201 McKinney Circle
Frederick, MD 21701
800-638-8437

Compensation in Nonprofit Organizations, 7th Edition
Abbot, Langer & Associates
548 First Street
Crete, IL 60417
708-672-4200

Association Executive Compensation Study
American Society of Association Executives
1575 I Street, N.W.
Washington, DC 20005-1168

National Summary:
Not-For-Profit Employment from the 1990 Consensus of Population and Housing (Preliminary Findings)

Independent Sector
1828 L Street, N.W.
Washington, DC 20036
202-223-8100

Compensation in Not-For-Profit Organizations
Coopers & Lybrand/Survey Research Unit
1301 Avenue of the Americas
New York, NY 10019-6013
212-259-2447

1994 Wage and Benefit Survey of Northern California Nonprofit Organizations
The Management Center
870 Market Street, Suite 800
San Francisco, CA 94102-2903

CAREER OUTLOOK

We are all worried about our working future, and this chapter opened with some troublesome examples of the changing face of employment opportunities in this country. As the global economy moves into the information age, there seem to be fewer traditionally "prime" jobs and more jobs in the low-paying sectors, many of them only "temp" or part-time positions. Those who have tried to comfort us claim the desirability of a greatly reduced work week that will allow people to pursue private pleasures or socially useful projects. Before this comes about, however, we will as a nation have to come to terms with a future in which the traditional place of private sector jobs no longer holds center stage in our economic and social life.

If you are considering the nonprofit arena as a good place to make a career and find value for your business degree, you may also find you have chosen the one sector of the economy where the opportunities won't diminish over time. In his 1995 book, *The End of Work: The Decline of the Global Labor Force and the Dawn of the Post-Market Era,* author and activist Jeremy Rifkin says that whether the issue is healthcare for an aging population, preservation of our nation's treasures, developing community projects, or fostering the arts, it is these person-to-person, nurturing skills that will be least vulnerable to replacement by computers, robots, bar scanners, and telecommunications technology. Scan the job-listing pages of a publication such as *Community Jobs* and try to reduce the job announcements listed there to digitalization or computerization. You cannot! These jobs are too complex, too difficult, requiring intimate contact between people. Though your role in these organizations may not be on the front lines of client/customer contact, it is the nonprofit organizations and their missions that will be among the elite, status-invested jobs of the future.

Already, we see the beginnings of a society with more of an emphasis on helping others. Your own college probably had an office of volunteer services that placed college students in community service sites such as senior centers, animal shelters, halfway houses, environmental clean-up projects, and other similar endeavors. Your high school or even grade school may have encouraged similar events and outreach for students. This trend is occurring as we as a nation learn of our citizenship with all peoples and our connection to the entire ecosystem of our planet.

An encouraging trend for nonprofits has been the growing number of for-profit firms that are "adopting" and sponsoring the efforts of nonprofits. Several things are indicated by this corporate interest. First, the valuable work of nonprofits is increasingly recognized and supported by the establishment. This corporate funding allows them to continue their work. Second, the corporations themselves become vested with some of the "halo" of good works that cloaks the nonprofit they sponsor, and that is, of course, good for business. Third, and most important, through the publicity of the corporation the nonprofit gains a far wider and more appreciative audience than they could on their own efforts. The following list is taken from a news report published December 12, 1994 by the Associated Press in the *Lansing State Journal:*

Some companies and the causes they support:

- ❑ **Ryka Inc.** Issues relating to violence against women.

- ❑ **Nike, Inc.** Tries to participate in the lives of American youth. The company has a $10 million program to develop sports and fitness facilities for youngsters without access to such centers and supports other youth programs such as the Boys and Girls Clubs of America.

- ❑ **Virginia Fiber Corp.** The paper mill gives 9 percent of its pretax profits to AmeriCares, a relief organization started by Virginia Fiber chief executive, Robert McCauley.

- ❑ **Avon Products Inc.** Works to promote breast cancer awareness using its cadre of 415,000 representatives nationwide. The program also extends to 10 other countries, where an appropriate women's health issue is chosen and promoted.

- ❑ **Reebok International Ltd.** Has aligned itself with human rights, first sponsoring Amnesty International's world tour eight

continued

---

continued

years ago and keeping involved with the rights group and the issue ever since.

❑ **The Stride Rite Corp.** Contributes to further inner city education and health.

❑ **Polaroid Corp.** Supports programs to fight violence against women; supports math and science teaching.

❑ **Liz Claiborne, Inc.** Campaigns to end violence against women.

❑ **Thom McAn Shoe Co.** Supports a school-to-work program and mentoring programs in five Worcester, Mass. public high schools.

STRATEGY FOR FINDING THE JOBS

A Three-Step Process

Let's outline a smart strategy to determine the best possible use of your skills in the nonprofit sector. As you work your way through these steps, you'll need to devote ample time to the completion of these activities. You'll need to think about your choices and to meet and talk with people regarding the various possibilities. Essentially, the strategy involves three steps: Making some important decisions, talking to people, and focusing your efforts. Let's take each step by itself.

STEP 1. Make Three Decisions.   First of all, realize your job search in the non-profit sector is not very different from any other job search. You'll need to begin by focusing your energy and your efforts so you aren't overwhelmed by information and options. The areas you can begin to make some decisions in are:

❑ What kinds of nonprofits you want to seek out

❑ Where you want to work

❑ How you will be positioning yourself as a candidate, based on your education and skills

Let's consider the factors involved in these decisions.

1. Be certain you believe in the mission. Nonprofits revolve around a mission more intensely than do many profit organizations. Whether the mission is aid to refugees, irrigation education, protection of abused children, equal justice, fair employment, or any of the thousands of other objectives, it should be something you are interested in and can remain interested in during your career. When it comes to hiring, nonprofits seek to establish the level of your commitment and the rationale for it. Understand their issues and decide which issues you most believe in and which might best sustain your enthusiasm, interest, and *passion.*

2. Determine where you want to work. This chapter has demonstrated an enormous variety of nonprofit jobs and a corresponding variety of work sites, from China to the inner city. What appeals to you? Are your concerns localized to your own town or city or your own state or region of the country? Are your concerns localized to a particular region of the United States, such as the Great Plains or the timberlands of the Northwest? Are you interested in South America, Asia, or Africa? Or do you want to be involved in a global issue involving the whole of the planet and our impact upon it? Answers to these questions will have much to do with not only the kind of organization you affiliate with, but also where that organization is located and where its operations are focused.

3. Position yourself to fit into the organization. Even within a particular niche of the nonprofits, there can be major differences in how people go about their work. Say, for example, you have selected the arts as an area you feel will sustain your career interests. Within the arts there are arts advocates, lobbyists, policy makers, educators, and a host of other positions, all requiring very different skills and using different ways of communicating and working together.

It's not a potential employer's job to figure out how you'll fit in their operation. You need to understand what that organization does and how you might best make a contribution to its mission. To make a winning presentation, use Chapter One, Self-Assessment, to analyze your skills and attributes, to reflect on your personality and work style, and to understand your communication preferences. Prepare yourself to present pertinent information about yourself to interviewers in a way they can appreciate. For example, if you are seeking a position with the Public Broadcasting Service (PBS), you should be aware that their activities include program acquisition and scheduling, educational services, advertising and promotion, audience research, broadcast and technical operations, development (fund raising), and engineering. If your strong skills are marketing/advertising and you have some good computer skills, you could look at opportunities in audience research and consumer behavior, or advertising and promotion, or special events and fund-raising and promotion activities.

STEP 2. Get Out and Meet People in Nonprofits. Start by meeting people who are working in your preferred nonprofit field in your own community area and then *network out* in increasingly wide circles to develop relationships with other professionals in this field. For example, perhaps your interest is in the environment, or more specifically, preserving natural wetlands and forest from development. Begin with your town administrator or planning board. Perhaps they belong to a national program that fosters the planting and replacement of lost trees in a community and provides grants for that purpose. Contacting national organizations can often lead you to more state-wide contacts in the specific areas of your interest.

The *Great Jobs* series repeatedly stresses the advantages of using your school's alumni network to meet people in your field. Some students prefer to contact alumni because they already share the same college experience and because alumni often have more commitment to helping students from their own schools than other people you may encounter. Certainly, my clients return again and again with stories of making instant friends with alumni in our network. They remark on the candor of our alumni contacts and the detailed information they are willing to provide. This process will help you find more contacts, more employment sites, and will also refine your interview content because as you search out your network, you learn more and more about the job, yourself, and how you can make the best fit between the two.

Review the chapter on networking (Chapter Six) to ensure you make the most out of every meeting. It will tell you how to prepare for each meeting and how to conduct interviews. It provides you with a variety of sample questions and explains follow up in order to keep your various contacts alive and fresh.

STEP 3. Focus Your Search.   Since you are spending significant time and money in a job search, you should narrow down your search and be more targeted. To accomplish that, you should do the following:

❑ Determine the type of mission(s) you are most interested in

❑ Decide on the geographic area of your search

❑ Determine one or two positions to seek in these organizations

❑ Set thresholds for entry-level income

In all likelihood, your final focus will be some blend of these four factors. Even with this starting focus, each informational interview will increase your knowledge in several ways. You'll learn the special vocabulary of the field, the unique challenges of the geographic location you've chosen, and you'll increasingly grasp the nature of the job you've targeted so that you become a sharper, more defined candidate.

POSSIBLE EMPLOYERS

Categories for the Nonprofit Sector

A taxonomy developed by Dr. Michael O'Neill divides the nonprofits into 11 categories:

1. Human and social service organizations

2. Mutual benefit organizations

3. Business, professional, farming, and labor organizations

4. Religious organizations

5. Scientific research organizations

6. Legislative, legal, political, and advocacy organizations

7. Health service organizations

8. Arts, cultural, historical, and community-educational organizations

9. Community development organizations

10. Private nonprofit educational organizations

11. Grantmaking organizations

You will find an abundance of material that you can use to locate possible employers in the nonprofit sector. Let's examine these resources—all of which contain employer information, in order, from the most general to the most specific.

General Descriptive Sources.   The reference works listed below are a good beginning because they give you a broad overview of the narrow areas of the nonprofit sector, how these organizations are structured, and what kind of employees populate them. Many of these resources will identify specific job titles and the duties and responsibilities associated with those positions, as well as the personal characteristics of the people chosen to fill them.

Career Opportunities in Art
Susan B. Haubenstock and David Joselit
1988
Facts on File Publications, Inc.
460 Park Avenue South
New York, NY 10016

Doing Well by Doing Good: The Complete Guide to Careers in the Non-Profit Sector
Terry W. McAdam
1988
Penguin Publishers
120 Woodbine Street
Burgenfield, NJ 07621
(now out of print, though still available in libraries and worth the search)

The Environmental Career Guide
Nicholas Basta
1991
John Wiley & Sons, Inc.
605 Third Avenue
New York, NY 10158-0012

Finding a Job in the Nonprofit Sector
The Taft Group
1991
A Division of Gale Research, Inc.
12300 Twinbrook Parkway, Suite 520
Rockville, MD 20852

Jobs and Careers with Nonprofit Organizations
Drs. Ron and Caryl Krannich
1993
Impact Publications
9104–N Manassas Drive
Manassas Park, VA 22111

Jobs in Arts and Media Management: What They Are And How to Get One
Stephen Langley and James Abruzzo
1989
American Council for the Arts
1285 Avenue of the Americas
3rd Floor
New York, NY 10019

The New Complete Guide to Environmental Careers
1993
The Environmental Careers Organization
Island Press
1718 Connecticut Avenue, N.W., Suite 300
Washington, DC 20009

Nonprofits' Job Finder
Daniel Lauber
1992
Planning/Communications
River Forest, IL 60305-1935

Opportunities in Environmental Careers
Odom Fanning
1996

VGM Career Horizons
4255 West Touhy Avenue
Lincolnwood, IL 60646-1975

Opportunities in Nonprofit Organizations
Adrian A. Paradis
1994
VGM Career Horizons
4255 West Touhy Avenue
Lincolnwood, IL 60646-1975

What Color Is Your Parachute?
Richard Bolles
1994
Ten Speed Press
P.O. Box 7123
Berkeley, CA 94707

Directories.   These excellent reference works are widely available and list organizations by type, by job category, and by geographic location. Many also contain bibliographies and resource lists that will offer additional, more specific information.

Alternatives to the Peace Corps: Gaining Third World Experience
Becky Buell and Kam Harnerschiag
1994
Food First/Institute for Food and Development Policy
145 9th Street
San Francisco, CA 94103

Directory of Internships in Youth Development
1993
The National Collaboration for Youth
1319 F Street N.W., Suite 601S
Washington, DC 20004

Good Works: A Guide to Careers in Social Change
ed. by Jessica Cowan
1991
Barricade Books
61 Fourth Avenue
New York, NY 10003

Great Careers: The Fourth of July Guide to Careers, Internships, and
Volunteer Opportunities in the Non-Profit Sector
ed. by Devon Cottrell Smith
1990
Garrett Park Press
P.O. Box 190B
Garrett Park, MD 20896

National Directory of Arts Internships
ed. by Warren Christensen
1988
National Network for Artist Placement
935 West Avenue, Suite 37
Los Angeles, CA 90065

The Peace Corps and More: 114 Ways to Work, Study, and Travel in the
3rd World
Medea Benjamin
1991
Global Exchange
2141 Mission Street, #202
San Francisco, CA 94110

Job Listings.   For a career counselor like myself, the list below is as familiar
and important as a group of good friends. We use them in the office daily as
they are excellent sources of information on potential career opportunities for
college graduates seeking to enter the nonprofit sector. Check them out. If
your career center doesn't subscribe to them, check your college or university
library or a major city library nearby. Your own college career center may be
able to arrange for you to use the services of another college that does subscribe through professional reciprocity. The hunt will be worth it.

Once you locate these job listings, use them to their best advantage. Any
issue tells you far more than simply what jobs are currently available. There is
editorial content that will inform you about current issues in the field, legislative initiatives, ethical challenges, and interesting profiles of nonprofit professionals. Read the back issues, too, and you'll expand your awareness of job
titles, job sites, and even possible salary figures growing. These job postings
lists can teach you about job sites you might not have considered, and even
though a job listing may be very old, if the job looks attractive to you, explore
similar nonprofits to ascertain their needs for that kind of employment.

Art Search: The National Employment Service Bulletin for the Performing Arts
Theater Communications Group
355 Lexington Avenue
New York, NY 10017

Arts Opportunities
The Career Planning and Placement Office
The Maryland Institute College of Art
1300 West Mount Royal Avenue
Baltimore, MD 21217

Association for Experiential Education
2885 Aurora, #28
Boulder, CO 80303-2252

AVISO
American Association of Museums
1225 I Street, N.W., Suite 200
Washington, DC 20005

The Chronicle of Philanthropy
P.O. Box 1989
Marion, OH 43305

COMMUNITY JOBS: The National Employment Newspaper for the Non-Profit Sector
ACCESS: Networking in the Public Interest
50 Beacon Street
Boston, MA 02116

Earth Work
P.O. Box 550
Charlestown, NH 03603

Environmental Opportunities
P.O. Box 670
Walpole, NH 03608

The Job Seeker (Environmental Jobs)
Route 2 Box 16
Warrens, WI 54666

The Nonprofit Times
Davis Information Group
190 Tamarack Circle
Skillman, NJ 08558

Opportunities in Public Affairs
110 Connecticut Avenue, N.W., Suite 700
Washington, DC 20036

On-Line Services Focusing on Nonprofits.   Want to go on-line? Here is a sample list of on-line networks. Some are commercial/consumer systems, but others are more focused on serving the nonprofit, social service, and public interest community.

American Online
Quantum Computer Services
8619 Westwood Drive Center
Vienna, VA 22182
Phone (800) 227-6364

CompuServe
500 Arlington Centre Boulevard
P.O. Box 20212
Columbus, OH 43220
Phone (800) 848-8199

DELPHI
General Videotex Corporation
3 Blackstone Street
Cambridge, MA 02139
Phone (800) 544-4005

ECHO
97 Perry Street #13
New York, NY 10014
Phone (212) 255-3839

Genie (General Electric Network for Information Exchange)
401 North Washington Street
Rockville, MD 20850
Phone (800) 638-9639

Prodigy
445 Hamilton Avenue
White Plains, NY 10601
Phone (800) 776-3449

The WELL (Whole Earth 'Lectronic Link)
27 Gate Five Road
Sausalito, CA 94965
Phone (415) 332-6106

Systems Serving Nonprofit and Public Interest Groups.

Arts Wire
1077 Treat Avenue
San Francisco, CA 94110
Phone (415) 826-6743

HandsNet
20195 Stevens Creek Boulevard, Suite 120
Cupertino, CA 95104
Phone (408) 257-4500

HandsNet is a national network of resources for social and economic change. Network tools include: *Federal Register* abstracts covering education; *OnLine News Clipping Service* which provides daily news briefs covering human services and justice topics; and fax capability. HandsNet's public forums on key human service issues are open to all members. Organizations with regional or national memberships can develop private forums to facilitate group work.

Institute for Global Communications (IGC)
18 DeBoom
San Francisco, CA 94107
Phone (415) 442-0220

The Institute for Global Communications (IGC) offers four computer networks: ConflictNet, EcoNet, LaborNet, and PeaceNet. ConflictNet provides telecommunications services to professionals and volunteers who work with organizations that promote peaceful resolution of disputes. EcoNet links people and organizations that work for environmental causes. LaborNet is the newest IGC network and provides information to labor representatives. PeaceNet connects activists and organizations involved in working for peace and human rights issues.

WIRE (Women's Information Resource & Exchange)
435 Grand Avenue, Suite D
South San Francisco, CA 94080
Phone (415) 615-8989
  WIRE publishes information on dozens of resources including: business, money, women's health, sports, *Newswires* (including White House press releases and stories about women around the glove), and *Political Progress* (up-to-date information on the changing political scene for women.

Possible Job Titles

Sample Job Titles in the Nonprofit Sector
(Taken from *Careers in the Nonprofit Sector: Doing Well by Doing Good,* by Terry McAdam. This is a virtual manual for those interested in nonprofit careers.)

Chief Executive Officer.   Responsible for directing the overall program and administrative activities of the foundation. Responsible for the effective use of financial and human resources of the foundation.

Controller.   Responsible for operation of financial and bookkeeping services, including preparation of financial analyses, income and expense reports, budgets, and governmental reports. May also be responsible for directing, purchasing, payroll, other financial operations.

General Counsel.   Responsible for directing the legal activities of the foundation. Responsible for coordinating legal matters with outside counsel, and for advising staff on legal matters pertaining to the foundation.

Program Director.   Responsible for investigating and evaluating grant proposals and/or carrying out in-house projects. In larger-staffed foundations, this may involve one subject area or geographic region. In smaller foundations, program officers are usually responsible for most aspects of the grantmaking process, including program research, proposal evaluation, and post-grant evaluation.
  Many job titles in the nonprofit sector are indistinguishable from the world of commercial, for-profit jobs. There are chief executive officers, marketing directors, nurses, doctors, lawyers, and more. We examined some positions earlier in this chapter that held job titles a business major could

easily identify and appreciate. But there are some job titles unique to the world of nonprofits. Many are listed below. In every case these are positions that are appropriate for people with business degrees.

Canvass director	Fund raiser
Case managers	Major donor field representative
Communications assistant	Outreach worker
Community organizer	Political activist
Energy advocate	Research assistants
Farm apprentice	Tenant organizer
Field assistants	Union organizer

RELATED OCCUPATIONS

By now, the direct correlations between nonprofit and for-profit organizations have been made more than once. The reader of this chapter should understand that not only are many jobs the same, many nonprofits have looked to the profit sector for management guidance and strategic initiatives. Goals of profit may be vastly different, but both profit and nonprofit organizations realize that only *well managed* organizations survive.

We have also seen that many nonprofits have created for-profit subsidiaries to generate income for their nonprofit initiatives. Many nonprofit museums, for example, have found a ready market and significant profits through selling fine arts and reproductions of museum pieces in museum stores, incorporated as for-profit subsidiaries and often administered by outside vendors. Profits are returned to the museum as income to support new museum ventures. This lessens some of the risks inherent in depending upon money from grants or the support of the public for all of a museum's funding.

A SAMPLE OF SOME LARGER NONPROFIT ORGANIZATIONS

This is a selected list, taken from the *National Directory of Nonprofit Organizations,* 1995, published by the Taft Group, 12300 Twinbrook Road, Rockville, Maryland.

American Ballet (NY, NY)
American Council for Nationalities Service (NY, NY)
American Enterprise Institute for Public Policy Program (DC)
American Film Institute (DC)
American Indian Heritage Foundation (Falls Church, VA)
American Philosophical Society (Philadelphia, PA)
American Printing House for the Blind (Louisville, KY)
American Society for the Prevention of Cruelty to Animals (NY, NY)
Amnesty International of the USA (NY, NY)
Association for Women in Science (DC)
Campaign for Human Development (DC)
Cancer Care (NY, NY)
Carnegie Council on Ethics and International Affairs (NY, NY)
Chicago Historical Society (IL)
Children's Hospital (Columbus, OH)
Children's Television Workshop (NY, NY)
Common Cause (DC)
Cooperative for American Relief Everywhere International (CARE)
   (NY, NY)
Courage Center (Golden Valley, MN)
Cousteau Society (Norfolk, VA)
Environmental Defense Fund (NY, NY)
Ethics and Public Policy Center (DC)
Food for the Hungry (DC)
Friends of the Earth (DC)
Gray Panther (Philadelphia, PA)
International Prison Ministry (Dallas, TX)
Lawyers Committee for Civil Rights Under Law (DC)
Literacy Volunteers of America (Syracuse, NY)
Metropolitan Opera Guild (NY, NY)
Mothers Against Drunk Driving (MADD) (Hurst, TX)
National Committee for the Prevention of Child Abuse (Chicago, IL)
Nature Conservancy (Arlington, VA)
Outward Bound USA (Greenwich, CT)
Partners for Livable Places (DC)
Pro Football Hall of Fame (Canton, OH)
Resources for the Future (DC)
Save the Children (Westport, CT)
Sierra Club (San Francisco, CA)
UNICEF, (NY, NY)
Union of Concerned Scientists (Cambridge, MA)

continued

continued

United Negro College Fund (NY, NY)
United Way of America (Alexandria, VA)
Volunteers of America (Metairie, LA)
Wilderness Society (DC)
YMCA, YWCA (NY, NY)

PROFESSIONAL ASSOCIATIONS

Professional associations remain a seldom-used but immensely valuable tool for job seekers. The organizations listed below have a vested interest in raising your level of general information about the career fields they represent. Most are very generous with their publications and providing answers to questions. Give them a try.

Association for Research on Nonprofit Organizations and Voluntary Actions
Route 2, Box 696
Pullman, WA 99163
Members/Purpose: Stimulates, coordinates, and aids the efforts of those engaged in voluntary action research, scholarship, and professional activity.
Training: Sponsors collaborative research proposals and projects on voluntary action topics.
Publications: *ARNOVA Newsletter.*

National Center for Nonprofit Board
2000 L Street, N.W., Suite 510
Washington, DC 20036
Members/Purpose: Seeks to improve the effectiveness of nonprofit organizations in fields such as arts and culture, conservation, religion, youth development, public policy, health and medicine, and social welfare by strengthening their governing boards.
Training: Offers assistance in organizing training programs, workshops, and seminars for nonprofit organizations.
Publications: Books and booklets, makes available audiotapes.

Nonprofit Management Association
315 West 9th Street, Suite 1100
Los Angeles, CA 90015

Members/Purpose: Seeks to further education and leadership capabilities in order to enhance both individuals and the management of the nonprofit organization.

Training: Provides opportunity to further education through information sharing and networking among members.

Society for Nonprofit Organizations
6314 Odana Road, Suite 1
Madison, WI 53719

Members/Purpose: Provides a forum for the exchange of information, knowledge and ideas on strengthening and increasing productivity within nonprofit organizations and among their leaders.

Training: Sponsors seminars and workshops on nonprofit management and leadership.

Publications: *National Directory of Service and Product Providers, Nonprofit World: The National Nonprofit Leadership and Management Journal, Society for Nonprofit Organizations—Resource Center Catalog.*

Volunteer Trustees of Not-for-Profit Hospitals
818 18th Street, N.W., Suite 900
Washington, DC 20006

Members/Purpose: Objectives are: to provide a trustee voice in policy making and legislative activities, and develop a communication network among trustees in order to provide the highest quality medical care at the lowest possible price.

CHAPTER FOURTEEN

PATH 5: RESEARCH ASSOCIATE— A STRATEGIC APPROACH TO THE MBA

While you're in college majoring in business, you are going to hear the MBA (Master of Business Administration) degree mentioned frequently. Many of your professors have received this degree on the way to their doctoral work in business. It has probably been frequently mentioned in your business textbooks, case studies, and profiles of successful businesswomen and men.

THINK AGAIN

However, not all MBA degrees are created equal, and MBA programs, curricula, and faculty can vary dramatically from school to school. The MBA degree has come under considerable scrutiny in the past 10 years, and there have been many news stories and journal articles discussing the increasing proliferation of MBA programs and the lack of quality in some of their program offerings, especially those from smaller schools. MBA programs are frequently evaluated and rated in the business press, and it is understood there is no comparison between the MBA degree offered by one of the larger, top 10 programs in the country, with a dedicated graduate faculty, and the offerings of a small, private, or state-supported college whose undergraduate faculty may be doing double duty in both the MBA program and undergraduate classes.

The Issue of Experience

Nevertheless, the MBA degree has much to offer the qualified business major and, in most instances, the degree can enhance your career. MBA programs place a high value on prior work experience when it comes to assessing the admission applications of a new class. Those employers that hire the graduates of MBA programs put an equally high premium on work experience. Some of that high salary the MBA earns in many cases is a reward for that expected experience. Would you want to be treated by a physician who had read all the right books but never had any patient contact before meeting you? Of course not! The MBA is no different than any other professional degree. There is an understandable expectation of experience to justify both the level of position and the salary.

An MBA without any business experience would actually hurt your career because employers are unwilling to hire and pay for an MBA degree without an accompanying high level of practical experience.

The job market is tough and is going to stay tough. For this reason, the MBA beckons all those business graduates who feel that getting the degree will add something to their resume and who hope the job market improves before they reenter it with the added credential of their new graduate degree. This is not a wise strategy because you continue to add unproven education without experience. Sadly, many of your peers who have taken MBAs with no real-world experience will tell you their salaries and job descriptions are little different from those of another employee with a bachelor's degree. In my own career counseling practice, I have seen this type of client all too frequently.

This chapter is all about making your decision to get an MBA a *thoughtful* choice, a choice that will not only enable you to get the most out of the degree, but also enhance your job prospects in the process.

WHERE ARE YOU IN THIS PICTURE?

First of all, consider one of the following scenarios to see if any fit your current thinking or situation:

Scenario 1: You've enjoyed your business major and done pretty well academically but you're not certain about exactly what kind of work you should look for. You're confused about what you can do in the work force and who will hire you.

Scenario 2: You're approaching graduation or you've just graduated. You've tested the job market and it doesn't seem like a good time to be employed. Jobs are hard to come by, low paying, and don't seem to value your degree. Maybe you think it would be better to stay in school, get an advanced degree, and then try the job market.

Scenario 3: Perhaps you've done the kinds of job search activities suggested in the opening chapters of this book and seen all the better jobs and big money go to those who have an MBA. You think, "Okay, I'll get an MBA," but you're worried about your own lack of work experience in a professional business environment. You wonder if you could get through the degree. You have to ask yourself if you have what it takes.

You may begin to feel as confused and frustrated as Shakespeare's Hamlet, wrestling over the question of whether or not to continue your education with an MBA or to get out of school and go to work. Certainly, given the uncertainties of the job market and the shifting paradigms of employers and employee bases, it might seem a wise investment to continue to add to your business education, to earn an advanced degree, and hope to make yourself more competitive than the typical undergraduate job candidate.

Graduate school has always been a popular option, for those who could afford it, when the job market is tight. Enroll in "B" school, wait a couple of years, and then hopefully enter the market at a more propitious time. The strategy is that, hopefully, not only will your chances of employment be better, but once you have an advanced degree you may be a candidate for more and different jobs than you would have been previously and at a higher salary.

THE "CATCH 22" OF NO EXPERIENCE

Business school officials want students who have work experience; such pupils learn more and contribute more to a dynamic classroom environment. MBA program curricula are built around adding to and enhancing the lessons with students' own personal experiences. When rising numbers of applicants for quality MBA programs created enough admissions competition, discerning MBA programs were able to require this work history for consideration for admission.

This work experience requirement obviously causes problems for the typical undergraduate applicant. For unless students without work experience are willing to enter lower-tier business schools that may have less demanding admissions requirements regarding work experience, they must somehow land excellent jobs rights from college. We all know those good jobs have been proven to be hard to attain without certain entry skills. The very top business students may qualify for employment at management consulting firms or financial institutions upon receipt of their bachelor's degree, but average students find they aren't competitive. What can you do?

Naturally, at this point, the clever student's intention turns to enhancing his or her attractiveness to an employer by getting an MBA. But you cannot get into the top MBA programs without first landing a good job. Since you intend your work experience to boost you into further schooling after a year or two on the job, you are in a weak position with a prospective employer. You are in a bind.

Interestingly, this is where the "experience catch" causes problems, not just for students but for the colleges they've graduated from. The value of your undergraduate business program is weakened by the lower quality of the employment you finally do secure on your way to the MBA. Your undergraduate program may not have been the boost to your job entry that you had hoped, nor does the degree appear to enhance your prospects for graduate school.

STRAIGHT TALK ON THE MBA

Let's identify some facts about MBA programs and their students that might be important to you in weighing the advantages and disadvantages of making a graduate school choice without experience.

First, many MBA students are older than the average new college graduate. A recent survey in the *Wall Street Journal's* special employment newspaper for college students, *Managing Your Career* (Winter/Spring 1995), demonstrates that on the average, the students in the graduating class of last year's MBA schools was 27.6 years old and had 4.5 years of professional work experience when they entered the program. More than 99 percent had some experience and 93 percent had worked for more than two years.

Second, many MBA students are there because they need the degree to advance in their organizations. They may, in fact, be funded by their employers, and they are likely to approach their studies with the seriousness, responsibility, and expectation of superior performance that you would associate with someone there under the aegis of their employer. For these students, graduate work is "part of their job" and they approach it with the same gritty determination they would approach any work project. They are aggressive about their education, assertive with their classmates, less interested in the social aspects of graduate school, and more focused on their performance.

Third, another very unique aspect of the MBA is the content of the coursework, which centers around case studies—written stories of actual business practices. Individually or in teams, graduate students take these cases apart, analyze them, and prescribe real-world solutions. This is almost impossible to do when your own business experience is limited to the kinds of employment available to undergraduates during the summer or on school breaks.

Fourth, while your undergraduate grades may be superior and you may have already gained some solid work experience, including an internship in business, it's important to realize most business schools utilize the work group to accomplish many assignments and projects. Even if you are a superior student, if you have had limited group work in college, you may not be ready for the hard-driving, highly organized, and demanding group work of the experienced businesspeople in your classes. That is a skill often learned on the job and you may find it hard to deal with the candid feedback on your performance by group members in addition to appraisals used by course instructors.

Finally, students who have a work history enter the graduate business school with a focus, be it sales, management, finance, real estate, law, or production. This focus enables them to target courses and focus their attention on the most relevant and useful material in the program. This is not apt to occur without the relevant work experience.

Gaining Admission to B School

For the candidate who approaches the admission office of a graduate business school, two elements of the application can be particularly important: a strong personal essay and an interview (even if not required). Both are good indicators of your readiness for an MBA program. With each, admissions committees will be looking for maturity, drive, and focus. The personal essay required by your application should clearly enunciate your:

❑ Motivation

❑ Goals

❑ Degree of readiness

An excellent guide to writing this essay is *How to Write a Winning Personal Statement for Graduate and Professional School,* by Richard J. Stelzer. Examining these issues in preparation for such a personal essay is a valuable experience in and of itself and may shed some light on the question, "To MBA or Not?" Further information on the application process can be found in *How to Get into the Right Business School,* by James L. Strachan.

If it is at all possible, even when not required, try to have a personal interview at the school. The interview will allow the school to question you and probe for the elements listed above and it will provide an opportunity for you to explain your decision to seek an MBA and to discuss your commitment to the world of business.

A Suggested Career Path to the MBA

Job Title

An ideal job for the business school undergraduate contemplating graduate school would be a position of some sophistication, reasonable salary, and yet, no expectation that you would stay there for very long. In fact, what would be even more ideal would be a position where the expectation *was* that you would leave (even *have to* leave) to return to graduate school. Such positions *do* exist. Typical position titles are research analyst or research associate (RAs) in management consulting firms, and financial analysts (FAs) at investment banks or investment banking departments of commercial banks. They may also be called business analysts, associate consultants, or just associates. The essential thing is that they all perform similar roles.

Most of these positions are in business consulting firms. These firms provide advice and services to other businesses. Some of these firms need help; they're in trouble over product development, staffing issues, profit and loss projections, or any of a host of complicated situations. Others are doing well and need assistance with coping with rapid growth; still others need help increasing profitability or efficiency. Consulting can be utilized by any business for any aspect of a business's operation. If you like business, you should enjoy consulting.

Job Duties

Generally, you will be doing library research, collecting data in organized forms, and conducting some data manipulations. Research associates or financial analysts assist in helping to put together proposals, case studies, or analyses designed to help the consultant's client solve their problems, determine future strategies, or implement programs. As you gain expertise, some responsibilities will be added, in most cases, having to do with additional and more sophisticated research capabilities, quantitative manipulation of data using computer software, and the presentation of findings to your work team.

There is a limit on what you can do, on the decisions you will be allowed to make and in how far you can go on your own. These positions have been structured for rapid turnover and for people to work *under* more senior positions who have those decision-making responsibilities.

Because these positions are designed to appeal to graduates contemplating advanced education, they are not designed to fulfill career aspirations. Though they come with a salary and benefits, they have more in common with internships than typical entry-level positions. In fact, these analyst positions are often part of special hiring programs. Since the job only lasts for two years, many entry-level candidates are recruited and hired, and the training and mentoring involved for the new analysts is considerable. The responsibilities are located in one individual or office that manages the research associate/analyst "program." The defined boundaries of the experience and the structure of the internal training process should be highly acceptable to the Bachelor's degree student seeking to gain valuable skills and experience before entering graduate school.

Strategic Advantages

Job candidates applying for these positions do not have to misrepresent their intentions of leaving for an MBA. In fact, if you should desire to stay, you would find upon investigation that senior responsibility and authority is reserved for the MBA, necessitating your obtaining an MBA anyway.

Many analysts do, in fact, return to the consulting firms and banks that initially hired them, *after* obtaining their MBA. At this point, they begin new career paths in positions with complicated titles such as "associate-to-consultant." These titles recognize they are on their way to the coveted consulting partnerships in the organization.

Whatever your choice upon coming to the close of your two years as a research associate, you are in a very different position than when you graduated from college. You have significant, important business experience that will have transformed the value of your undergraduate degree. You are well situated to apply to one of the top graduate business programs and feel confident about your ability to succeed.

Whatever graduate program you do enter, you arrive better prepared to make the most of the degree. When you graduate with your MBA, you offer your new employer excellent justification for a responsible, decision-making position with all the appropriate rewards of such a job.

AN ALTERNATIVE STRATEGY

Perhaps in reading through this strategy, you've begun to have some doubts about its suitability in your case. Though you agree with the proposition, you don't feel like the ideal candidate. Your objections might be on any number of grounds: your grades in college may not have been good enough for you to be competitive for some of these consulting positions; or maybe your objection is you are not interested in resettling for any amount of time in the urban areas occupied by this type of business; or it may be that the nature of the work of research associates as described does not interest you. You still have options.

The basic premise of this book has been to suggest the importance of acquiring "portable" skills; that is, skills that you can carry from job to job. Content skills are pertinent to one job and not easily transferable to another. Portable skills follow you throughout your career. In today and tomorrow's ever-changing job market, portable skills offer you the best measure of job security.

Suggesting the research analyst path *before* you get an MBA accomplishes two things: you gain those important portable skills from the job itself, and you guarantee success in the MBA program and after you graduate.

But if, for the reasons listed above or perhaps other reasons, this path to the MBA isn't for you, you can still accomplish the same goals in a slightly different way by seeking out positions after graduation that provide the same kind of preparation as the consulting firms do, but without the same intensity of competition or the geographic restrictions or the job/task definitions. Let's look at some recent job announcements for positions that would be ideal for a recent business graduate who has an MBA program in their future:

Financial analyst: Join us, the largest natural gas distribution company in the state. We currently have a challenging opportunity available for a financial analyst with a bachelor's degree and excellent PC skills.

Budget analyst/nonprofit: To provide financial oversight of mental health and substance abuse programs. Resp. incl. tracking revenues & expenses, preparing budget reports, devel. spending plans w/prog. administrators. B.A. knowledge of spreadsheets & WP req'd.

Market analyst: As a key member of our marketing team focused on wholesale gasoline operations, you'll collect and interpret market data, advise management about market trends and critical regional market activities, develop and analyze rebate/reward sales programs, and track/report competitive information. To qualify, you should have a BA/BS in Marketing, excellent PC and creative skills; Windows-related software proficiency—Quattro Pro for Windows 5.0 and the ability to manage multiple projects simultaneously.

These are, of course, career positions and not the two-year, self-liquidating kinds of positions described in the career path. You will need to honestly negotiate and express your intentions about advanced education and work out a solution with your employers to ensure that, if you do decide to leave for graduate school, you leave with excellent recommendations and the possibility to return. You may decide to go to graduate school at night and hold on to your position. In fact, the employer may offer you educational benefits as an inducement to that course of action. And, of course, you may find your job so interesting, with so many possibilities for personal enrichment that you decide not to go to graduate school, at least for the foreseeable future. Whatever your decision, you will have begun to build upon your undergraduate education with valuable work experience that benefits both your career and any possibility of future professional education.

WORKING CONDITIONS

If you are working for a consulting firm of the size that can afford a number of research or financial associates or an investment bank or investment department of a commercial bank large enough to have such a department, you should be thinking in terms of a major metropolitan area or the highway belt around such an area. This is where you will find the concentration of employers hosting these kinds of positions.

As a career counselor, I have discovered there are a variety of reactions to living in a metropolitan area—some people love the idea and others don't. Most will admit, however, that metropolitan living offers more *choices* than any other locale, more choices in living, more choices about shopping, more choices in entertainment, and many more opportunities to meet people.

It's good to note that many fine graduate schools of business are also located in these major population zones, and that may prove convenient when it comes time to move ahead in your strategic plan to enter an MBA program.

What's It Like to Work in Consulting?

There is no "typical" day for a research associate or financial analyst in consulting or investment banking. However, while there may be no daily routines (and that in itself may be an attraction for you), the following activities and roles played are fairly constant over time.

Information Resourcing. These associate positions all require finding answers, usually under pressure of time and cost. To succeed, you need to be inventive, be good on the phone, and believe you can do it. In most consulting and investment decisions, information needs to be of high quality and recent. Providing that information will be a big part of your daily job. Your day will probably begin by scanning several newspapers, watching for business and market information that might prove helpful. Begin that newspaper reading practice now. It'll come in very handy in your MBA program.

Financial analyst positions at investment banks or in the investment department of larger banks monitor the performance of particular stocks and securities on the world's stock exchanges and stay well informed about the industries they track. Generally, you will focus on one or two industries in this kind of position.

Julie DeGalan, one of the creators of the *Great Jobs* series, is fond of saying that the answer to any question is only "two phone calls away." She has demonstrated this time and time again, sometimes quite dramatically in delivering the needed information. The persistence and positive attitude that underlies a philosophy of only "two phone calls away" would serve the research associate and financial analyst well in their jobs.

Travel.   Long distance travel is more a function of the research associate in the consulting industry than the analyst in investment banking. Some entry-level consulting positions can involve a grueling amount of travel. Just as the problems are global, clients can be global as well. Consultants leave the United States every day for China, Latin America, and Eastern Europe. Many of our largest consulting firms and investment banking services have had a strong European presence for decades. This increasingly far-flung demand for consulting/analyst services gives an edge to the individual with language skill and/or cultural sensitivity. Both research and financial analyst positions can involve significant out-of-the-office time in meetings with and working on-site with clients. To succeed, you need to be flexible and willing to get up and go. When you are on-site with the client, there tend to be correspondingly long days, because your client knows you aren't going home, but to a hotel.

Analysis.   Designing or running complicated computer models to evaluate corporations or monitor stock price movement or daily work with numerous databases to retrieve important information will consume much of your time. You will need to become familiar with all kinds of statistical digests, annual reports, Securities and Exchange Commission documents, spreadsheets, and financial market reports.

Whether you need to analyze the investment potential of a foreign firm, the comparable company activity pursuant to a merger, or the involved preparations prior to a public offering of stock, you will encounter data that needs to be transformed into usable information by your analysis. This information will then become the basis for the consulting team's action plan for the client.

This manipulation and understanding of data will provide some of the most valuable experience you can bring to your MBA program. It is perhaps one of the most crucial skills for graduate work; and your ability to transform "data" into "information" should help to make your progress through the MBA program a smooth one. You will have an advantage over many of your peers, even those with business experience, because as a consulting associate or financial analyst you are working for so many different clients on so many different projects that you will develop a broad understanding of resources and relevant techniques.

Presentation.   In a consulting firm, the work is underwritten by client fees. Though you may be working on several different projects simultaneously, all your work is client directed and available to the client for examination and review. Attractive presentation of materials is a skill you will begin to appreciate in consulting. The presentation may be a carefully prepared written document with charts and graphs (demanding mastery of software products) or it may be a public presentation with overheads, handouts, and your explanations of your material as well as responses to questions. Creativity, quality work with deadlines, and skills with a variety of presentation techniques are what you will take away from this experience. This will be valuable in your MBA program and later in your career.

> **FACT:** These presentations are often group endeavors and done to serve the client, not those presenting. It'll be a good lesson for you and a challenge for some to keep their egos under control and to think of the overall effect of the presentation on the client. There are no "stars."

Teamwork.   As a research associate or analyst, all of your work supports more senior staff people who have the major responsibility for the success or failure of a client contract. Consequently, a team approach is important in everything you'll do. You'll learn to clearly communicate your activities to your team members in order to avoid overlaps, misunderstandings, and wasted effort on anyone's part. This team approach will stand you in good stead in your MBA program.

> **FACT:** These teams are no longer just internal, but now include members of the management staff from your clients. It's a successful strategy that commits the client early on to implementation of the team's recommendations.

TRAINING AND QUALIFICATIONS

Let's begin with a rather general statement of training for RAs and FAs from the *Occupational Outlook Handbook for 1994–95,* published by the U.S. Department of Labor, Bureau of Labor Statistics.

> There are no universal educational requirements for entry-level jobs in this field. However, employers in private industry prefer to hire those with a master's degree in business administration or a discipline related to the firms' area of specialization. Those individuals hired straight out of school with only a bachelor's degree are likely to work as research associates or junior consultants, rather than full-fledged management consultants. It is possible for research associates to advance up the career ladder if they demonstrate a strong

aptitude for consulting, but, more often, they need to get an advanced degree to do so.

Employers of these positions will be looking for people with some very specific qualifications. A strong candidate will possess very strong quantitative, analytical, and communications skills. They will be able to work in fast-paced, demanding environments, and they will need to demonstrate achievements such as a high GPA, sophisticated academic and part-time work experience, and extracurricular leadership positions.

FACT: Listening is a critical skill in dealing with clients. If you don't see the problem the same way, you're wasting your time in devising solutions! Consulting is about communication.

SKILLS AND REQUIREMENTS

Consulting is done in a wide variety of contexts by some of the most prestigious firms in the world. While most consulting falls under the rubric of management consulting, there is a diverse set of other areas where consulting is provided. Broadly speaking, the job requirements are as follows:

- People skills: High
- Sales skills: Medium
- Communication skills: High
- Analytical skills: Extremely High
- Ability to synthesize: High
- Creative ability: High
- Initiative: Medium
- Computer skills: Medium
- Work hours: 50–90/week

EARNINGS

Starting salaries in consulting positions (analyst position) with a bachelor's degree, after bonus, range from $30,000 to $50,000. Starting salaries with an MBA degree (associate position) range, after bonus, from $40,000 to $125,000. These salaries vary with firms and with the region of the country you are in. The national average salary level reported by *Money* magazine in 1992 was $82,309. What you need to remember in reading these very generous salary figures is that these firms have their employees under tremendous scrutiny. If you don't perform, you'll be let go. This remains true even as you climb the salary ladder. Many of these firms have very specific expectations for when employees should be achieving certain levels of performance. When you see high earnings such as these, you shouldn't be surprised that the following are true: 1) getting hired will be correspondingly difficult, and 2) you will work very hard, indeed, for that salary.

US News and World Report reports the following median salaries in consulting:

Research associate	$ 30,400
Entry-level consultant	41,800
Management consultant	89,200
Senior consultant	120,100
Junior partner	120,100
Senior partner	194,000

An informal survey of new employees in various consulting firms showed dramatic variability in salaries. The following numbers are representative of what we found among new hires.

Representative Starting Salaries in Consulting (1994)

Andersen Consulting (MBA, Systems Consulting)	$ 46,000
Cornerstone Research (BBA, Litigation Consulting)	$ 40,000+
EDS (MBA, Management Consulting)	$115,000 + loaded laptop
Gemini Consulting (MBA, Strategic Consulting)	$ 80,000
Management Consulting (MBA, Strategic Consulting)	$ 75,000 base + $20,000 bonus
McKinsey (BBA, Strategic Consulting)	$ 42,000
McKinsey (MBA, Strategic Consulting)	$ 90,000 (+$15,000 signing bonus)
McKinsey (MBA, Associate, 1–2 years)	$150,000–200,000

CAREER OUTLOOK

The consulting industry has really been growing in the last few years. Two outcomes of that growth have been: 1) companies today are more likely to "buy" from among this growing array of specific consulting services to solve problems, rather than hire permanent staff to accomplish the same things, and 2) firms who hire associates on these two-year programs find the turnover keeps their permanent staff vital, energetic, and competitive.

Add to that list the volatile business environment in the 1990s that has challenged even smaller corporations with issues of global competition, dramatic technological advances, and an endless stream of new thinking and practices for organizational structure. Faced with this kind of dizzying environment, it's no wonder management cries, "Get us a consultant!"

FACT: Industry analysts track a consulting industry growing by leaps and bounds through the 1990s. Hiring is and will continue to be an active process and strong demand is anticipated to continue. *Consultants News* reports over 80,000 consultants sold or provided over $17 billion dollars worth of advice in 1993.

STRATEGY FOR FINDING THE JOBS

If you've decided you want to enter an MBA program after first taking a position as a financial analyst or research associate, you're already further ahead in finding one of those jobs than you think! Why? Just as you've made a decision to seek an MBA at some point in your future by first acquiring some valuable "portable" skills, potential employers have determined that they want employees who have direction and goals in their lives. You will be setting yourself apart from countless other graduates with your ability to articulate your life plan and future aspirations. Even if the individuals talking with you don't entirely agree with the specific details of your decisions, they will respect the thinking and planning that you've done and realize it sets you apart from your contemporaries.

If you want a consulting position, don't start by looking through the "Help Wanted" section of your paper. Consulting firms do not advertise or publish entry-level research associate or financial analyst positions. Why not? These are *highly* selective positions and there are limited numbers of them. Furthermore, consulting firms and investment banking organizations assume that one indication of a candidates' suitability for this kind of role will be their ability to seek these positions out on their own.

To make this easier, I have developed an extensive listing of consulting firms that will facilitate a good beginning to your search activities. Additionally, the articles cited are a selection from recent periodical literature focusing on consulting. They will give you a good sense of what's happening in the industry. They will also give you additional names of potential employers and provide you with an excellent basis for an in-depth interview with these kinds of employers! Finally, the list of directories will lead you to hundreds of other possible employers of various types and sizes.

Possible Employers

Ten Leading Firms in Consulting (*Business Week*, June 25, 1994)

Andersen Consulting, 33 West Monroe Street, Suite 16-E, Chicago, IL 60603, (312) 372-7100. 1993 revenues: $2,876 million. Number of consultants: 22,500. Recent clients: Astra/Merck, Caterpillar.

A.T. Kearney, 222 West Adams Street, Chicago, IL 60606, 312-648-0111. 1993 revenues: $340 million. Number of consultants: 1,250. Recent clients: Aetna, GM, Sears.

Booz Allen & Hamilton, 101 Park Avenue, New York, NY 10178, 212-697-1900. 1993 revenues: $800 million. Number of consultants: 4,600. Recent clients: Proctor & Gamble, Volvo.

Boston Consulting Group, 1 Exchange Place, 30th Floor, Boston, MA 02109, (617) 973-1200, Fax: (617) 973-1399. 1993 revenues: $340 million. Number of consultants: 1,250. Recent clients: Aetna, GTE, NYNEX.

Coopers & Lybrand, 1301 Avenue of the Americas, New York, NY 10019, (212) 259-1000. 1993 revenues: $1,351 million. Number of consultants: 7,650. Recent clients: Allied Signal, H.J. Heinz, Quaker Oats.

CSC Consulting, Cambridge, MA [or 5500 Wayzata Boulevard, Suite 1100, Minneapolis, MN 55416, (612) 593-1122]. 1993 revenues: $470 million. Number of consultants: 2,500. Recent clients: Agway, Amoco.

Gemini Consulting, 55 West Wacker Drive, Chicago, IL 60601, (312) 332-6100. 1993 revenues: $1,351 million. Number of consultants: 1,700. Recent clients: Dupont, Union Carbide.

McKinsey & Co., 55 East 52nd Street, New York, NY 10022, (212) 446-7000, Fax: (212) 688-9521. 1993 revenues: $1,300 million. Number of consultants: 3,100. Recent clients: American Express, AT&T, Mellon Bank.

Mercer Management Consulting, New York NY, [or 2300 North Street, N.W., Washington, DC 20037, (202) 778-7000]. 1993 revenues: $134 million. Number of consultants: 600. Recent clients: British Rail, Chemical Bank, Sara Lee.

Monitor, 25 1st Street, Cambridge, MA 02141, (617) 252-2000. 1993 revenues: $190 million. Number of consultants: 340. Recent clients: AT&T, Pacific Telesis.

SELECTED ARTICLES

"The Craze for Consultants: How Management Can Get Its Money's Worth," *Business Week,* July 25, 1994, p. 60–66.

"The Ever-Bigger Boom in Consulting," *Fortune,* April 24, 1989, p. 113.

"Inside Andersen's Army of Advice," *Fortune,* October 4, 1993, p. 78. Decries Andersen Consulting's approach, its training, and its use of a common methodology for systems consulting.

"Let's Go for Growth," *Fortune,* March 7, 1994, p. 60. Describes a popular 1990s business strategy: high growth. Good background reading for an interview in consulting.

"Lock the Doors. It's EDS," *Business Week,* September 19, 1994, p. 36. Describes the aggressive strategy of EDS in the management consulting business. EDS's goal is to have 5,000 to 7,000 new consultants in the next five years. EDS plans to hire 250 MBAs in 1995.

"The McKinsey Mystique," *Business Week,* September 20, 1993, p. 66. Describes the workings of top-of-the-line McKinsey & Co. ("The Firm") and close relations with corporate America.

"The Selling of a B-School Grad," *Business Week,* March 28, 1994, p. 146.

OTHER RESOURCES INCLUDING DIRECTORIES

The Career Guide: Dun's Employment Opportunities Directory. This gives an alphabetic listing of corporations and investment banks explaining career opportunities, personnel requirements, training and career development practices, benefits and addresses.

Consultants and Consulting Organizations Directory, 1994. Gale Research, Detroit, MI, (800) 877-GALE. This comprehensive directory lists over 20,000 businesses and individuals who consult for businesses and government.

Consultants News. Kennedy Publications, Templeton Road, Fitzwilliam, NH 03447, available from the Consultants Bookstore at (603) 585-2200. This publication covers the industry of management consulting, covering recent trends and who is growing.

Directory of Management Consultants. Kennedy Publications, Templeton Road, Fitzwilliam, NH 03447. Available from the Consultants Bookstore at (603) 585-2200. This excellent directory lists consultants of all kinds and gives specialties, locations, and phone.

Harvard Business School Career Guide: Management Consulting. Harvard Business School Press, 1994. Lists job descriptions in leading consulting firms including contact persons for MBA students and phone numbers. An invaluable resource. Cost: $19.95. (617) 495-6700.

Nelson's Directory of Investment Research, 1995. Nelson Publications, 1 Gateway Plaza, P.O. Box 591, Port Chester, NY 10573. A superior source of firms that hire investment analyst type positions. Investment banks, investment departments and brokerage houses.

Approaching Specific Consulting Firms

There's no question that breaking into the top firms like Bain, McKinsey, and Mercer will be a challenge. These firms target top schools and hire heavily from the same pool. On the other hand, superb firms such as Andersen Consulting are large yet easier to crack. Andersen has hired thousands of consultants on college campuses and are regular recruiters at the top job fairs as well.

> **FACT:** Get ready for interviewing of a different color! Many consulting firms will present you with case studies to quickly read and comment upon as part of your interview process. This process demonstrates how fast you think on your feet and how inventive you are, important aspects of the kind of work you're being hired to do.

Looking for employers in the fields of investment banking and consultant requires a resource that gives you a "big picture" look at industries. One of the best is a book by Leila K. Kight, *Getting the Lowdown on Employers and a Leg Up on the Job Market.* It will help you do basic research on industries, employers, and government agencies. Kight teaches you valuable techniques to use other research sources wisely, too.

KEY JOB AREAS IN CONSULTING

Many consulting firms specialize in specific kinds of consulting or have specific areas of expertise in the field. Below are some examples of this, along with the names of firms utilizing that approach.

Strategic Consulting

These consultants help with strategic planning for the subsequent two to five years. Consultation might include choosing a strategy for growth, making suggestions for restructuring, providing international expertise, suggesting acquisitions or divestitures, and/or revitalizing leadership. While not applying fixed "recipes," some consulting firms are known for having a specific perspective. Gemini Consulting, for example, suggests that businesses transform themselves using the "four Rs": *Reframing* corporate issues, *Restructuring* the company, *Revitalizing,* and then *Renewing* the organization and its people. Prominent firms in strategic consulting include:

A.T. Kearney	Chicago, IL
Andersen Consulting	Chicago, IL
Bain & Co.	Boston, MA
Booz Allen & Hamilton	New York, NY
Boston Consulting Group	Boston, MA
Coopers & Lybrand	New York, NY
Gemini Consulting	Morristown, NJ
McKinsey & Co.	New York, NY
Mercer Management Consulting	New York, NY
Monitor	Cambridge, MA

Business Process Re-engineering Consulting

An important trend in business in the last five years is the enormous push to increase productivity through improving business processes. Business process re-analysis and design has been important to the following firms:

Boston Consulting Group	Boston, MA
Coopers & Lybrand	New York, NY
CSC Consulting	Cambridge, MA

Systems Consulting

Consultants provide firms with services that involve specialized knowledge, a fresh perspective, and a high level of expertise. It would be hard to find an area which fits this description better than that of systems consulting. These consultants offer advice to organizations about the optimal configuration of their information systems, the integration of their information systems, the introduction of client-server computing, and the purchase of hardware and software. Prominent players in this market include:

Andersen Consulting	Chicago, IL
Cap/Gemini America	Morristown, NJ
CSC Index	Cambridge, MA
Digital Consulting	Maynard, MA
EDS	Plano, TX
Ernst & Young	Chicago, IL
IBM	Armonk, NY
Technology Solutions	Chicago, IL

Human Resources Consulting

Some of the most important and sensitive decisions in any firms involve who to hire, how to compensate and motivate them, and how to develop their skills. Human resource consultants offer advice on such things as compensation and benefits packages, pension funds, benefits of a diverse workforce, and employee development programs. Some leading human resource consultants are:

Automated Concepts	Chicago, IL
Hewitt Associates	Lincolnshire, IL
Wyatt Group	Chicago, IL
Towers Perrin	Chicago, IL

Litigation Consulting

The complexity of litigation has increased significantly in recent decades. As a result, the demand by law firms for litigation support has risen dramatically. Litigation consultants provide this support by working with attorneys to map out case strategies, develop courtroom exhibits and tactics, and provide economic analysis of the advantages or disadvantages of litigation. This position requires good analytical and problem-solving skills. Some of the many firms in this business include:

Charles River Associates	Boston, MA
Cornerstone Research	Menlo Park, CA
Economic Analysis Corporation	Los Angeles, CA
FinEcon	Los Angeles, CA
Law & Economics Consulting Group	Emeryville, CA
Litigation Sciences	Los Angeles, CA
Micronomics	Los Angeles, CA
National Economic Research Associates	White Plains, NY
Price Waterhouse	Los Angeles, CA and New York, NY

Finance Consulting

Financial consultants provide financial advice to corporations and money managers. This advice may involve pricing of securities, strategies for creating shareholder value, business valuation, economic forecasts and analysis, and/or suggestions for treasury management. Firms involved in this growing area include:

A.B. Laffer & Associates	Los Angeles, CA
Alcar Group	Chicago, IL
Andrew Kalotay Associates	Sea Cliff, NY
Boston Consulting Group	Boston, MA
Houlihan Lokey Howard & Zukin	Los Angeles, CA
Ibbotson Associates	Chicago, IL
McKinsey & Co.	New York, NY
Stanford Consulting Group	Menlo Park, CA
Stern Stewart & Co.	New York, NY
Treasury Management Associates	Aurora, CO
Wilshire Associates	Los Angeles, CA

Possible Job Titles

Associate Consultant   Financial Analyst
Associates   Research Analyst
Business Analysts   Research Associate

Beyond B School

If you do decide to pursue the idea of two years of professional experience before business graduate school, either with a consulting firm or some alternative choice of your own devising, one obvious place to turn once you've achieved that graduate business degree is back to your original employer.

And that does happen frequently. Generally, the work, the compensation, and the level of management expertise is worthy of your commitment and your advanced education. The very qualities that drew you to these experiences as solid preparation for your MBA are still valid for your work post-MBA.

One word of caution here. If you do return to your original employer after graduate school, you'll find things have, naturally, changed. At the same time, you, too, are no longer the same job candidate. You're older, you're wiser, and you have expectations of a position and responsibilities both commensurate with your new degree and built upon your previous experience. It will be your job to point out that you are no longer the same job candidate. If, during the interview process, you determine you are still being viewed as the trainee you were before, you might do better to look elsewhere and start with a fresh slate.

With an MBA and solid work experience in a consulting firm or investment banking organization, before and/or after securing your graduate degree, there is always the temptation to consider going solo as a consultant.

> **FACT:** It's not easy to make it on your own as a consultant. If you're busy with a client, where do you find the time to market yourself? If you're alone, your only credibility comes from clients, some of whom may want to remain anonymous and are unwilling to be part of your advertising effort. Only one in ten solo consultants lasts a decade.

An enhancement to the solo consultant is attaining the designation of Certified Management Consultant (CMC). For information on achieving this designation, contact: **Institute of Management Consultants,** 230 Park Avenue, Suite 544, New York, NY 10169

As your career progresses, another important consideration for going solo is keeping up a good network of contacts. In your work as an associate with a consulting firm or as a financial analyst in an investment bank and even during your MBA, you will become acquainted with numerous other talented individuals who will rise in their respective businesses, and it is important to stay in touch with them. They may be future customers.

FACT: A new trend is *relationship consulting.* Working with a company over many years, on retainer, to ensure continued monitoring, discussion, and implementation of ideas without the bother of renegotiating or beginning a new history with a consulting firm over and over.

PROFESSIONAL ASSOCIATIONS

Professional associations remain the "hidden treasure" for job seekers. These organizations have a vested interest in raising the general information level of recent graduates about the career fields they represent. Most are very generous with their publications and providing answers to questions. Give them a try.

American Association of Healthcare Consultants
11208 Waples Mill Road, Suite 109
Fairfax, VA 22030
Members/Purpose: Serves as a resource for healthcare providers; offers continuing education to members. Provides information concerning the role of hospital/health consultants
Publications: Membership directory.

American Association of Medico-Legal Consultants
Barclay Rittenhouse Square
Philadelphia, PA 19103
Members/Purpose: National medical malpractice screening panel. Members are physicians and attorneys united for medical malpractice screening, peer review, medical and hospital risk management, and medical audits.

American Association of Political Consultants
5335 Wisconsin Avenue, N.W., Suite 700
Washington, DC 20015
Members/Purpose: Regular members are corporations and individuals who devote a major portion of their livelihood to political counseling and related activities. The association provides a vehicle for the exchange of information, resources, and ideas among its members.
Publications: Membership roster, newsletter.

American Association of Professional Consultants
9140 Ward Parkway
Kansas City, MO 64114
Members/Purpose: Professional consultants. Aids and guides members in the improvement of their professional abilities.
Publications: *The Consultant's Journal, The Consultant's Voice,* membership directory.

American Consultants League
1290 Palm Avenue
Sarasota, FL 34236
Members/Purpose: Full- and part-time consultants in varied fields of expertise. Provides assistance to consultants in establishing and managing the business component of their consultancies.
Publications: *Consultants Directory, Consulting Intelligence, How to Mass Market Your Advice, The Consultants Malpractice Avoidance Manual.*

American Society of Agricultural Consultants
8301 Greensboro Drive
McLean, VA 22101
Members/Purpose: Strives to maintain high standards of ethics and competence in the consulting field
Publications: Newsletter.

Association of Managing Consultants
521 5th Avenue, 35th Floor
New York, NY 10175
Members/Purpose: Professional management consulting firms who serve all types of business and industry.
Training: Sponsors specialized education dealing with professional development.
Publications: *Directory of Membership, Journal of Management Consulting,* newsletter.

Association of Master Business Administration Executives (AMBAE)
c/o Beth R. Cantor
AMBA Center
227 Commerce Street
East Haven, CT 06512
Members/Purpose: Private corporation by Master of Business Administration executives to serve their professional career and financial needs.
Training: Conducts seminars.
Publications: *AMBA Network,* quarterly. Newsletter. *MBA Employment Guide,* semiannual, *MBA Industry Reports,* periodic.

Council of Consulting Organizations
521 5th Avenue, 35th Floor
New York, NY 10175
Members/Purpose: Individual management consultants who work privately or in consulting firms that meet the institute's requirements.
Publications: *Directory of Members.*

Independent Computer Consultants Association
11131 South Towne Square
Suite F
St. Louis, MO 63123
Members/Purpose: Promotes professionalism within the industry; increased awareness in the general business community of the products and services available and provides members with group benefits.
Training: Conducts educational programs.
Publications: *The Independent, Tax and Handbook for Consultants and Clients.*

MBA/Business Executives: American Management Association
130 West 50th Street
New York, NY 10020
Members/Purpose: Seeks to broaden members' management knowledge and skills.
Training: Conducts the Extension Institute, a private self-paced study program and Operation Enterprise, a young adult program for high school/college level students. Offers courses, workshops, and briefings.
Publications: *Compensation and Benefits Review, Compflash, Management Review, Organizational Dynamics, The President, Project Update, Supervisory Management, Management Solutions, Supervisory Sense,* and *Trainers Workshop.*

Society of Professional Business Consultants
621 Plainfield Road, No. 308
Willowbrook, IL 60521
Members/Purpose: Persons engaged in rendering business consultant services to physicians and dentists. Provides members with educational information to upgrade their effectiveness as professionals.
Publications: *The Consultant,* newsletter, roster.

ADDITIONAL RESOURCES

ABI/Inform on Disc
UMI–Data Courier, Inc.
620 South Fifth Street
Louisville, KY 40202

Advertising Career Directory
Visible Ink Press
Gale Research Inc.
P.O. Box 33477
Detroit, MI 48232

AHA Guide to the Health Care Field
American Hospital Association
P.O. Box 92683
Chicago, IL 60675-2683

American Association of Homes for the Aging
1129 20th Street, N.W., Suite 400
Washington, DC 20036

American Bank Directory
McFadden Business Publications
6195 Crooked Creek Road
Norcross, GA 30092

American Salaries and Wages Survey
Gale Research Inc.
P.O. 33477
Detroit, MI 48232

America's Corporate Families
Dun & Bradstreet Information Services
899 Eaton Avenue
Bethlehem, PA 18025

America's Federal Jobs
JIST Works, Inc.
720 North Park Avenue
Indianapolis, IN 46202

America's Top Medical and Human Services Jobs
JIST Works, Inc.
720 North Park Avenue
Indianapolis, IN 46202

Audio Video Market Place
R.R. Bowker Co.
245 West 17th Street
New York, NY 10011

The Banking Job Finder
Mainstream Access, Inc.
Prentice–Hall, Inc.
Englewood Cliffs, NJ 07632

The Best Towns in America
Houghton Mifflin Co.
222 Berkeley Street
Boston, MA 02116

Best's Insurance Reports
A.M. Best Co.
Oldwick, NJ 08858

Black's Medical Dictionary
A & C Black
81 Adams Drive
Totowa NJ 07512

Blue Book Digest of HMOs
National Association of Employers on Health Care Action
P.O. Box 220
Key Biscayne, FL 33149

The Boston Globe
The Globe Newspaper Co.
135 Morrissey Boulevard

P.O. Box 2378
Boston, MA 02107

Braddock's Federal-State-Local Government
Braddock Communications
909 North Washington Street, Suite 310
Alexandria, VA 22314

Burrelle's Media Directory
Burrelle's Media Directories
75 East Northfield Road
Livingston, NJ 07039

Business and Finance Career Directory
Visible Ink Press
A Division of Gale Research Inc.
835 Penobscot Building
Detroit, MI 48226-4094

Business Rankings Annual
Gale Research Inc.
P.O. Box 33477
Detroit, MI 48232

CAM Report: Career Movement and Management Facts
Priam Publications, Inc.
P.O. Box 1862
East Lansing, MI 48826

The Career Guide: Dun's Employment Opportunities Directory
Dun & Bradstreet Information Services
899 Eaton Avenue
Bethlehem, PA 18025

Career Information Center
Macmillan Publishing Group
866 Third Avenue
New York, NY 10022

Careers Encyclopedia
VGM Career Horizons
NTC Publishing Group
4255 West Touhy Avenue
Lincolnwood, IL 60646

Careers in Business
Careers in Communications
Careers in Computers

Careers in Finance
Careers in Government
Careers in Health Care
Careers in Social and Rehabilitation Services
VGM Career Horizons
NTC Publishing Group
4255 West Touhy Avenue
Lincolnwood, IL 60646

Careers in the Nonprofit Sector: Doing Well by Doing Good
by Terry McAdam
The Taft Group
5130 MacArthur Boulevard, N.W.
Washington, DC 20016

Careers in State and Local Government
Garrett Park Press
Garrett Park, MD 20896

The Chronicle of Higher Education
1255 Twenty-Third Street, N.W.
Washington, DC 20037

College Placement Council Annuals
62 Highland Avenue
Bethlehem, PA 18017

College to Career: The Guide to Job Opportunities
by Joyce Mitchell
The College Board
Box 866
New York, NY 10101

Community Jobs:
The National Employment Newspaper for the Non-Profit Sector
ACCESS: Networking in the Public Interest
50 Beacon Street
Boston, MA 02108

Companies That Care
by Hal Morgan and Kerry Tucker
Simon & Schuster/Fireside
Simon & Schuster Building
Rockefeller Center
1230 Avenue of the Americas
New York, NY 10020

The Complete Guide to Public Employment
by Ronald Krannich and Caryl Krannich
Impact Publications
4580 Sunshine Court
Woodbridge, VA 22192

Computing and Software Design Career Directory
Gale Research Inc.
P.O. Box 33477
Detroit, MI 48232

Consultants and Consulting Organizations Directory
Gale Research Inc.
P.O. Box 33477
Detroit, MI 48232

Consultants Directory
Dun & Bradstreet Information Services
899 Eaton Avenue
Bethlehem, PA 18025

Consultants News
Kennedy Publications
Templeton Road
Fitzwilliam, NH 03447

The Corporate Address Book
by Michael Levine
A Perigee Book
G.P. Putnam's Sons
200 Madison Avenue
New York, NY 10016

County Executive Directory
Carroll Publishing
1058 Thomas Jefferson Street, N.W.
Washington, DC 20077

Credit Union Directory and Buyer's Guide
United Communications Group
4550 Montgomery Avenue, Suite 700–N
Bethesda, MD 20814

Current Jobs for Graduates
Current Jobs in Writing, Editing & Communications
Plymouth Publishing, Inc.
P.O. Box 40550

5136 MacArthur Boulevard, N.W.
Washington, DC 20016

Developing a Lifelong Contract in the Sports Marketplace
by Greg Cylkowski
Athletic Achievements
3036 Ontario Road
Little Canada, MN 55117

Dialing for Jobs: Using the Phone in the Job Search (video)
JIST Works, Inc.
720 North Park Avenue
Indianapolis, IN 46202

Dictionary of Holland Occupational Codes
Consulting Psychologists Press, Inc.
577 College Avenue
Palo Alto, CA 94306

Dictionary of Occupational Titles
U.S. Department of Labor
Employment and Training Administration
Distributed by Associated Book Publishers, Inc.
P.O. Box 5657
Scottsdale, AZ 86261

Directory of American Firms Operating in Foreign Countries
World Trade Academy Press
50 East 42nd Street
New York, NY 10017

Directory of American Research and Technology
Reed Reference Publishing
121 Chanlon Road
New Providence, NJ 07974

Directory of Bond Agents
Standard and Poor's Corp.
25 Broadway
New York, NY 10004

Directory of Corporate Affiliations
National Register Publishing
121 Chanlon Road
New Providence, NJ 07974

Directory of Directories
Gale Research Inc.

P.O. Box 33477
Detroit, MI 48232

Directory of Management Consultants
Kennedy and Kennedy, Inc.
Consultants News
Templeton Road
Fitzwilliam, NH 03447

Directory of Manufacturers
Dun & Bradstreeet Information Services
899 Eaton Avenue
Bethlehem, PA 18025

Directory of National Environmental Organizations
U.S. Environmental Directories
P.O. Box 65156
St. Paul, MN 55165

DISCOVER
American College Testing
Educational Services Division
P.O. Box 168
Iowa City, IA 52244

Earth Work
Student Conservation Association
P.O. Box 550
Charlestown, NH 03603-0550

**The End of Work: The Decline of the Global Labor Force and the Dawn
of the Post-Market Era**
G.P. Putnam's Sons
New York, NY

Effective Answers to Interview Questions (video)
JIST Works, Inc.
720 North Park Avenue
Indianapolis, IN 46202

Employer's Expectations (video)
JIST Works, Inc.
720 North Park Avenue
Indianapolis, IN 46202

Encyclopedia of Associations
Encyclopedia of Business Information Sources

Encyclopedia of Medical Organizations and Agencies
Gale Research Inc.
P.O. Box 33477
Detroit, MI 48232

Environmental Industries Marketplace
Gale Research Inc.
P.O. Box 33477
Detroit, MI 48232

Environmental Opportunities
Environmental Studies Department
Antioch/New England Graduate School
Keene, NH 03431

Equal Employment Opportunity Bimonthly
CRS Recruitment Publications/CASS Communications, Inc.
60 Revere Drive
Northbrook, IL 60062

Federal Career Opportunities
Gordon Press Publishers
P.O. Box 459
Bowling Green Station
New York, NY 10004

Federal Jobs Digest
Breakthrough Publications
P.O. Box 594
Millwood, NY 10546

Federal Times
6883 Commercial Drive
Springfield, VA 22159

Flying High in Travel
John Wiley & Sons
605 Third Avenue
New York, NY 10158

Folio: The Magazine for Magazine Management
Six River Bend Center
911 Hope Street
Box 4294
Stamford, CT 06907

Foreign Consular Offices in the United States
U.S. Department of State
Washington, DC 20520

Foundation Grants to Individuals
The Foundation Center
79 Fifth Avenue
New York, NY 10003

Gale Directory of Publications and Broadcast Media
P.O. Box 33477
Detroit, MI 48232

Getting the Lowdown on Employers and a Leg Up on the Job Market
by Leila K. Kight
Ten Speed Press
P.O. Box 7123
Berkeley, CA 94707

Good Works
A guide to careers in social change
Edited by Donna Colvin
Barricade books
61 Fourth Avenue
New York, NY 10003

Government Job Finder
by Daniel Lauber
Planning/Communications
7215 Oak Avenue
River Forest, IL 60305

Graduate Management Admissions Test
Graduate Management Admission Council
P.O. Box 6108
Princeton, NJ 08541

Graduate Record Exam
Graduate Record Examinations Board
Educational Testing Service
P.O. Box 6000
Princeton, NJ 08541

Great Careers: The Fourth of July Guide to Careers, Internships, and Volunteer Opportunities in the Nonprofit Sector
Garrett Park Press
P.O. Box 190B
Garrett Park, MD 20896

Green at Work
by Susan Cohn
Island Press
Suite 300
1718 Connecticut Avenue, N.W.
Washington, DC 20009

Handbook for Business and Management Careers
VGM Career Horizons
NTC Publishing Group
4255 West Touhy Avenue
Lincolnwood, IL 60646

Harrington-O'Shea Career Decision Making System
American Guidance Service
4201 Woodland Road
P.O. Box 99
Circle Pines, MN 55014

Harvard Business School Career Guide:
Management Consulting
Harvard Business School Press
Cambridge, MA 02138

Harvard Gazette
Harvard Office of News & Public Affairs
Holyoke Center 1060
Cambridge, MA 02138

Healthcare Career Directory
Visible Ink Press
Gale Research Inc.
P.O. Box 33477
Detroit, MI 48232

Health Care Job Explosion!
Careers in the 90's
by Dennis V. Damp
D-Amp Publications
P.O. Box 1243
Coraopolis, PA 15108

Hoover's Handbook of American Business
The Reference Press
6448 Highway 290 E, Suite E-104
Austin, TX 78723

Hospital Market Atlas
SMG Marketing Group, Inc.
1342 North LaSalle Drive
Chicago, IL 60610

Hospitals Directory
American Business Directories, Inc.
5711 South 86th Circle
Omaha, NE 68127

How to Write a Winning Personal Statement for Graduate and Professional School
by Richard Stelzer
Peterson's
P.O. Box 2123
Princeton, NJ 08543

Human Services Career Connection
372A Broadway
Cambridge, MA 02139

Index of Majors and Graduate Degrees
College Board Publications
Box 886
New York, NY 10101

Infotrac CD-ROM Business Index
Information Access Co.
362 Lakeside Drive
Foster City, CA 94404

InternAmerica
The Internship Newsletter and News Service
105 Chestnut Street, Suite 34
Needham, MA 02192

International Jobs and Careers, The Complete Guide to
by Ron and Caryl Krannich
Impact Publications
9104-N Manassas Drive
Manassas Park, VA 22111

International Television Association Membership Directory
International Television Association
6311 North O'Connor Road, LB 51
Irving, TX 75039

Internships 96
Peterson's Guides
P.O. Box 2123
Princeton, NJ 08543

Job Bank Series:
  Atlanta Job Bank
  Boston Job Bank
  Chicago Job Bank
  Dallas-Ft. Worth Job Bank
  Denver Job Bank
  Detroit Job Bank
  Florida Job Bank
  Houston Job Bank
  Los Angeles Job Bank
  Minneapolis Job Bank
  New York Job Bank
  Northwest Job Bank
  Ohio Job Bank
  Philadelphia Job Bank
  St. Louis Job Bank
  San Francisco Job Bank
  Seattle Job Bank
  Washington, DC Job Bank
Bob Adams, Inc.
260 Center Street
Holbrook, MA 02343

Job Hotlines USA
Career Communications, Inc.
P.O. Box 169
Harleyville, PA 19438

The Job Hunter
The National Bi-Weekly Publication for Job Seekers
Career Planning and Placement Center
University of Missouri–Columbia
100 Noyes Building
Columbia, MO 65211

Job Opportunities in Business
Job Opportunities in Health Care
Peterson's
P.O. Box 2123
Princeton, NJ 08543

The Job Search Handbook for Educators: ASCUS Annual
Association for School, College & University Staffing
1600 Dodge Avenue, S-330
Evanston, IL 60201

Job Seeker's Guide to Private and Public Companies
Gale Research Inc.
P.O. Box 33477
Detroit, MI 48232

The Job Seeker's Guide to Socially Responsible Companies
by Katherine Jankowski
Visible Ink Press
A Division of Gale Research, Inc.
835 Penobscot Building
Detroit, MI 48226-4094

Jobs for People Who Love Travel
Impact Publications
9104 North Manassas Drive
Manassas Park, VA 22111

Kennedy's Career Strategist
1150 Wilmette Avenue
Wilmette, IL 60091

Libraries, Information Centers and Databases in Science and Technology
Reed Reference Publishing
121 Chanlon Road
New Providence, NJ 07974

Manufacturing Directories
Tower International
588 Saco Road
Standish, ME 04084

Marketing and Sales Career Directory
The Career Press Inc.
P.O. Box 34
Hawthorne, NJ 07507

Medical and Health Information Directory
Gale Research Inc.
P.O. Box 33477
Detroit, MI 48232

Merriam Webster's Medical Dictionary
Meriam Webster Inc. Publishing
Springfield, MA 01102

Million Dollar Directory: America's Leading Public and Private Companies
Dun & Bradstreet Information Services
899 Eaton Avenue
Bethlehem, PA 18025

Moody's manuals
Moody's Investors Service
99 Church Street
New York, NY 10007

Myers-Briggs Type Indicator
Consulting Psychologists Press, Inc.
3803 East Bayshore Road
Palo Alto, CA 94303

National Ad Search
National Ad Search, Inc.
P.O. Box 2083
Milwaukee, WI 53201

National Business Employment Weekly
Dow Jones & Co., Inc.
P.O. Box 300
Princeton, NJ 08543

National Directory of Internships
National Society for Internships and Experiential Education
3509 Haworth Drive, Suite 207
Raleigh, NC 27609

National Directory of Non-Profit Organizations
Gale Research Inc.
P.O. Box 33477
Detroit, MI 48232

National Directory of Private Social Agencies
Croner Publications, Inc.
34 Jericho Turnpike
Jericho, NY 11753

National Directory of State Agencies
Cambridge Information Group Directories, Inc.
7200 Wisconsin Avenue
Bethesda, MD 20814

National Human Services Employment Biweekly
13137 Penndale Lane
Fairfax, VA 22033

National JobBank
Bob Adams, Inc.
260 Center Street
Holbrook, MA 02343

National Trade and Professional Associations of the United States
Columbia Books Inc.
1212 New York Avenue, N.W., Suite 330
Washington, DC 20005

Nelson's Directory of Investment Research
Nelson Publications
1 Gateway Plaza
P.O. Box 591
Port Chester, NY 10573

The New Complete Guide to Environmental Careers
Island Press
Suite 300
1718 Connecticut Avenue, N.W.
Washington, DC 20009

NewsLinks
International Schools Services
15 Roszel Road, P.O. Box 5910
Princeton, NJ 08543

Non-Profit Job Finder
Planning/Communications
7215 Oak Avenue
River Forest, IL 60305

Occupational Outlook Handbook
Occupational Outlook Quarterly
U.S. Department of Labor
Bureau of Labor Statistics
Washington, DC 20212

Occupational Thesaurus
Lehigh University
Bethlehem, PA 18015

O'Dwyer's Directory of Public Relations Firms
J.R. O'Dwyer Co. Inc.
271 Madison Avenue
New York, NY 10016

Online Systems for Nonprofits
by Barbara Gersh
available through:
CompuMentor
89 Stillman Street
San Francisco, CA 94107

The 100 Best Companies to Sell For
by Michael Harkavy and The Philip Lief Group
John Wiley & Sons
605 Third Avenue
New York, NY 10158

The 100 Best Companies for Gay Men and Lesbians
by Ed Mickens
Pocket books
A Division of Simon & Schuster, Inc.
1230 Avenue of the Americas
New York, NY 10020

The 100 Best Companies to Work for in America
by Robert Levering and Milton Moskowitz
A Currency Book published by Doubleday
Bantam Doubleday Dell Publishing Group, Inc.
666 Fifth Avenue
New York, NY 10103

101 Challenging Government Jobs for College Graduates
An Arco Book
Prentice Hall Press
New York, NY 10023
(out of print, but can be found in many career libraries)

Opportunities in Banking
Opportunities in Federal Government Careers
Opportunities in Health and Medical Careers

Opportunities in Hospital Administration
Opportunities in Human Resources Management
Opportunities in Marketing
Opportunities in Nonprofit Organizations
Opportunities in Personnel Management
Opportunities in State and Local Government
Opportunities in Telecommunications
Opportunities in Television and Video
VGM Career Horizons
NTC Publishing Group
4255 West Touhy Avenue
Lincolnwood, IL 60646

Peterson's Grants for Graduate Students
Peterson's Guides to Graduate Study
Peterson's Internships
Peterson's
P.O. Box 2123
Princeton, NJ 08543

Places Rated Almanac
Prentice Hall General Reference & Travel
15 Columbus Circle
New York, NY 10023

Professional Career Series:
  Advertising
  Business
  Communications
  Computers
  Health Care
  High Tech
VGM Career Horizons
NTC Publishing Group
4255 West Touhy Avenue
Lincolnwood, IL 60646

Professional Careers Sourcebook
Gale Research Inc.
P.O. Box 33477
Detroit, MI 48232

Professional's Job Finder
Planning/Communications
7215 Oak Avenue
River Forest, IL 60305

Profitable Careers in Nonprofit
John Wiley & Sons
605 Third Avenue
New York, NY 10158

Public Relations Career Directory
Gale Research Inc.
P.O. Box 33477
Detroit, MI 48232

Public Relations Journal
Public Relations Society of America
33 Irving Place
New York, NY 10003

Regional, State, and Local Organizations
Gale Research Inc.
P.O. Box 33477
Detroit, MI 48232

Research Centers Career Directory
Gale Research Inc.
P.O. Box 33477
Detroit, MI 48232

Security Dealers of North America
Standard and Poor's Corp.
25 Broadway
New York, NY 10004

SIGI PLUS
P.O. Box 6403
Rosedale Road
Princeton, NJ 08541

The Skills Search (video)
JIST Works, Inc.
720 North Park Avenue
Indianapolis, IN 46202

Sports Market Place
Sportsguide
P.O. Box 1417
Princeton, NJ 08542

Standard Directory of Advertising Agencies
Reed Reference Publishing

P.O. Box 31
New Providence, NJ 07974

Standard and Poor's Register of Corporations
Standard and Poor's Corp.
25 Broadway
New York, NY 10004

State Executive Directory
Carroll Publishing Co.
1058 Thomas Jefferson Street, N.W.
Washington, DC 20077

State Government Research Directory
Gale Research Inc.
P.O. Box 33477
Detroit, MI 48232

Stedman's Medical Dictionary
Williams & Wilkins
428 East Preston Street
Baltimore, MD 21202

Strong Interest Inventory
Consulting Psychologists Press, Inc.
3803 East Bayshore Road
Palo Alto, CA 94303

The Tough New Labor Market of the 1990s (video)
JIST Works, Inc.
720 North Park Avenue
Indianapolis, IN 46202

U.S. Industrial Outlook
Superintendent of Documents
P.O. Box 371954
Pittsburgh, PA 15250
(S/N 003-009-00618-0)

U.S. News and World Report
2400 N Street
Washington, DC 20037

The Video Register & Teleconferencing Resources Directory
Knowledge Industries Publications
701 Westchester Avenue
White Plains, NY 10604

Ward's Business Directory of Corporate Affiliations
Gale Research Inc.
P.O. Box 33477
Detroit, MI 48232

What Can I Do with a Major in . . . ?
by Lawrence Malnig with Anita Malnig
Abbott Press
P.O. Box 433
Ridgefield, NJ 07657

Where the Jobs Are: A Comprehensive Directory of 1200 Journals Listing Career Opportunities
by S. Norman Feingold and Glenda Hansard-Winkler
Garrett Park Press
P.O. Box 190
Garrett Park, MD 20896

Who Audits America
Data Financial Press
P.O. Box 668
Menlo Park, CA 94026

World Chamber of Commerce Directory
P.O. Box 1029
Loveland, CO 80539

Y National Vacancy List
YMCA of the USA
101 North Wacker Drive
Chicago, IL 60606

INDEX

ABI/INFORM On Disc (CD-ROM), 52
Accepting employment, 85
Accomplishments/achievements
    section, of resume, 35, 37
Account manager, 167–68
Action verbs for resume, 28–30
Activities section of resume, 31–32
Administration, 194–95
Admission marketing director, 168
Advancement, 148–49
Affiliations section of resume, 31–32
Allied healthcare personnel, 180
Alumni career connections, 155
Alumni network, 50, 63–64, 133–34
American Salaries and Wages Survey (3rd
    edition), 13
America's Corporate Families, 51
Analysis, 228
Appearance, 77–78
Application statement (graduate
    school), 102
ARTSearch, 55
Assistant buyer/buyer trainee, 153

B school. *See* MBA
Benefit package, 128

Best Towns in America, 12
Black's Medical Dictionary, 170
Board and Administrator, 199, 201
Bob Adams, Inc., 52–53
Bookstore, for job search, 59
Boston Globe, 56, 152
Brinkerhoff, Peter C., 188
Broadcast letter, 37–39
Budget analyst, 226
Budget worksheet, 10–11
Business organizations, for research, 57
Business process re-engineering
    consulting, 236
Buyer/merchandising trainee, 146–47,
    152

Campus job postings, 155
Capabilities section, of targeted resume,
    37
Career counselor, 57
*Career Guide: Dun's Employment
    Opportunities Directory,* 52
Career Information Center, 49
Career libraries, 59–60
Careers Encyclopedia, 49
"Careers '96," 156

Career-specific directory, 53
Case, John, 56
Chamber of Commerce, 54, 57, 65
Chief executive officer, 214
Client contact, 125
College alumni network, 63–64
College Board, 98
College Placement Council, 151
College Placement Council Annual: A Guide to Employment Opportunities for College Graduates, 55
College teaching, 94
College to Career: The Guide to Job Opportunities, 49
Collegiate Employment Research Institute, 152, 173
Commission plan, 127–28
Communication skills, 87, 119–20, 177
Community Jobs, 55, 188, 198, 202, 211
Companies That Care, 52
Competitiveness, 125
Computerized job search service, 59–60
Consultants News, 232
Consulting. *See also* Research associate
  career outlook, 232–33
  job areas in, 236–39
  job titles in, 239
  as path to MBA, 224–25
  professional associations, 240–43
Consumer behavior, 158
Contact list, 63–66
Content-bound jobs, 180
Control buyer, 158
Controller, 214
Cooperative education, 155
Corporate Address Book, 157
Cost-of-living index, 12–14
Councils on Business and Industry, 57
Cover letter, 40–43
  broadcast letter instead of, 37–39
Culture, of organization, 190
Current Jobs for Graduates, 54
Customer knowledge and contact, 119

Dartnell Corporation, 126
DeGalan, Julie, 227
Demographics, 174
Department manager, 153
Dialing for Jobs: Using the Phone in the Job Search (video), 56
Dictionary of Occupational Titles (DOT), 47, 48
Directories, 179, 209–10
Divisional merchandise manager (DMM), 152

Economic needs, 10–14
Education section of resume, 26–27, 35, 37
Effective Answers to Interview Questions (video), 55
Employer directory, 51–52
Employers, 78
  in consulting, 233–34
  in healthcare, 178–79
  in nonprofits, 206–7, 215–17
  in retailing, 159–61
  in sales, 132–34
  used in networking, 65
Employer's Expectations (video), 55
Employment agency, for research, 57–59
Encyclopedia of Associations, 66
Encyclopedia of Business Information Sources, 157
End of Work: The Decline of the Global Labor Force and the Dawn of the Post-Market Era, 202
Entrepreneurship, 149–50
Environmental Opportunities, 55
Equal Employment Opportunity Bimonthly, 12
Executive director, 169, 190, 190–91
Executive search firm, 57
Executive training programs, 148
Experience/employment section of resume, 27–30, 35, 37
Experiential diary, 16–17

Federal Career Opportunities, 54
Federal Jobs Digest, 54

Feedback
  from follow-ups, 86–87
Finance consulting, 238
Finances, and healthcare field, 175
Financial analyst (FA), 113, 224, 226
Follow-up
  after networking or interviewing,
    83–87
Foreign language proficiency, 177
Fortune, 158
Forward integration, 141
Foundation Center, 103
Foundation Grants to Individuals, 103

General counsel, 214
General merchandise manager (GMM),
  152
General objective statement, 25
Geographically-based directory, 52–53
*Getting the Lowdown on Employers and a
  Leg Up on the Job Market,* 235
Goals, 14–15, 178
Graduate Management Admission Test
  (GMAT), 100
Graduate Record Exam (GRE), 100
Graduate school, 64, 93–104
  application statement, 102
  determining need for, 96–97
  financial aid, 103
  finding the right program, 98–102
  motives, 94–98
Grants for Graduate Students, 103
*Great Careers: The Fourth of July Guide
  to Careers, Internships, and
  Volunteer Opportunities in the
  Nonprofit Sector,* 188, 210
Great Jobs series, 206, 227
Green Marketing Alert, 142
Guides to Graduate Study, 98–99

*Handbook for Business and Management
  Careers,* 49
Harrington-O'Shea Career Decision
  Making System (CDM), 76
Head hunter, 57
Heading, of chronological resume, 23

Health maintenance organization
  (HMO), 167
Healthcare, 109–11, 165–84
  career outlook, 174–75
  definition of career path, 167–70
  earnings, 173
  job hunting strategy and checklist,
    175–78
  job sources, 178–79
  job title and related occupations,
    180–81
  professional associations, 181–84
  training and qualifications, 172–73
  working conditions, 170–72
Hidden job market, 62
Home care contract administrator, 167
Home healthcare, 175
Hospital administration degree, 172
*How to Get into the Right Business
  School,* 223
*How to Write a Winning Personal
  Statement for Graduate and
  Professional School,* 102, 223
Human resources consulting, 237

Index of Majors and Graduate Degrees,
  98
Industry-focused objective, 26
Information resources for job search
  identifying, 51–56
  locating, 56–60
Information resourcing position,
  227–28
"Informercial." *See* Self-promotion
  tools
Infotrac CD-ROM Business Index, 52
Inside sales, 122–23
Institute of Management Consultants,
  240
Interest inventory, computerized, 46–47
Internship information, 64, 155
Internships 1996, 155
Interviewing, 64, 74–82, 130–31
  content, 78–82
  closing, 84
  preparation for, 75–78

Job Bank series, 52–53
Job description research, 48–49
Job directory, 46–48
Job fairs, 133, 156–57
Job Hotlines USA, 54
Job Hunter, 54
Job offers and package, 88–92
Job Opps '95 Health Care, 175
Job posting publications, targeted, 54–55
Job search preparedness, 20–21
Job Seeker's Guide to Private and Public Companies, 52
Job sites and organizations, 63
Job titles, 44–60
Job vacancy notices, 64
Journal keeping, 3

Kight, Leila K., 235

Length, of chronological resume, 25
Letters of recommendation, 101–2
Listening, 116
Litigation consulting, 237–38
Longer-term goals, 14–15

Malnig, Anita, 47
Malnig, Lawrence R., 47
Managing Your Career, The College Edition of the National Business Employment Weekly (Wall Street Journal), 95, 157, 222
Market analyst, 226
Marketing, 122–23
   contract, 129
Marketing and Sales Career Directory, 133
Marketing/retail clubs, 154
MBA (Masters in Business Administration), 93–96, 219–27
   career path to, 224–25
   gaining admission, 223
   strategy, 112–13
Media relations and special events, 168
Medical terminology, 170
Membership services, 192–93

Merchandise analyst, 159
Merchandising, 143–44
Merriam Webster Medical Desk Dictionary, 170
Million Dollar Directory: America's Leading Public and Private Companies, 51
Money magazine, 231
Moody's, 51
Museum work, 215
Myers-Briggs Type Indicator (MBTI), 76

National Ad Search, 54
National Business Employment Weekly, 54
National Directory of Nonprofit Organizations, 215
National Job Bank, 53
National Trade and Professional Associations of the United States, 66
Negotiation
   of job offer, 89–91
Network contact record, 66–67
Networking, 49–50, 61–73, 178, 205–6
   beginning process of, 69–72
   preparation for, 63–69
   questions to ask and answer, 70–72
   shutting down, 72–73
   using present and former supervisors in, 64–65
Newspapers, 133
Nonpaid employment, 31
Nonprofit organizations, 111–12, 185–218
   career outlook, 202–4
   career path, 190–95
   earnings, 198–202
   employers, 206–7, 210–12, 215–17
   job finding strategy, 204–6
   job titles and related occupations, 214–15
   professional associations, 217–18
   training and qualifications, 197–98
   working conditions, 195–97

Objective
    of chronological resume, 23–26
    of functional resume, 35
    of targeted resume, 35–36
*Occupational Outlook Handbook for
    1994–95,* 49, 96–97, 153, 229
Occupational Thesaurus, 47
Offers
    comparing, 91–92
    reneging on, 92
Offices of New Business Development,
    57
On-campus recruiting, 156
100 Best Companies to Sell For, 52,
    112–13, 128
*100 Best Companies to Work For in
    America,* 52, 157
On-line services, nonprofits, 212–13
*Opportunities in Nonprofit
    Organizations,* 52
Opportunities In . . . (VGM series), 53
Outplacement service, 58–59
Outside sales, 122–23

Periodicals and newspapers, in job
    search, 54
Periodicals with classifieds, 179
Personal interviews, 131–32
Personal traits, 3–8
    needed in sales, 120–21
Personal values, 4, 8–10
Peterson publications, 98–99, 103,
    155, 175, 176
Places Rated Almanac, 12
Portable skills, 123
Position-focused objective, 26
Preferred skills, 19
Presentation, 228
Principles of nonprofit organizations,
    188–89
Problem solutions for resumes, 30
Product classification, 123–24
Product knowledge, 118–19
Productivity, 125

Professional associations and
    organizations, 57
    in consulting, 240–43
    in healthcare, 181–84
    in nonprofit organizations, 217–18
    in retailing, 162–64
    for sales, 135–39
    used in networking, 65–66
Professional Career Series (VGM), 53
*Professional's Job Finder/Government Job
    Finder/Non-Profits Job Finder,* 52
Program director, 214
Programming, 192
Promotability, 119
Public health degree, 172
Public library, for research, 56–57
Public relations, 193–94
Publications, 193

Reality testing, 95–96
Reference books, for job titles, 47
Reference works, for nonprofits, 207–9
References on resume, 33, 35
Referent power, 131
Reframing, 236
Regional fact books, 57
Rejection (graduate school), 103–4
Related courses section of resume, 27
Relationship consulting, 240
Relocating, 64, 90
Renewing, 236
Repetitive employment with same
    employer, 30
Research associate/analyst (RA), 113,
    219–43. *See also* MBA
Researching business careers, 44–60
Resources, additional, 244–68
    on consulting, 234–35
Restructuring, 236
Resume/cover letter, 22–43
    broadcast letter, 37–39
    chronological, 23–30
    functional, 33–35
    purpose, 22–23

questions and answers about, 31–33
for retailing, 157
solutions to problems with, 30
targeted, 35–37
used in interviewing, 76–77
Retailing, 96, 108–9, 140–64
career outlook, 153
definition of career path, 146–48
earnings, 151–53
employers, 159–61
interview tips, 158–59
job hunting strategy, 154–57
job titles/related occupations, 161–62
professional associations, 162–64
training and qualifications, 150–51
working conditions, 148–50
Revitalizing, 236
Rifkin, Jeremy, 202
Rorech, Maureen, 157

Salary
requirements, 4, 10–14
vs. commission, 126–28
Sales career path, 106–8, 114–39
career outlook, 128–29
definition, 121–24
earnings, 126–28
employers, 132–34
job finding strategy, 129–32
job specifications, 118–21
job titles and related occupations, 134
professional associations, 135–39
training and qualifications, 125–26
working conditions, 124–25
Sales management trainee, 147
Sales staff, 153
Self-assessment, 2–21, 124–25, 148, 205
reviewing, 63
seven-step process, 3–20
used in interviewing, 75–76
Self-promotion tools, 67–69
Shadowing, 64
Shop manager, 158
Skill base, 15–20, 81–82

Skills Search (video), 55
Small Business Administration (SBA), 57
Smith, Devon Cottrel Smith, 188
Social & Behavioral Sciences Jobs
   Handbook, 54
Software, for resume creation, 57
Sports Market Place (Sportsguide), 53
Sports Market Place 1996, 133
Stalling strategy, 95
Standard and Poor's Register of
   Corporations, 52
Stedman's Medical Dictionary, 170
Stelzer, Richard J., 102, 223
Store management, 145, 147
Strachan, James L., 223
Strategic consulting, 236
Strong Interest Inventory (SII), 76
Summary of qualifications statement, 26
Supervisors, present and former, 64–65
Systems consulting, 237

Tangible/intangible products, 123–24
Teamwork, 229
Technical sales, 123
Technology, 174–75
Telephone interviews, 64, 131
Temping, 157
Thank-you note, 84–85
Tone words, 69
Total Quality Management (TQM), 190
Tough New Labor Market of the 1990s
   (video), 56
Travel, 150, 228
Turnover, 108

U.S. Centers for Disease Control and
   Prevention, 166
U.S. Department of Labor, 96–97,
   153, 174, 229
Bureau of Labor Statistics, 153, 174,
   178, 229
Underdeveloped skills, 19–20
handling during interview, 81–82
US News and World Report, 231

Values, personal, 8–10
Verbs, action, 28–30
VGM career series, 49, 52, 53
Videos, for job search, 55–56, 59
Visitors' guides, 57

Wall Street Journal, 54, 95, 157, 222
Want ads, for job titles, 47–48
*What Can I Do with a Major In…?
How to Choose and Use Your College
Major,* 47
*Where the Jobs Are: A Comprehensive
Directory of 1200 Journals Listing
Career Opportunities,* 54

Work environment, 175
Work settings research, 49
Work values, 9
Working conditions, 8
for consulting firm, 227–29
in healthcare, 170–72
in nonprofits, 195–97
in retailing, 148–50
in sales, 124–25
Workplace risk issues, 172
World Chamber of Commerce Directory, 54

Y National Vacancy List, 55
Yellow pages directory, 65